Is the world getting weirder, or am I ha

Have you ever seen anything like it in

Here is the story of the orange ogre in the big white house, a sparkly princess and some stoned geese.

There are rockets and robots and cars in space.

Hold tight, it's a bumpy ride.

06.01.18

Imperfect recall

Poor Donny is grumpy. He needs a Farley's Rusk and a rattle.

A nasty man has been saying nasty things and the leader of the free world is in a huff.

If it were just the book Fire and Fury, that looks likely to save struggling book shops the whole world over, it might be bearable.

His side could say that it is simply a collection of tittle-tattle and lies written to make money from the boffo box office that is Donald Trump.

The President could refute the suggestions contained within its pages that he is incompetent and not bright enough for the post by tweeting that he is "like, really smart".

And that is exactly what he did.

He added that his, like, smartness is one of his two greatest assets, the other being his mental stability.

Any suggestion to the contrary was a hoax on the American public and that "the Democrats and their lapdogs, the Fake News Mainstream Media, are taking out the old Ronald Reagan playbook and screaming mental stability and intelligence".

Probably not the best example to highlight. Ronald's own son said that his father had Alzheimer's while in office and Reagan was formally diagnosed with the disease in 1994.

A real, like, smart person would have picked a better example.

Unfortunately for all of us who live in Donny's world, it is not just the ramblings of the current President and the book of the year that suggests we have a problem.

A Yale University psychiatry professor has met with members of Congress to discuss President Donald Trump's mental health.

To paraphrase, she thinks he is out of his tiny orange mind.

Dr Bandy X. Lee, a name I am not making up, believes that the President is 'unravelling' and that he poses a 'public health risk' by being in office.

She is an expert on violence, but there is no proof that Trump is predisposed to aggressive outbursts.

Well, there were the tweet-storms against other world leaders and fellow politicians and celebrities and models and sports people and the threat to punch a dissenter in the face and saying that others should be roughed up, and the time when he told an audience to "knock the crap out of" anyone objecting at his rallies, and that he would pay for the assailant's legal fees, and when said he loved the old days when protesters would be carried out on a stretcher.

But apart from that there's no evidence that he has a propensity for violence.

In December last year, Dr Lee gave a presentation in Congress on why Trump's presidency was an 'emergency' to a group of Democrats and one lone Republican senator who was presumably lost and couldn't find the exit.

She said 'From a medical perspective, when we see someone unravelling like this, it's an emergency.'

Lee told the New York Daily News. 'We've never come so close in my career to this level of catastrophic violence that could be the end of humankind.'

She might have been referring to Trump's boast about his nuclear button, which, like everything else about him, he insists is the biggest.

He has boasted that he has the biggest buildings and big genitals and a big nuclear arsenal and only the latter is verifiably true.

America does have the world's biggest nuclear arsenal and Trump can set it off in a fit of pique if Melania swats his hand away again.

There is no button on his desk, as he claimed. The launch procedure involves a briefcase called the "football" that is attached to a man who follows the President everywhere he goes.

If Kim Jong-un calls him fatty, Trump can beckon the man over and enter the codes that are delivered to him every day.

These codes are what they call "the biscuit".

Donny has been told not to eat the biscuit.

For security reasons, the biscuit has several fake codes, so the President has to memorise which are the correct ones.

And that is where things get a lot more comfortable for all of us without access to a fall-out shelter.

We can all relax now.

The chances of him recalling something like that are pretty slim.

I bet he couldn't remember where he left his giant orange bottom.

07.01.18

Peas in a pod

Toby Young is a right-wing controversialist that has been appointed to the board that regulates universities.

This has given people cause for concern because of his comments in the past about women and minorities.

Boris Johnson is our chief diplomat, his position is that all those dolly birds and pooftahs should get a grip and stop whining.

He did not say that, I made that up. But would you be at all surprised if he had?

Boris said that Toby Young possessed just the sort of caustic wit that made him perfect for the job.

Examples of that wit were bulk-deleted by Toby Young from his Twitter account the moment people started to point them out.

They were mostly about the size of women's breasts and insults about the poor and gay people.

This is what passes for caustic wit in Boris Johnson's world because that is exactly what he writes too.

In 1996, while a journalist for the Telegraph, Johnson went to the Labour conference and wrote "the 'Tottymeter' reading is higher than at any Labour Party conference in living memory".

He wrote, "Time and again the 'Tottymeter' has gone off as a young woman delegate mounts the rostrum."

Good word that: "mounts".

I bet he got a tiny bulge of excitement when he came up with that one.

It was a time when he noted that women's allegiance was shifting to the Labour party.

His position was that this was not because of a more inclusive stance by Labour, but because Labour was improving in the polls and women's "natural fickleness" meant they were following the sweet smell of success.

They couldn't help themselves, small brains you see.

When Johnson edited the Spectator magazine, despite complaints, he pinned a Pirelli calendar to the wall, which means that Boris Johnson was 14 years old when he edited the Spectator.

When he left, he wrote to his successor that if Kimberly Quinn, who was then the Spectator's publisher, came by with some helpful suggestions for boosting circulation, he should "Just pat her on the bottom and send her on her way."

In 2005, while campaigning to become the Conservative MP for Henley in the general election, he told voters that "voting Tory will cause your wife to have bigger breasts,"

In 2012, while hosting the London Olympics as mayor, Johnson told his readers of the "magnificent" experience of watching "semi-naked women playing beach volleyball ... glistening like wet otters."

You could be forgiven feeling that people like him are a bit emotionally stunted – maybe it was the single-sex private school education.

He seems to be still in his uniform, pulling pigtails on the bus.

It is not just women in his cross-hairs, as you can imagine – the stunted juvenile mind would not stop there.

Writing in the Spectator in 2000, Johnson attacked what he called "Labour's appalling agenda, encouraging the teaching of homosexuality in schools, and all the rest of it.", compared gay marriage to bestiality and wrote of "tank-topped bumboys" blubbing that Peter Mandelson had left the government.

No wonder he thinks that his close personal friend Toby Young is ideal for the board of the university regulator, the body that is supposed to have students' welfare at its heart.

It is just the sort of snorting good wheeze that a modern day Just William would come up with.

13.01.18

Not Doing the Lambeth Walk

Donald Trump has cancelled his visit to London.

He heard the Queen was not going to pick him up at the airport and relay him to the palace in a glorious, gilded procession and he threw a tantrum and called off his arrangements.

That's not true. I made that up, apart from the tantrum part.

He was going to open the new US embassy: ribbon cutting, smiling, waving, speechifying, that sort of thing.

This is not Virginia though, where he is more popular than Star Wars. He would not have been greeted by cheering local yokels in Make America Great Again hats.

Our locals had other things in mind. That is probably the reason for his absence.

When he went to Saudi Arabia, Israel, France, Poland, Germany, Japan, South Korea, and 'Jyna' he would not have been able to understand the insults thrown at him, but here they would be shouted in English, and he has almost mastered that language.

The Twitter spats he has had with London's mayor Sadiq Khan and Theresa May, the rudeness shown him by Boris Johnson and pretty much all of our politicians that have expressed an opinion and the abuse he gets on social media from the good people of this land probably did not help either.

However, none of those people are to blame, according to the man himself.

The real culprit preventing Ancient Orange from coming to open America's newest and spangliest embassy is, of course, the notorious Kenyan Muslim terrorist Barack Hussein Obama.

Obama is from a period of what seems like ancient history, when the leader of the free world did not sit in bed at 6.30 in the evening stuffing Big Macs in his face and picking Twitter fights with former Miss Worlds.

Donny said it was Oback Arama's fault that he's not coming to good old Britainland because Obama sold the old US embassy in Mayfair for what he called 'peanuts'.

Very bad deal, hugely bad, everyone says so, I can tell you that.

Also, the new embassy is in an 'off location', which means there isn't a McDonald's within lumbering distance.

The man doesn't want to go to an off location – why should he? He needs 'me time' at his golfing resorts.

It's not like it's part of the job for a President to open the new embassy in the country they have the famous Special Relationship with.

This has nothing to do with the fact that he wouldn't get the full state visit and hang out with the royals and get driven around in a gold carriage and wouldn't be met with cheering fans wherever he went. What on earth would give you that idea?

All the pomp and appurtenances of wealth and status mean nothing to Donny, as you will know if you have ever seen pictures of him ascending his golden tower in his golden elevator to his golden apartment.

He released a statement, by which I mean he sent out a message on Twitter, like a 12 year old.

It said: 'Reason I cancelled my trip to London is that I am not a big fan of the Obama administration having sold perhaps the best located and finest embassy in London for 'peanuts', only to build a new one in an off location for $1.2billion. Bad deal. Wanted me to cut ribbon – NO!'

The capitalised 'NO' with an exclamation mark is priceless. You can hear him stamping his tiny feet three thousand miles away.

This petulant strop is more about his approval ratings, which have set the bar so low for American presidents that to get lower, the next one would have to limbo under it.

By the way, would you care to guess what his predecessor's approval rating is?

It is 63% at the time of writing.

They are like yin and yang – Donny is on 37 and Obama is on 67. Complete opposites.

In this country, though, it is worse. In Britain, Trump is about as popular as dandruff - a full 77% of Britons dislike him.

Darth Vader gets a better score than that.

14.01.18

La Maladie du NHS.

The NHS is in such a state that the best hospital in Britain is in France.

The entirely unexpected onset of winter has plunged the health service into its yearly crisis. Someone should buy the authorities a calendar, with the cold months highlighted in blue, so they can plan for their arrival.

There is a government target of seeing people in A&E within four hours, a time period known as: not nearly quickly enough.

If you have your head lodged in a saucepan, or a garden implement sticking out of your torso, it would be quite nice to be attended to faster than it takes to watch the extended version of The Lord of the Rings.

Sadly, this is not possible due to entirely predictable unforeseen circumstances.

The Shadow Health Secretary, Labour's Jonathan Ashworth said that the Prime Minister had lost control of the NHS.

This is a statement from the opposition to the Prime Minister of the day that comes along as regularly as Christmas.

To help ameliorate the calamitous state of the NHS, patients in Kent that are still mobile are being advised to hop on a ferry and hot-foot it to Calais, where they will seen *tout de suite*.

The French hospital is being run in conjunction with the British health service and the treatment you will receive is practically the same as here, with a few small changes.

In France, for instance, you will not be kept in an ambulance in the car park while a bed is found for you to die on and hospital corridors will not be full of people on trolleys waiting for a ward, like a scene in M*A*S*H.

Furthermore, in the French hospital, every doctor and nurse is fluent in our mother tongue. That is how you will be able to tell where you are when you wake up from your operation – in France, everyone speaks perfect English.

And instead of trailing across the ward to the one toilet by the door, and sharing a bathroom with twenty other people, you will be stationed in your own room, with an en-suite, which in French is called an "en-suite".

The Calais hospital is described as a modern facility, with 500 beds and it serves French food.

It seems a shame that you have to be ill to go there.

Relatives and friends can book rooms for themselves in the hospital while they are visiting their loved ones. They cost just £35 a night and meals are £7.10.

The best bit is the wait time for treatment. Compared to Britain, there isn't any. Four weeks for your surgical procedure that has just been cancelled in Kent.

Oddly, this excellent offer is not being taken up. The Kent authorities are having to re-advertise the service because so few have availed themselves of the opportunity.

Maybe the people of Kent would rather die a slow death in the south of England than recover speedily in the north of France.

It could be that they don't like the idea of waking up to a continental breakfast.

Maybe they insist on the full English or nothing, which might be why many of them are needing hospital treatment in the first place.

It seems odd that it has come to this, especially after Theresa May declared that the NHS would be better prepared for winter than ever before.

It is difficult to know what she meant by that. Perhaps she has become confused. Maybe she needs a check-up.

If she gets on the Eurostar, I know a place that could fit her in straight away.

20.01.18

Burning and building bridges.

As part of the government's drive to deal with the consequences of asking the people what they think, Theresa May welcomed her French counterpart, President Emmanuel Macron, for a chit-chat and what journalists call a "slap up meal".

The meal was in a place that boasts a Michelin star.

That's classy. The likes of me can only dream of eating in an establishment recommended by people who make tyres.

For dessert, Mrs M chose the Humble Pie.

She was told in no uncertain terms that: no we can not have a bespoke deal, no the finance racket that we Brits depend on will not get special treatment and yes we will have to pay an extra £45m to titivate the Calais camp where migrants collect before Sellotaping themselves to the underside of lorries to make it the promised land.

Can you imagine how desperate they must be if Dover looks better than where they have come from?

May's agreement for the extra £45m to strengthen border security in France lies at odds with the 11% cut she made in border security in Britain, the 1,000 border security posts she axed and the 20,000 police officers she cut since 2010, both as PM and Home Secretary.

She seems to be pulling in two opposing directions on every issue she faces.

As the PM was both distancing herself and cementing ties with the "unelected bureaucratic socialist experiment that is Europe"

(Copyright N Farage), Boris Johnson was paddling in another direction, entirely his own.

Typically off-message and eager to hog the limelight, Bozo of the F.O. raised the prospect of building a bridge or road tunnel between Britain and France.

Half the Tory party want to burn bridges and he is suggesting we build one.

He said it out loud to the French at one of the meetings they had during that highly successful UK/France summit at which we bravely capitulated to their every demand and picked up the bill for lunch.

Boris said: 'They are two of the world's biggest economies and they are linked by a single railway. It is ridiculous.'

To remedy this ridiculousness, he plans a mighty span that will forge a new connection between the two old enemies, just as we are looking elsewhere to fashion partnerships.

Trade deals between us and the continent are being torn up, our Brexiteers are jetting off to the planet's furthest most countries to secure business contracts to replace the EU ones we are cancelling and Boris Johnson is planning to yoke Britain to France in order to glue together a relationship that is in the divorce courts.

Have the hair mousse fumes gone to his head?

Apart from anything, building a bridge to bolster ties between France and the UK sounds a lot like thwarting The Will of the People.

Just ask the man on the Southend omnibus what he thinks about building a bridge to let Johnny foreigner over here more easily and he'll spit out his dentures.

This is not the first time Boris has talked up a new connection.

In private conversations at the 2016 Tory Party conference in Birmingham, he said: 'If you wanted to show your commitment to Europe, is it not time for us to have further and better economic integration with a road tunnel?

Two years ago he was all for MORE economic integration.

Tunnels are very expensive, however, and we don't have any funds to spend on anything that is not a palace occupied by our Queen or our MPs, or that is not a weapon of mass destruction, so it will have to be a bridge.

It will probably be dubbed the Boris Bridge.

That alone is a pretty good reason not to have one.

Another is that the Channel is the busiest shipping lane in the world. About 600 ships pass through the gap between us and France every day, and unless the bridge will be one long unsupported span, it will need huge beams sunk into concrete to hold it up.

Ships will crash into these on the hour, every hour.

Then there is the wind – the road bridge over the Thames at Dartford is closed for high winds about once a month and it is closed either completely or partly due to crashes about once every day.

Can you imagine what will happen as the traffic from one end tries to get its head around driving on the wrong side of the road, in the perpetual wind and rain of the Dover Straight?

We could twin this genius transport idea to the other one from Office Boris, the cable car over the Thames.

I bet most people in London have forgotten it is there – still catering for the same 16 regular users and at a cost of only £60m.

Besides, is this the same country that can't fix the potholes in the road, can't provide a policeperson to investigate a crime against you even if it is happening right now, or operate on you in anything other than an emergency for lack of money?

Where are we going to get the billions it would cost for a bridge that long – borrow it from the Germans?

It's a good job Foreign Secretary Boris isn't in charge of anything important or we'd really be in trouble.

21.01.18

Sound-ish of mind and body

It is one year since Donald Trump spoke to the few thousand people ("millions and millions of people") assembled in Washington to see him inaugurated as The Worst President Ever ("The Best President Ever, no-one could be more presidential, believe me").

In the intervening time, he has achieved so much.

He has managed to pick fights with Australia, China, Russia, Iran, Syria, Yemen, Afghanistan, Mexico, Canada, North Korea, Sweden, Europe in general, Germany in particular, the Republican Party and the Democratic Party, the FBI, the CIA, the NSA, most of his staff, the National Basketball Association, the National Football Association and various Miss Worlds, celebrities, actors, athletes, politicians, comedians, TV stations, all past Presidents except "the great Abe Lincoln" and all news media except his fans at Fox News.

All that and he has still managed to fit in golfing every other day.

It must be that whirlwind of activity that has kept him so trim.

The Whitehouse doctor gave President Trump his routine physical and declared that he was in great shape for someone who eats burgers in bed and takes a golf cart to travel down the hall to the loo.

I made that up. He actually said that the President is in excellent health and, (despite what your eyes may tell you), he is not obese.

The stats say that a man of 6 feet 3 inches, weighing 239 pounds achieves a 29.9 score on the Body Mass Index, which is classed as simply overweight.

A score of 30 BMI would mean that Ancient Orange would be classed as obese.

It is the only thing related to large size that Donny does not want associated to his name.

The problem is that, while statistics don't lie, the information that goes into the making of them can.

The internet is full of helpful examples, posted by concerned citizens, of men who are six feet three inches and weigh 239lbs who do not resemble the walking dough ball that is the leader of the free world.

Trump would have to have hollow legs if he were to get away with claiming he tips the scales at that score.

Old joke alert: Speak-Your-Weight machines would say "one at a time" if he were to mount one.

Of course, if Trump was just an inch shorter than advertised, he would fail the obesity test too. Unfortunately, his New York drivers licence states that he is not 6 foot 3 inches, only 6 foot 2.

Pictures of him standing next to Barack Obama, who really is 6 foot 2 show them to be the same height.

So, it is possible that Trump and his physician are being economical with at least one of his measurements.

The doctor also announced, completely unbidden, that Trump is free of "cognitive issues".

This also seems unlikely, as the list of his furious assaults on multiple targets listed above would attest.

Apparently, he scored the maximum 30 out of 30 on the Montreal Cognitive Assessment test.

This a test that you are supposed to pass with flying colours, consisting as it does of identifying pictures of lions and being able to draw a clock face.

As though to reinforce the message, the Whitehouse doctor said, "He is very sharp. He's very articulate when he speaks to me".

Really? Now we are straying into the realms of the ridiculous.

If so, it is certainly a side to Trump that the rest of the world is yet to see.

Why would he keep all that sharpness and articulacy to himself?

26.01.18

Donny Does Davos

Donald Trump arrived at the gathering of the world's elite like he was recreating Apocalypse Now.

He flew in low out of the rising sun and about a mile out, he put on the music.

In the film of his life, Wagner's Valkyrie would boom out, with lyrics added specially for the incoming storm: me me me me me, me me me me me, me me me ME me, me me me me...

He had never been invited when he was just a "businessman".

This must have hurt: his face pressed against the glass, always smudging it orange on the outside.

Now he was allowed inside because of an historical mistake in the American voting system.

He lumbered in, sucked the air out of the room and immediately broke into his routine of berating the press (so fake) and crowing about the size of the crowd (biggest ever, I can tell you that, they never had such a big crowd, everybody says so).

He posed with other world leaders, looking like he had no idea or remote interest in who the people on either side of him were.

When they spoke, they remained static. Trump swayed from side to side. He seems incapable of standing still, like a three year old.

It looked like any moment he would grab his tinkle and rush off stage saying he needed a wee-wee.

Theresa May was on child minding duty. Trump had recently seen The Darkest Hour and told the PM that she could be the new Churchill. Maybe he meant she would be driven to drink.

This was the first awkward meeting since Trump threw a strop when Mrs M corrected him about re-tweeting far right nonsense about Muslims.

Trump kept up that gale of verbosity that prevents anyone else in the room from getting any limelight.

Bloomberg News recently reported that, according to current and former UK government officials, Mrs May finds it impossible to get a word in on the few occasions they have spoken by telephone.

Trump simply opens his mouth and the words gush out like water from a garden hose and he leaves the PM less than ten seconds to respond before talking over her and embarking on another self-eulogising monologue.

If you are not talking about Donny, Donny isn't listening.

The speech he delivered to the gathering at Davos was what they call low-key for this President.

He stuck to the script that someone else had written for him and refrained from extemporising or throwing out free hats.

The "liberal elite fake-news mainstream media" were effusive in their praise. They could not believe that he managed to get through the event without straying from his prepared remarks or declaring war on China or North Korea or Iran or CNN.

They were also mightily disappointed. That is why the crowds at Davos were so large.

They hadn't come to see Bongo out of U2 tell us how to organise the affairs of a music making corporation to achieve maximum tax efficiency and they weren't there for a lesson in I-told-you-so from Tony Blair.

The throng had assembled to watch a giant orange gorilla throw his poop around his cage.

He thought it was an indication of his popularity. Actually, it was an indication that the human race, even the elite ones, have not moved past enjoying Bedlam as an amusement.

Melania was nowhere to be seen.

Her unmoving, granite features had hardened further on being subjected to the endless coverage of Trump's alleged affair and subsequent hush money paid to the porn star Stormy Daniels.

As though to underline what it must be like to be married to the man, the first lady had chosen to visit a holocaust museum at home rather than take a free, five star, VIP trip to a glamorous resort in the Swiss Alps with her husband.

27.01.18

The Russians are coming!

Her Majesty's Principal Secretary of State for Defence, Gavin Williamson, has warned that a Russian cyber-attack on Britain's electricity supply could cause 'thousands and thousands' of deaths.

The Defence Secretary brought his considerable military experience, forged from his exemplary career in the armed forces to come to that conclusion.

Just kidding, he just made it up and blurted it out.

As far as I can tell, from conducting extensive research over the course of at least five minutes, Gavin Williamson has no military background of any kind whatsoever.

He used to work in a pottery firm that made plates and he keeps a tarantula in his office, so he was the obvious choice to be selected head of the Ministry of Defence.

If the enemy were to come after us with a ceramic dinner service, he'd be our man.

The Defence Secretary alerted us that Moscow has been photographing power stations and may be planning to damage the British economy and infrastructure.

This hot news must have come from a briefing note that had been sent in 1947. He's only just received it.

He said that Russian President, Vlad the Insaner, could target interconnectors, which link power between countries, potentially leaving millions of homes without electricity.

He could have said that the Russians might also target our train lines, leaving countless commuters stranded at home but Southern Rail has already done that.

Or he could have alerted us to a Russian plan to blow up the Moon or send a woman with daggers in her shoes to kick James Bond to death.

Literally anything could happen, and he wants to make sure we know that.

Mr Williamson said: 'The plan for the Russians won't be for landing craft to appear in the South Bay in Scarborough and on Brighton Beach… they are going to be thinking, 'How can we just cause so much pain to Britain?'

'Damage its economy, rip its infrastructure apart, actually cause thousands and thousands and thousands of deaths, but actually have an element of creating total chaos within the country.'

I would say that it is job done on that score.

Fomenting chaos is why they co-opted a bunch of oily charlatans and plied them with dodgy Russian money and used armies of internet trolls to seed discord with Brexit.

The pound tanked, we're all fighting with each other and our leaders are desperate to make trade deals with anyone that will sign one – and as you know, all the best deals are made from a position of weakness.

If that was the Russian's plan, it was executed with German efficiency.

Meanwhile, the head of the Army said Britain needed to 'keep up' with Putin's growing military strength or see our ability to take action 'massively constrained'.

So, at a time when the council is turning off the street lights and letting the roads go to pot and the NHS is refusing anyone that's not an emergency and the police won't come to your house for a burglary and has given up on shoplifters, all for a lack of cash, the thing on which we need to be spending more of the money we don't have is ever more exciting ways to kill people?

It couldn't possibly be that the military budget review is being written and everyone concerned is trying to ensure that no one gets a slice of their pie?

It all looks a bit like the Ministry of Defence just wants to shore up its case for the money to keep rolling in.

If the military's income is cut though, and the Russians do invade, at least Gavin could sick his spider on them.

02.02.18

Going for tea to China

The latest stop on Great Britain's glorious world tour of genuflection was in the Far East.

Mrs M. went to China to prostrate herself at the feet of the ruling emperor to beg forgiveness for the Opium Wars and see if she can't drum up a bit of trade on the other side of the planet to make up for the predicted shortfall caused by turning our backs on trade with our next door neighbours.

It went very well. They didn't arrest her once, and she came back with vague promises of business to be done.

Unfortunately, Britain cannot enter into any contractual obligation until we are free of the pernicious influence of the Evil European Unelected Socialist Superstate, so any pronouncements of deals made are a little premature, but the PM was in need of a good news story.

For the cameras, Mrs M made a perfunctory ten minute speech, light on concrete proposals, and drank a cup of (Chinese) tea.

The British delegation announced that the trip was a great success, truly this was the dawn of a global Britain, we are open for business, and all that old flannel.

Investment and trade deals worth a reported £9bn were trumpeted. There were no details forthcoming because there aren't any.

It was a vague promise that at some point in the future, if the wind is blowing in the right direction, the Chinese might invest but there seems little for them to buy here that the Qataris don't already own.

And anyway, we already do $79bn worth of business with them a year.

That trade is conducted on terms that were negotiated on behalf of the 512 million people of the EU, the most powerful trading block on earth.

Why would the Chinese offer us 65 million Britons better terms than those?

It's not as though being in the EU is holding us back either, Germany sells six times as much to the Chinese as we do.

What can we sell to them that they don't already buy from us, and vice versa?

It's not like we make much that they would want, apart from weapons of mass destruction and they seem to be self-sufficient in those as it is.

We could offer them the services of our banking racket but they appear to have that covered too.

The PM flew round half the world to make nice to the country that her security services say is a threat to our nation and came back with little to show for it.

At least she did not have to suck up to a mass murdering dictator and claim "shared values", as Liam Fox had to do in the Philippines.

That was a low point in the history of the nation.

In China, Theresa May did not have any problems with bringing up the human rights abuses of her hosts, in that she did not mention them at all.

You can't go to a place to ask for some loose change and also lecture them on arresting political opponents, lawyers and activists and the frequent use of torture, or chastise them for executing more people than the rest of the world combined.

The state controlled Chinese media congratulated the Prime Minister for ignoring the "nagging" and not bringing any of that up.

Instead, May confined herself to flattery and enthusiastic remarks about how lovely everything was.

We may have turned into an ethically vacuous grovelling lick-spittle on the world stage but at least we are getting our country back!

At home, the Brexiteer Ultras celebrated the great news of opaque assurances of future dealings.

They only just resisted the urge to wrap themselves in the flag, have a multiple patriot-gasm and announce that the Chinese need us more than we need them.

03.02.18

No ethics please, we're British

The Saudis are coming. Someone had better beat the dirt out of the red carpet.

We might not be able to afford to perform life-altering hip, knee and eye treatments on the NHS but we will certainly raid the bank to ingratiate ourselves with the new ruler of the House of Saud.

The Crown Prince Mohammed bin Salman will jet in to meet what are described as "senior royals".

That means you can relax Meghan, stand down Kate, this is a job for Granny.

Question: The Queen is always wheeled out to glad-hand the Saudis because

a) we think they are just our sort of people,

b) they have a celebrated record on human rights, or

c) they own all the money in the world that Amazon doesn't have.

There will probably be British protests over Saudi Arabia's human rights record and its conduct in the three-year Yemen civil war but the Queen will keep quiet and the government won't say a thing.

If the Saudis didn't live on a sea of sand where billions of years ago a mighty forest once stood and then died and turned into oil, they would be selling camel milk for a living and we wouldn't return their calls.

That is the essence of Britain's ethical foreign policy – we'll roll over and you can pat our stomach but only if you're loaded.

And this bloke is very loaded indeed.

As we are leaving the EU, our banking fraternity are making noises of disgruntlement. They will not countenance losing any money to Brexit, so it is very important for UK plc to bung them a bone.

The Saudi state oil group Aramco is the world's biggest and it is floating 5% of its value. Every stock market on earth wants a piece of that $2 trillion worth of action.

It would mean a waterfall of cash for any company that can insert itself into the process.

The fees to make it happen would amount to $1bn.

Imagine how much in bonuses that would pay for.

Never mind that the rules of the London Stock Exchange demand that at least 25% of any sovereign controlled company is offered in stocks to qualify for a listing.

Do you imagine that Donald Trump would be stymied by rules to encourage the Saudis to bring their business to the New York stock exchange?

Rules are for losers.

When the Prince arrives, we will ignore the anti-Iran stuff and the anti-Qatar stuff and the Yemen bombing and the subjugation of women and the medieval beliefs and terrorists that the Saudis are exporting to the world.

Meanwhile, British lawyers have submitted complaints to the UN human rights council on behalf of more than 60 Saudi human rights and political activists who were detained last September and in some cases have since disappeared.

We don't mind doing business with people like that because they have a pile of cash you could climb up to reach the Moon.

Should we secure their trade, there will dancing in the streets in the City of London.

There won't be any on the avenues of Saudi Arabia though, because that's against the law.

I am not making that up - this week, urgent demands were issued by the governor of Asir province, Prince Faisal bin Khaled that a couple filmed dancing in a street in the city of Abha should be investigated and arrested.

Last year, a 14 year old boy was arrested by the Saudi authorities for violating the public morals by dancing the Macarena outside, where people could see him.

Last month, a popular TV host in the country was arrested for "dabbing" on stage, a dance move that the Saudis say promotes a "narcotic culture".

The performer says he got carried away.

I should think he was - carried away in the back of a windowless van.

And what do these actions and the rest of their abuses of what we call basic human rights make them?

Nice people to do business with.

10.02.18

The wrong sort of billionaire.

The usual suspects went ape this week when it was revealed that a super-rich, foreign dwelling, off-shore based financier is using some of his vast wealth to attempt to engineer an exit from Brexit.

The right-wing press went into a fury that you could have spotted from the car that Elon Musk just sent to Mars on the world's most powerful rocket.

The force that missile created was as nothing compared to the splenetic rage that greeted the news that The Man Who Broke The Bank Of England, George Soros, is inveigling his way into the push for freedom from the evil empire of the EU.

The reason that the right went berserk is that the only outsiders they want interfering with our politics are THEIR super-rich, foreign dwelling, off-shore based financiers.

Practically every major donor to the Brexit cause has some tax efficient, accounting wheeze which registers their business address on a moon circling Uranus.

It's what rich people do to ensure that only we little people pay taxes.

Oddly, among those gilded elites, George Soros is the only one that has spoken up about how unfair it is that he pays so little in tax.

That's right – a billionaire actually wants to pay more tax to help society.

And he puts his money where his mouth is.

In another slap in the face to the hard right, Soros has spent huge funds on destabilising dictators and autocrats in his native Hungary as well as the Ukraine and Georgia.

He has used his billions on promoting civil rights and democracy and has given more money to charity than almost anyone else who has ever lived - £18bn of his £23bn fortune.

His foundation, Open Society, is the third biggest charitable body in the world and works globally to, as it puts it, "build vibrant and tolerant democracies".

He's spreading human rights and freedom and democracy. Clearly this madman must be stopped.

The Sun newspaper put it like this: "A RECLUSIVE billionaire with powerful friends, a track record for helping to topple governments and a wife half his age surely belongs in a Bond film."

They don't do self-reflection or irony at The Sun, unless that was a fantastic, dangerously overt dig at their own proprietor.

I doubt it. They weren't talking about a right-wing billionaire meddler, they were talking about a left-wing billionaire meddler – the worst kind!

The Mail, Telegraph, Sun and Express all railed at the 87-year-old George Soros for poking his nose into our affairs.

The thinking appears to be that he does not live here, he is not registered to pay tax here, so Brexit is none of his business.

Just one small point: the recent leaking of the Paradise Papers, which showed once again the lengths to which the rich and shameless go to secrete their wealth in off-shore bolt-holes, featured pretty much all of the leading players in Camp Brexit.

Much of the millions that poured in to the anti-EU campaign came from some decidedly dodgy characters who are no strangers to the ways of the secretive, tax averse, foreign based, wealth management business.

But the right wing press happens to agree with their viewpoint, so that's OK by them.

Relatively speaking, it seems like small change that Soros has donated £400,000 to the pro-EU campaign group, Best For Britain.

The group stands accused of using social media to try and convince us that leaving the EU might not be in our best interests.

My God – using social media to make a political argument!

No right-wingers would ever stoop to such tactics, just ask those keen promoters of Brexit, the foreign based, tax efficient, un-meddlesome Donald Trump and Vladimir Putin.

10.02.18

A problem with gas

British shale gas companies have said the business will finally begin in earnest this year, after last year passed without any serious fracking going on.

Industry insiders insist this year will mark that start of the process of hydraulic fracturing to extract gas trapped underground in shale rock.

In other news...new research suggests fracking is linked to breast cancer.

A US study found that chemicals used in the high-pressure extraction of oil and gas cause mutations in adult mice's mammary cells.

It is the same uncontrolled cell division that causes cancerous tumours in humans.

You may be thinking that they probably made the mice swim in a concentrated soup of the stuff to get those results, but no - the cell division happened when mice were exposed to the equivalent level of chemicals found in the drinking water of areas affected by fracking,

You may have seen the documentary footage of Americans lucky enough to be in fracking areas setting fire to their kitchen tap water. Who would have thought that drinking a flammable liquid could be bad for you?

Fracking involves drilling down into the earth before squirting a high-pressure mixture of poisonous chemicals into it to release all that delicious gas and oil stored in the rocks.

Campaigners say the use of potentially cancer-causing chemicals in fracking may contaminate local water supplies.

Concentrating selfishly on the health aspects of the process shows that they clearly do not appreciate the important point about this, which is how much money the frackers can make from it.

The protesters are wasting their time.

You know they are going to start fracking, no matter what, because according to the British Geological Survey, Britain is sitting on shale gas deposits that could supply the UK for 25 years.

There's a pile of untapped money you could fill a gasometer with in a swathe of land from Lancashire to Yorkshire and Lincolnshire.

They will probably be eyeing up locations near you, if they haven't already.

The public aren't keen – just 13% totally support it, but I bet 100% of those 13% don't want it happening anywhere near them.

Fortunately, the government will step in and protect us, just like they did with the car emissions scandal.

Oh, that's right, they didn't.

To prevent a repeat of that outrage, car manufacturers that cheat emissions tests are to face multi-million-pound fines in the future.

The key words in that sentence are the last three.

The government has leapt into action to protect us and punish wrong-doers by saying that they have no laws to prosecute the car giants for one of the biggest public health scandals of all time.

Apparently there is no law to prevent companies from poisoning the public deliberately in order to make more money.

If only there was, the government would definitely do something about it, don't you worry.

The Americans seem to have found a way – they have fined Volkswagen $4.3bn for their deeds.

We have fined them nothing at all.

Still, that same British government says that fracking is completely safe and there is nothing to worry about.

That's good enough for me!

I might buy a fire extinguisher for the kitchen sink though, just in case.

17.02.18

Times up for Tories?

It used to be that you could buy your own home if you had a normal job. People that worked as teachers and office managers, plumbers or drivers could afford to buy a place to call their own.

Even nurses used to be able to afford one and doctors could have one with its own front door on a street in Chelsea.

These days, you would need to a doctorate in mathematics and have sold your soul to work in a hedge fund to get a house in SW3.

Twenty years ago, when young middle-class professionals used to rave all weekend to house music, they were twice as likely to get their own place as their modern equivalents who strive all weekend to buy a house.

A report by the Institute for Fiscal Studies said that just one in four young middle-income families now owns their own home.

It was two in three in the 1990s.

It means people with ordinary jobs are now stuck renting into their thirties, or forties, or forever.

This is very bad news for the Conservative Party.

The Tories are not building enough homes, just like the government before them and the one before that.

In fact, Britain has not built enough homes in pretty much any year since the Second World War.

As usual, short termism is the cause. Successive governments have reneged on their duty to provide shelter for all and simply aimed their policies at those who already had one: older people.

Unfortunately for the Tories, time does not stand still and those older people are falling off life's conveyor belt and are not being replaced with new home owners.

Young people are now as likely to own their own home as they are to vote Tory, and that's the problem for the party in blue.

The young used to vote for left wing parties and gradually shifted to the right over time.

You care about people more when you are young and you haven't had the joy of life beaten out of you.

When you're young you are starry-eyed about the possibilities available to you and not yet miserable that life has not come up to your expectations; you have hopes and dreams and you haven't yet given up hopes of fulfilling them.

So the young vote left - the caring wing of the political spectrum.

When they got old though, they'd acquired things that they wanted to protect, and that's when they used to start to vote for right-wing parties.

When they have a house and a pension and assets, people tend to vote Tory because that's the kind of party that will be more likely to let them hang on to their wealth and not distribute it for the benefit of others less fortunate.

That equation is now broken.

Young people aren't buying houses and they don't have pensions and they haven't gathered any wealth.

Why would they start voting for a right-wing party, if they don't have anything to protect?

It is likely that they will continue to vote for left wing parties, unless someone comes along and persuades them that the reason they haven't done well is not the stupid government or the evil multinationals, or the way the tax laws are written by and for the rich, it is the fault of someone below them on the ladder of life, and that's where so-called populism comes in.

The Tories need to give people easily identified minorities to hang the blame on – if only there weren't so many foreigners vying for houses and cheap foreign labour, who are more eager and work harder, or just generally people "comin over 'ere", then they would be able to have their own home.

That is the message they need to promote to keep the young on-side.

In short, they need to do a Donald Trump.

He blamed the Mexicans but we have the EU and as long as Theresa May doesn't do anything to stem the flow of immigrants, it just might work.

But she is currently engaged in doing just that.

And when the immigrants stop coming, who will the young be persuaded to blame then?

Anyone want to bet against Jeremy Corbyn becoming our next PM?

18.02.18

Marking your own homework.

How much do you value your own work?

How do you think you are doing?

What would you give yourself out of ten?

If you are Britishly modest and self-effacing, then you will probably have thought something along the lines of: I am doing quite well, not bad really and I would give myself a six...maybe a seven out of ten on a good day.

But what if I put it like this: how much money do you think you should be earning?

What if you were allowed to set your own pay? How much would you value your efforts then?

Exactly.

You would be stinking rich by this time next week. And that is precisely why university vice-chancellors make so much.

A freedom of information request by the University and College Union, which represents university staff, found that 95% of university leaders are either members of their own remuneration committee or entitled to attend their meetings.

Vice-chancellors are paying themselves inflated salaries via "shadowy" remuneration committees meeting in secret behind closed doors.

They have read of bankers doing that and they think that just because they don't really do much for a living, why shouldn't they get telephone number salaries too?

The FOI request also asked institutions to send full minutes of the most recent meeting of their remuneration committee.

Almost none of them complied, for obvious reasons.

Don't worry though, because the body that represents vice-chancellors is on the case.

The Committee of University Chairs published guidelines on executive pay just last month. It stated that VC's should not sit on their own remuneration committees.

So, problem solved, case closed, move along please, nothing to see here.

Except for one small detail: it's voluntary.

Vice-chancellors can voluntarily refuse to sit in on the meeting that sets their own pay and not vote stratospheric wage rises for themselves.

But why would they?

If you could set your own salary, why would you voluntarily choose not to?

Some vice-chancellors think they're worth half a million quid a year, and they say so, and they get it.

Student's degrees might be costing them an arm and a leg, and they may not be able to pay the debt off for years, if ever, and the qualification they come out with might not be worth much because the quality of teaching is not reflected in the cost of their degree, but not to worry – at least there's one person making a ton of money out of it.

That is one reason why their tuition costs over 9 grand a year – so that the ceremonial leader of the institution that is putting them in debt for the rest of their lives can go on living in the manner to which they have recently become accustomed.

And it is only recently that this has happened

The average pay for vice-chancellors in 2005/06 was £165,105 plus pensions and accommodation and expenses and etc.

That went up by 56% over the next decade to £257,904 in 2015/16.

Don't fret though, because the body that regulates universities is on the case.

The Office for Students has just come into being and is tasked with representing the interests of students.

They will certainly address this spiralling wage bill for executives who preside over institutions that have decidedly mixed results on student satisfaction.

Unfortunately, its own chief executive, the person in charge of regulating the vice chancellors, is the former chief lobbyist for...the vice-chancellors.

22.02.18

Digging in for the 'do.

There's is a school in Great Yarmouth that was doing very badly. Its exam results were some of the worst in the country.

They recorded pass rates of just 30% in English and Maths at GCSE, which would be great if those pupils wanted to become radio talk show hosts, for example, but pretty much useless for anything else.

So they did something about it. They appointed a new headmaster, renowned for his tough approach to discipline.

His thinking is that if students are paying attention to what he teacher says, rather than gawping at their phones or doing their make-up, they might learn something.

In order to instil the right attitude, new head teacher, Barry Smith, announced to the parents that certain hairstyles were not acceptable in school.

He sent out a letter to the families before Christmas saying that the new rules will be applied from the 26th of this month, giving them over eight weeks to comply.

Of course, the parents were fully supportive of these demands, recognising that their off-springs' education was of the utmost importance.

Just kidding – they had a purple fit of rage that Stevie Wonder could have seen through walls.

They said, "Dahnchoo tell me what to do wiv my kids...it's my right, I can do what I want", or words to that effect.

It's not as though the haircuts are worth fighting over. They are as comically hideous as any adopted by 15 year-olds since teenagers were invented.

Specifically, the cut in question is what the kids call the "Meet me at McDonalds".

Presumably, this is because the sort that sports such a 'do hangs out there, stuffing their fat faces with cow parts and grease, as a between-meals snack, wiping their hands down their nylon track suits, checking their hair in the reflection in the window, texting their mates to see what they have doing since they last texted them ten seconds ago, and spitting.

This particular cut is mostly close shaved with a long perm on top, cascading over their squinty little eyes.

They look like they've been caught in an explosion in a pubic hair factory – it is short at the sides and curled and piled on top like they're wearing a poodle as a hat.

That may ring a bell. It is the same haircut worn by the New Romantics of the 1980's.

Acts like Boy George and Adam and the Ants used to wear it.

Parents are digging their heels in, demanding their right to send their kids out looking like Kajaoogoo!

They must think that their progeny will all grow up to be famous, so why do they need to learn things?

Posting a letter about it on social media, one mother said it was 'absolutely ridiculous'.

Another said: 'You can't take time off sick as it affects your education...but they will happily send you home because they don't like your hairstyle.'

No, they won't...they will send your child home if you don't obey a school rule that you've known about for two months

Another said: 'I think it is all getting silly now, a hairstyle does not affect a child's learning.'

But an attitude against the school you're in will.

It is not the first time that this headmaster has come against the immovable object that is a parent's fury at someone trying to help them overcome their stupidity.

Mr Smith previously threatened to deprive pupils of their mobile phones, and asked that they follow the teachers with their eyes when in class.

In other words: pay attention, this stuff might be boring and won't affect your ability to be a reality television star but on the off-chance you don't win the lottery, it's important.

Hard to believe that they needed telling that, but the school's dismal exam record before he got there suggests that the new head should be given all the encouragement the parents can muster.

After all, learning something in class might be the only hope their children have of leaving Great Yarmouth.

24.02.18

Insulting without trying

In this parallel, through-the-looking-glass universe of weirdness that we are living in now, what someone says on the internet is news and the reaction of others to that original message is also news.

In the interests of going with the flow, here's a good one:

A Conservative association has reportedly been "slammed" over a tweet suggesting that families unable to live off £10 a week were 'indolent or dysfunctional'.

Saying they've been slammed sounds like some livid bug-eyed giant picked the whole place up and smashed it in to the ground – and I suppose that's just what happened.

The bug-eyed giant being the combined force of the incensed on Twitter, which seems to be the repository of all that is raging and screaming and furious.

A post from the Bath Conservative Association addressed food poverty among the less well off in the area and cited the food campaigner Jack Monroe's blog about struggling to feed her child.

It read: 'The reality may be indolent or dysfunctional parents or more likely parents who simply don't know how to feed their children well. If absolutely-not-a-Tory Jack Monroe could feed herself & her child for £10 a week - not easily, but adequately - most people can.'

That message, posted on the official Twitter feed of the Bath Conservative Association was immediately disowned by...the Bath Conservative Association.

Why distance themselves from it? Why would anyone think that it was outrageous that the Tory party would be dismissive and arrogant about the desperate poor?

I thought that was their thing.

You know...Labour are all about the workers down t'pit and the Tories are for the evil landowner in the big house at the top of the hill.

Just look at that cartoon top-hatted toff Jacob Rees-Mogg – would you be entirely surprised if his afternoon tea was made from orphan's tears?

The Tories are so comically moustache twirlingly nasty that they even have to keep denying that they are the nasty party.

The Greens do not have to keep denying how nasty they are and neither do the Lib Dems or the Monster Raving Loony Party, despite the fact that they have the words "monster" and "raving" right there in their name.

So who could be remotely surprised that a Conservative association would think insulting things about those less fortunate than them, saying that those mothers who cannot feed themselves and their child on £10 a week are indolent or dysfunctional?

I thought that's what the Tories believed, but I may have that wrong.

They may be the nice party and I am mixing them up with someone else.

The best part was their apology – and I am not making this up - they apologised for what they said was: "a single thoughtless tweet on food poverty, not intended to insult"!

Calling poor people indolent and dysfunctional was not meant to insult them?

That's about the most thick-headed thing I've ever heard – and if they are upset that I would say that, then I'm sorry, I didn't mean "think headed" to be insulting.

02.03.18

Collapsing in the face of adversity

On the east coast of the USA, they have just experienced a winter storm. They called it a "bombogenesis".

"Snowmageddon" was already taken and "All Out Thermonuclear Stormtastrophe" seemed over the top even for weather forecasters.

Boston suffered a four foot storm surge that led to people kayaking to work through flooded streets and lorries were swept away by waves.

Winds of hurricane velocity brought two feet of snow and two million people were without power.

In Great Britain, a light dusting of the white stuff caused the entire country to fall flat on its face, as it does every time it snows a very little here.

Commuters were the first to suffer.

Railway stations in London urged workers to abandon the office and make their way home before 3pm. They turned people away and closed the platforms at 8 in the evening.

People were stranded in town with no way to get home. They were the lucky ones. At least they could repair to the pub.

Rail passengers mutineered outside Lewisham station when their service came to a halt and prised the doors open to make their escape on the live tracks.

The electric rails had to be shut off and Southeastern Railways had to plead with the remaining travellers to stay on board because a lot of dead people on the line might hold up the service even more.

One train that did manage to leave Waterloo came to a halt and stayed still for ten hours.

Still, it could have been worse – over 50 people were stranded on a train headed for Weymouth for 15 hours without heating or toilets.

One man was pictured sleeping on the luggage rack. Others took their minds off their predicament by dancing to the music of Madonna.

The driver locked himself in his compartment and refused to come out, or explain what was going on, or when their ordeal might end.

Cruelly for those on board, at about 2.30 in the morning, the train did judder into action, moved about a foot and then stopped again.

That must have seemed like they were being tortured.

Meanwhile, the roads were without incident as drivers were taking extra care in the terrible conditions.

Of course I am kidding. Kent police, for instance, received 100 calls about car crashes in the space of 30 minutes and the AA said over 13,000 "incidents" had occurred since the bad weather hit.

Thousands of drivers that had ignored the "don't travel unless absolutely necessary" warnings were stuck on roads brought to a standstill by blizzards and accidents.

Hospitals cancelled even more operations than normal and ambulance crews pleaded for the help of 4x4 owners to get them to where they needed to be.

Ten thousand properties were without power in the South West, the army was called out to rescue trapped drivers in Hampshire, the RAC were called to over 8,000 breakdowns, hundreds of flights were cancelled from airports in London, Edinburgh, Dublin and Bristol and supermarket shelves were stripped bare by panic buyers .

Can you imagine what would have happened if we'd had a bombogenesis? The entire country would have flipped upside down and would be sinking and on fire.

The worst is now over, though, and we can congratulate ourselves on getting through it.

This will never happen again. Until next year when a perfectly ordinary winter day brings to this first world country the sort of chaos that would shame a third world one.

03.03.18

It's war! Heel spurs notwithstanding.

President Donald Trump - that still sounds weird, over a year after he took office.

It's like saying: Prime Minister Dale Winton. It will never seem normal.

Anyway, Ancient Orange has done the one thing he has omitted so far in his race to be the most popular president ever, ever, ever. He has started a war.

Of course, there were his Twitter wars with various celebrities, sports stars, Miss Worlds, families of dead soldiers, fellow Republicans, journalists, staff, ex-staff, sexual abuse accusers, foreign dignitaries, foreign countries and television programmes, but they don't count.

There was the war on guns that he prosecuted for the five minutes between the latest school mass shooting and the meeting he took with a representative of the gun lobby, who reminded him of the thirty million reasons why he should allow the weapons manufacturers to sell whatever they want to whomever will buy them.

Those reasons were green and all had a picture of George Washington on one side and were given to him by the gun lobby to help him to beat Hilary

Those were not real wars. This war is for real. Not so real that he would fake a growth on his heel bone to get out of. Not the shooting kind. The money kind.

In a series of tweets that started before 6am, presumably from the golden throne, he started a trade war with America's chief trading partners.

The leader of the free trade, globalisation-is-good party said he will slap 25% tariffs on foreign steel and 10% on aluminium.

He explained, in capitals with exclamation marks, that he was doing this because the way other countries were treating America was UNFAIR!

And if these other countries didn't like what he was doing and responded with their own tariffs on US goods, then he promised "RECIPROCAL TAXES".

"Reciprocal" might be the longest and most complicated word that he has ever tweeted. That is a measure of how upset he is pretending to be.

In Donny's explaining, he is protecting the US metals industries and the forgotten working men. In reality, he is desperately attempting to boost his popularity in the blue collar states, which are somehow not yet 100% in support.

VERY UNFAIR!

The grown-ups in the Whitehouse and his party were aghast. They will have to set their morning alarms earlier to catch him before he does anything else unscripted and unsupervised.

They must have thought they had successfully advised him against this decision.

Gary Cohn, his top economic adviser, reportedly threatened to resign if he went ahead. Treasury Secretary Steven Mnuchin told Trump that the stock market gains he loves to boast about would collapse and Defence Secretary James Mattis, told him that a trade war would hurt U.S. relationships with its allies.

Like a puppy, however, if you leave him unsupervised, he will pee on the carpet.

Trump said that trade wars are a good thing and easy to win.

What he knows about business you could write on his bald spot with a paint roller.

The kind of trade war he is proposing will hurt the very same types who show up to his rallies sporting gun holsters and Make America Great Again hats.

Tariffs is another word for taxes and they are paid by the people doing the consuming, not the people doing the manufacturing.

The yeehas doing the whooping and hollering when he says things like "lock her up" and "gonna build a wall" will be the ones out of pocket when the price of everything from toasters to cars goes up as a result of this war.

And when Canada and China respond with tariffs on, say, US farm exports like corn and beef, then it is the rural poor – his base support – that will suffer the most.

The British steel industry will not get off lightly either. It is only just surviving and profit margins are low.

Theresa May may live to rue the day she helped him down that very scary, tiny little ramp when she went to prostrate herself in front of him at the Whitehouse.

If this is a special relationship, what's a not special one like?

10.03.18

What rubbish!

In order to stem the tide of thrown away plastic, the government has proposed a latte levy.

As usual, our leaders merely proposed the idea and then did nothing. Doing nothing is what they are good at.

If doing nothing were an Olympic event, every four years our government would be on the podium, tears in eyes, watching the Union flag being raised while that dirge about giving our best stuff to the queen rings out.

Theresa May has probably figured that such a tax on single-use coffee cups is not something the public are passionate about, so it is fairly safe to place it on the not-to-do list.

The phrase "latte levy" might be the problem.

It sounds like the most middle class, entitled, soft southern thing you have ever heard. It's like proposing a Barbour wax jacket tax or a tariff on truffles from Fortnum & Mason.

The benign name hides an awful truth, though. In this country, we throw away almost a half a million plastic lined paper coffee cups every day, of which about 0.25% are recycled.

Despite that, having weighed the options, ministers have rejected calls for a latte levy on takeaway coffee cups to reduce the amount of waste they create.

The government has bravely decided to do nothing about a problem in case the electorate doesn't like it.

The same thing happened with the plastic bag tax.

Once introduced, it reduced the number of plastic bags given out and thrown away by 85%.

The government likes to take great credit for that but it waited an embarrassingly long time before it acted, timidly waiting to see what happened in other countries to see whether governments overseas were hauled over the coals by a furious electorate who were denied their placcy bag rights.

Denmark was one of the first to adopt the idea, as you would expect.

Aren't they always so perfect?

The Danes introduced a plastic bag tax in 2003. It took our government 12 years to catch up, so desperately frightened they were about making any sudden moves.

Ireland introduced a levy on throwaway bags a year earlier in 2002, so its not as though we didn't have an English speaking example nearby to follow.

We were one of the last countries on earth to make the change – China, Australia, Brazil, Mexico, France, Bangladesh, Belgium - you name it they did it before we did.

We were pathetically slow to catch up, and the government is still gripped by a paralysis, a desperate fear of doing something that might get them bad press or a thumbs down emoji on Twitter.

The chair of the environmental audit committee, accused the government of talking warm words but taking no action on Britain's terrible record of recycling.

We recycle about 44% of household waste in England, according to the government's own figures, about the same rate as two years ago.

In Wales, they manage over 57%, so it can be done but only if those in power feel the need to act.

Environment secretary Michael Gove feels no such need. He again failed to introduce a plastic bottle deposit scheme, despite Theresa May saying that she was declaring war on single-use plastic.

Not so much war as capitulation.

She said she was considering policies including a tax on takeaway containers.

Saying she might do something cancels the need to, you know, actually do something.

The other way to avoid action is to have a consultation. They take ages and by the time they report their findings, the likelihood is everyone will have forgotten all about the issue and will be concentrating on something else.

A consultation by the Department for Environment, Food and Rural Affairs (Defra) on a plastic deposit scheme was carried out last autumn but the government has not published it.

There's money well spent.

Another consultation announced in November by the chancellor, Philip Hammond, into taxes and charges on takeaway packaging and plastic bottles has yet to be launched three months later.

In the meantime, ministers can excuse not doing anything because they don't want to prejudge the findings of the consultation.

The environmental audit committee's key recommendation on reducing coffee cup waste was the introduction of a 25p levy to help fund recycling measures.

That would help change behaviour, might help create less waste and be a benefit to us all in the present and the future.

Instead of that risky endeavour, ministers have chosen to ask coffee companies to voluntarily print an anti-littering message on their throw away cups.

That's our forward thinking, all-action, go-getter British government in action.

10.03.18

A robust response

The Foreign Secretary announced that Britain would not hesitate to impose a new punishment on Russia if it was found to be responsible for the suspected attack on Russian spy Sergei Skripal in Salisbury on Sunday.

That might have carried more weight if our Foreign Secretary was not Boris 'Bozo of the F.O.' Johnson.

He's the man that got stuck on a zip-wire and flattened a ten year old in a rugby 'friendly' on a diplomatic trip to Japan.

It is doubtful that he puts the willies up Vladimir Putin.

And besides, he threatened a new punishment, which implies that we are already punishing them. What does that entail? Overcharging them for mansions in Chelsea?

If Russia is found to be behind the poisoning of its ex-agent, the very serious repercussions that Bozo is considering include a partial boycott of the World Cup in Russia this summer.

At first, I thought that seemed cruel to the footballers who dreamed of representing their country in their inevitable defeat to the Germans in the quarter finals on penalties.

That is not what he has in mind though.

The partial boycott that Boris is cooking up would mean that our footballers would travel without their diplomatic outriders.

He's threatening Russia with an absence of official British hangers-on at their World Cup.

That'll teach 'em!

Mr Johnson said: 'I think it will be difficult to see how, thinking ahead to the World Cup this summer, I think it would be difficult to imagine that UK representation at that event could go ahead in the normal way. We will certainly have to consider that.'

That is the firm action of a confident British government.

Furthermore, we could refuse to send the Russians an Easter card or we could cut back on our vodka consumption.

Bozo of the FO insisted any attempt to kill on British soil 'will not go unsanctioned or unpunished'.

Recent history tells us otherwise.

Did we do anything about Alexander Litvinyenko who was killed on British soil in 2006 by polonium, which could only have come from a nuclear reactor, thereby sending a message that a state was behind it?

A judge said was probably approved by President Vladimir Putin.

Then there was Russian millionaire Alexander Perepilichnyy, a key witness in a £140million tax fraud investigation, collapsed in November 2012.after he ingested gelsemium – a very rare toxic plant found only in China,and a known method of assassination by Russian contract killers.

Did we do anything then?

A radiation expert who investigated the 'assassination' of Alexander Litvinenko was found dead in a mysterious suicide five months after a trip to Russia.

No action on our part.

The Foreign Secretary told MPs the Government would stand up for the 'lives, values and freedoms' of people in Britain.

But apparently not if it means actually doing anything.

Shadow defence secretary Diane Abbott warned ministers not to allow 'London and the Home Counties to become a kind of killing field for the Russian state'.

Defence Secretary Gavin Williamson repeated warnings of the military threat from Russia, warning Putin had 'hostile intent' toward Britain.

He said that the Kremlin had developed a much more aggressive posture towards the UK in the past 12 months and the country should not sit submissively by.

But that's what we're good at.

Boris Johnson told the Commons: 'I can reassure the House that should evidence emerge that implies state responsibility, then Her Majesty's Government will respond appropriately and robustly.'

How will Vladimir Putin sleep after hearing that?

Quite soundly I would imagine.

16.03.18

A sternish response

The Russian government stands accused of poisoning people in this country. This is very serious. The only people who are allowed to poison people in this country are the British government.

Just ask the 3,400 servicemen who were used as human guinea pigs for nerve agent experiments at our top secret Porton Down chemical weapons facility in Wiltshire. If you can find any of them still alive, that is.

Porton tested more human subjects with nerve gas, for the longest period of time, than any other scientific establishment on earth.

The substance that killed Kim Jong-un's half-brother in Malaysia – the ultra-deadly VX nerve agent – that was ours. We invented that.

What we don't know about deadly chemicals you could write on a CS gas canister.

So we know a poisoning when we see it and if it was a Russian victim, it stands to reason it was a Russian state perpetrator, no proof needed, case closed, off to war.

Not a real war, of course, a pretend war of stern speeches and diplomatic toing and froing.

We must show Vlad that we are very cross but not so cross that he and his oligarch chums take all of their money out of the country.

We want them to feel chastised but not so much that they stem the stream of billions of dodgy roubles that grease the wheels of the money laundering operation that the banks and the legal and accounting firms in the Square Mile specialise in. To say nothing of the high-end estate agents in the pricier parts of prime central London.

We want to give them a yellow card, not have them pick up the ball and storm off home.

To that end, Mrs May deployed Her Majesty's Principal Secretary of State for Defence, also known as head of the Ministry of Defence.

That is an impressive brace of titles.

You might expect, that as the trumpets sound and the Secretary of State for Defence is announced, around the corner would hove a person of impressive stature, an individual to be reckoned with, a person that would give the collywobbles to any Johnny Foreigner that wanted to mess with us.

And it is true – Gavin Williamson, our Defence Secretary, is a very impressive figure, in that he looks quite tall.

He has the crooked mien of a man who has spent his life stooping through doorways.

As a figure of international power and capability, however, he is as imposing as our other top diplomat, that roly-poly jolly figure of fun, Bozo of the F.O., our Foreign Secretary.

On the Russian poisoning, the Defence chief squeaked that Russia should "go away and shut up".

He looked like a 14 year old telling off his annoying sister for reading his diary.

The Russians looked at this outburst and could barely contain their laughter.

They wheeled out the Russian Ministry of Defence spokesman Major-General Igor Konashenkov, who looks like he rips the heads of grizzly bears, just for the fun of it.

He said, that our Gavin was speaking like a "market wench", which I think is an insult, and that "The rhetoric demonstrated today by the head of the British Defence Ministry Gavin Williamson is remarkable for his extreme degree of intellectual impotence".

He was not finished – the Major-General announced that Mr Williamson is a disgrace to Britain and is acting like a pre-pubescent schoolboy.

Ouch. That must have hurt.

You may be thinking, as the Russians surely are: who is this Gavin Williamson?

Well, he was elevated to the post of the Defence Secretary in November 2017 by the Drear Leader Theresa May.

This came as something of a surprise to many as he has very little military background.

He may have once owned an Action Man, but that's about it.

On the other hand, he does have a BSc in Social Sciences from the University of Bradford and did once work for a company that makes pots, so at least he has that valuable experience.

Plus, he keeps a tarantula in his room.

And what kind of person keeps a tarantula in their room?

That's right – a pre-pubescent schoolboy.

17.03.18

Who's playing footsie with the Russians?

Jeremy Corbyn was accused of being an "apologist for Russia" after suggesting that it might be the actions of a responsible government to acquire some actual evidence of wrongdoing before it starts hostilities with a despot in charge of nuclear weapons.

The Labour leader's not capturing the mood of the nation, intoned the press. We want punishment first, evidence later, they said.

He's thwarting The Will of the People!

I know that it is suddenly fashionable to attend to the mood of the populace by those that wanted us out of the EU, but they would not be saying that if they had lost the referendum, and it isn't really the basis of a coherent government strategy.

If we went to enact the will of the people at every turn, then we would be at war with Germany, in expectation of them beating us in the forthcoming World Cup, and Ant would be Prime Minister and Dec would be the Secretary of Defence.

I think the Russians probably did poison their ex-spy but I can't prove it and neither can the government.

We don't even know how they were poisoned, or where, so how can we possibly know with great certainty who poisoned them?

We can assume the Russians did it, but then we assumed that Saddam Hussein had weapons of mass destruction that could deliver catastrophe to London in less than 45 minutes, or your money back.

We assumed the world's economy was going great guns 5 minutes before the start of the biggest recession in history.

We assumed that the American people would elect a stable genius. Only that assumption was correct though, and we know that because he told us so himself.

The story of the poisoning has curiously morphed into the story of Jeremy Corbyn's failure to back the government in leaping to expensive conclusions and of being too enamoured of the Russians.

He is a communist after all.

Well, he isn't, as far as I can tell and neither is Vladimir Putin.

If either main political party can be accused of cosying up to Russia, it is surely the Conservatives who have more evidence against them.

It is true that Labour have more money coming in from unions than any other source but that is hardly a surprise. They are supposed to be the party of the working man and woman.

Yet this fact is constantly touted by the press as being somehow suspect. In May 2017, the Telegraph reported that Labour's General Election campaign was being funded almost entirely by union donations. Disgraceful!

Compare the amount brought in by both parties during the election campaign last year.

A record £40m of donations poured into British politics in the three months before the election.

The Conservative party raised almost £25m while there was only £9.5m for Labour.

Furthermore, the bulk of Labour's income came from unions but most of the Tory party's funds came from wealthy individuals and companies.

There was £1.5m from JCB, the company linked to a Conservative peer who also helped fund the Brexit campaign.

A hedge fund manager, a theatrical impresario, and the founder of the giant Addison Lee taxi firm all gave over £1 million each.

Political donations of over £7,500 must be registered by name. Eleven percent of those donations to the Tories came from people with fancy titles.

Which sounds as though it would be more likely to enact the will of the greatest number of people - a party funded by organisations that represent millions or one bankrolled by a few vastly rich individuals?

The Unite union represents 1.4m people – Sir and Lady Bufton Fortescue-Smythe represent only themselves.

But it is worse than that.

While the Labour leader is accused of being too close to the Russians, it is the Conservatives who are surfing on a tide of roubles – three million pounds worth since 2010.

In 2015 an analysis by Deutsche Bank suggested that since the mid-1970s much of the new money that has washed through the Tory supporting City of London has come from one country in particular: Russia.

They said a good deal of the £133bn of dodgy money that comes through London's banks is related to Russia.

But don't take their word for it - in December 2017 our own National Crime Agency said as much as £90bn of criminal money is laundered through the UK each year.

In 2016, the Financial Times said an insider at a Swiss bank warned Britain's financial watchdogs that bankers in its UK office were offering services that could facilitate tax evasion and money laundering.

He also told the US authorities. The Americans took it very seriously. The British merely said that they were concerned and then did nothing.

As far back as 2011, the Financial Times reported that Tory MPs' desire to cut the 50p top rate of income tax is because rich City donors are so close to the party.

The Tories are funded by the banks and the banks are enjoying standing under a waterfall of iffy money coming from Russia.

The leader of the Labour Party isn't the red under the bed.

It is the leader of the Conservative Party that is embarrassingly pink.

24.03.18

Petty in pink

I just got my new passport.

I'm not going anywhere but it was going to expire, so I thought I had better re-new it, just in case I win the lottery and can go on holiday, or I need proof of age when buying the lottery ticket in the first place.

Imagine my surprise when what arrived was not a handsome blue we've-got-our-country-back proper British passport, but a dark red one with the words European bloomin' Union at the top, above where it says United Kingdom of Great Britain.

Above it!

We don't want to be forced to carry pink identification, as that Tory MP Andrew Rossindale pointed out.

And it didn't make him a preposterous twit for saying that something is pink that is obviously a dark red burgundy.

Pink is a colour with connotations, and I think that's what he was going for when he said, "The humiliation of having a pink European Union passport will now soon be over and the United Kingdom nationals can once again feel pride and self-confidence in their own nationality when travelling, just as the Swiss and Americans can do"

Andrew Rossindale, Conservative MP, is the same top-notch parliamentarian that used his time in office to table an early day motion calling for the national anthem to be played at the end of the day on BBC1, like in the good old days.

I expect he represents excellent value for money for the taxpayer – he's just the sort of fellow we need in high office, bending his considerable talents at solving the big issues of the day.

Let's leave aside the fact that if the pride of the country depends on the shade of its travel documents then we are in a very sad place indeed.

Let's also gloss over the truth that we could have had the blue colour all along; there are no rules about that in the EU. Our government chose to have burgundy, it was not a stipulation from Brussels.

The issue of the day is that the new passport printing contract did not go to a British company. The government selected a Franco-Dutch firm for the contract because it saved the British public the not insignificant amount of £120m.

Shares in the suspiciously foreign sounding De La Rue, the maker of the UK's current burgundy passports, fell after it heard the news.

The rabid right-wing press wrapped themselves in the flag and had a patriot-gasm.

The papers that are owned by off-shore trusts to reduce their tax liabilities in this country spied an opportunity to posture as the saviours of British Britain.

If they cared so much, you might think they would not go to such lengths to deprive the country of so much desperately needed tax.

It's a puzzler.

What is not puzzling is that the government was doing its duty to save the public a vast sum that could be better spent on, oh I don't know, the NHS for instance, or weapons of mass destruction.

A bad use of public funds would be to spend it on a specific business, that made £58m in profit last year, at the expense of the competition.

It would also set a dangerous precedent if they did.

Should we now subsidise every home grown company to protect it from foreign competitors?

That sounds like it would put up the prices of everything.

Besides, if the public do not support British business, why should the government do so with the public's money?

We don't buy British clothes and we don't buy British cars, or fridges or phones or stereos or televisions or computers.

We don't even buy British apples – 70% of the apples we eat are imported.

The reason we don't buy British is because we don't like what we produce and it's more expensive than the alternatives.

Why on this one thing – passports - a thing most of us will hardly ever use, do we get all jingoistic and protectionist?

I know why the press do it – that old refrain of "I love my country more than you do" sells papers and lets them claim the nationalistic, moral high ground, where their tax-avoiding owners do not belong.

The readers of those papers have no such excuse though.

We stopped buying British a long time ago and thought nothing of it.

The result is that shops closed, companies were sold overseas, businesses went bust and factories were shuttered.

It's a bit late to claim buyer's remorse and demand Britain first now.

24.03.18

Famous Fop Goes Fishing.

Nigel Farage went fishing this week, sporting a brown pin-striped suit, cufflinks, a spotted silk tie and a melancholy look on his face.

He didn't quite get the hang of it – you're supposed to pull live fish from the river and put them in the boat, not arrive with dead fish and throw them in the water.

Still, practice makes perfect – if at first you get it all wrong, read a manual. He could bone up on it while being fitted for a sou'wester.

The act of fishing itself was not the issue. As it was our Nige, the issue was, of course, the EU.

The Prime Minister, Mrs M, has agreed to remain within the EU's Common Fisheries Policy for around 20 months after Britain's glorious exit on March 29, 2019.

Farage needed to display his displeasure. He has a history of showing the utmost concern for the plight of the British fishermen, having gone to fully one of the 42 meetings of the EU's Fisheries Committee, of which he is a member.

One out of 42. That shows commitment to the cause.

He highlighted to the attending press that we should think of all those fish that are ours by right that will be caught by representatives of the Unelected European Socialist Superstate.

What no-one seemed to question was our right to those fish.

Why are the fish ours?

Fish don't vote, they don't have nationality, they move about – why do they become ours the moment they swim to within a certain arbitrarily determined distance from our coast?

Why aren't they Iceland's? If they swim past Iceland before they get here, then they should be caught by their country of origin shouldn't they?

If refugees come to Europe, people say that they should stay in the first country they arrive in, so why is it the opposite for other species?

The fish aren't British any more than the air that crosses the country is British – they belong to Europe because that's where most of them get born and live and die.

And besides – according to government figures, 3 of the top 5 most valuable UK fisheries are for shellfish – prawns, scallops and crabs.

They live nearby, don't move about like other fish and we have almost complete control over them. We have exclusive access to waters six miles from our coasts.

We don't like that stuff much though. We export 85% of it, mostly to...the EU.

The British consumer prefers the white, bland fish that swims further out, in what not even the most ardent patriot would call our waters.

British fishermen feel ignored and fear for a dying industry but pretty much every manual labourer could say the same over the past 40 years.

Coal miners, ship builders and factory workers have all suffered job losses, or the total collapse of their industries.

Fishing has been affected but not as much as some trades.

According to the government's own figures, there were an estimated 11,757 fishermen in 2016, down 9 per cent since 2006.

What manual industry hasn't seen a 9% fall in employment since 2006?

In 2016, UK vessels landed 701 thousand tonnes of sea fish (including shellfish) into the UK and abroad with a value of £936 million. This represents a 21 percent increase in value, compared with 2015.

Fish imports are more or less what they were in 2006 and exports are more or less the same too.

If you dangled that state of affairs in front of the British steel worker, they'd take it hook, line and sinker.

30.03.18

My rocket's bigger than your rocket.

Vladimir Putin test fired Russia's new Sarmat intercontinental ballistic missile this week. He got it on video, so we could celebrate the launch too.

This supposedly 'invincible' hypersonic weapon can duck and weave its way to the intended target, thus outwitting any response from clunky old western military defence systems, which can't duck and think weaving is for sissies.

Putin looked as pleased with himself as anyone could without actually bursting out laughing.

The jaunty black and white chequered rocket popped out of the ground like a whack-a-mole, paused as though to check its route, then blasted off into the sky so as to rain down his displeasure on anyone he can't kill by poison.

It is a hypersonic weapon, has a speed of Mach 20, and can carry about ten tonnes of Russian ill will.

That is not the full extent of their new weaponry though. The Russians also showed off the Avangard hypersonic glide vehicle, which sounds like something Superman might use when he's too tired to fly.

Each one of those can sport a nuclear warhead that could give a country a headache they would never recover from.

The Russians have a name for it. They have dubbed their newest, most special weapon "Satan".

I am not making that up.

Vladimir Putin is not a fan of the subtle approach.

It's like Vlad is auditioning to be the next James Bond villain.

He said his new missile strikes 'like a meteorite, like a fireball', and then he crossed the bridge in his underground lair over the shark tank while stroking a fluffy white cat.

Or he could have been strangling it. Hard to tell.

While Russia has called its monochrome missile the name of the most evil thing of our imagination, NATO has gone in the opposite direction, as though to reassure us.

They have named it "Snowflake".

Doesn't that sound comforting? Who was ever hurt by a snowflake?

It is the description given by usually old people to describe usually young people of a sensitive disposition that they disagree with.

It is a term of derision: "bloomin' snowflakes worrying about pollution – it's just a bit of lead in the air – cancer never 'urt no one" or, "bloomin' snowflakes worrying about offending people, we never minded about offence when I were a lad – bullying never 'urt no one" - that sort of thing.

This particular snowflake is reportedly so robust a thing that in order to intercept it, at least 500 American counter missiles would be needed.

Or at least that's the claim of the chairman of Russia's Defence and Security Committee.

But then he would say that wouldn't he?

This was Putin doing his usual hard-man routine before the sham elections that he unsurprisingly won because all of the people who could challenge him were either in jail or dead.

This rocket boasting is playing to his Let's Make Russia Great Again rhetoric.

Why change a successful formula?

The large fly in his ointment is that the US outspends the next nine countries combined on military hardware.

If you didn't know any better, you could be forgiven for thinking that Putin and Trump going back and forth with the military willy-waving is just an excuse to throw vast sums of public money at their friends and donors running the weapons manufacturers that are the only ones that will benefit from all this.

Sometimes, it really is all about the money, honey.

31.03.18

The forecast calls for raining fire.

Just when you thought it was safe to go out in the garden, after the Beast from the East and the Pest from the West, we discover that a Chinese space station called the Tiangong-1, is falling from the sky.

China's top scientists calculate that it will re-enter the earth's atmosphere at precisely 11:30am BST, on Easter Sunday.

Or it could be sometime on Saturday, or conceivably on Monday. They really don't know. And they don't know where it will land either.

Apart from that, they have everything under control.

Tiangong is Chinese for "heavenly place" and that is where it will send you if it hits you in the face.

But don't worry – if the impact doesn't kill you, it has a number of highly toxic chemicals on board that should do the job, if a little more slowly.

It has Hydrazine on board, for instance.

It is a chemical included in rocket fuel that causes irritation of the eyes and throat, and dizziness.

You what else causes dizziness? Getting bonked on the noggin by ten tonnes of space junk going at 18,000 miles an hour.

Areas that could be hit include, but are not limited to: New York, Barcelona, Beijing, Chicago, Istanbul, Rome and Toronto.

Without actually looking it up and doing the maths, I can estimate that's about 100m people in the firing line.

There's more: when the station does eventually enter the atmosphere it could unleash a 'series of fireballs' and there is no good scenario that you can write that includes the word "fireballs".

If scientists do not yet know where the space station will crash, they certainly don't know where the fireballs will land, but other than that, there's nothing to be concerned about.

Tiangong-1 is now rubbing against the Earth's outer atmosphere and it is dropping out of orbit by about 2.5 miles a day, unless it is crash landing at the moment I am writing this.

At about 43 miles above the surface, it will begin its re-entry.

That word "re-entry" sounds like an orderly process but this will be a careering tangle of red hot metal, like a thunderbolt from a furious mythical god.

Fortunately, the European Space Agency said the chances of it hitting an actual human are small.

The odds of being struck by space debris are one in 1.2 trillion, said an ESA space debris expert, which is an actual job, and not just something I made up.

Happily, nobody has ever died from being hit by space junk falling back to Earth.

There was an incident in a Western Australian town called Esperance in 1974, when a piece of the Skylab fell to the ground and the local authorities fined NASA for littering.

That's actually true.

NASA refused to pay. Maybe they claimed it wasn't littering, they had merely parked it there.

I hope the Chinese don't park anything near you.

Better stay indoors, just in case.

06.04.18

Hoping for a good master

Elon Musk sounds like a cheap aftershave aimed at the teenage market: "cover yourself with the penetrating, insistent scent of Elon Musk and you will be beating the babes off with a stick. Requires no gym work. Also thins paint."

But Elon Musk is not to be found on the shelves of Superdrug, he pops up wherever there is a leap forward in sci-fi-like technology.

He is the chap behind PayPal, the method by which you can confidently buy things online that you don't need, with money you haven't got, without having your details stolen by a Russian bot.

We liked that so much that he quickly amassed all the money in the world that hadn't been reserved for Bill Gates.

With that cash he invented solar panels that look like proper tiles and not some hideous roofing mistake that was left there by the builders. And he makes the most desirable electric cars, one of which he sent into space on his own rocket.

He has made one of the world's largest fortunes from computers and technology, so you would think that he would be comfortable with the idea of artificial intelligence (AI), but he is not.

The Tesla billionaire has repeatedly warned us of our impending demise at the hands of out of control robots and AI.

Indeed, it is reported that a South Korean University is already developing a secret robot army that could give North Korea's Kim Jong-un a bad haircut, or completely destroy humanity, depending on its programming.

Musk's latest alarm is of immoral robot leaders from which humanity can never escape.

We are already up to our eyeballs in immoral leaders, so it's not such a stretch.

In a new documentary called 'Do You Trust This Computer?' by Chris Paine, Musk talks about the possibility of an authoritarian government building an AI system that outlives its creator and keeps the people under permanent oppression.

He is so concerned about it that he has paid for the film to be free on YouTube for the weekend but you have to provide your own popcorn, which seems a bit tight for a man worth $21bn.

He said that mankind could create 'an immortal dictator from which we would never escape.'

If that sounds ridiculous, just imagine how much of their personal wealth Donald Trump or Vladimir Putin would give for such a device.

For us to avoid this apocalyptic scenario, Musk says our governments must learn about the dangers, take on board the urgency to regulate artificial intelligence and act now for the benefit of future generations.

To reduce what he called this 'fundamental risk to the existence of human civilisation', we need the authorities to bring in laws to stop humanity from being outsmarted by computers.

Unfortunately, politicians aren't going to immerse themselves in the dull task of learning what computers are capable of; there's no immediate upside for them.

There's no votes in preventing something happening in the future.

There are only votes in fixing a problem that has already occurred.

Best of luck with that when the problem is that The Terminator is spraying machine gun fire at anyone that comes near it.

Short-termism is the problem, as usual.

Elon Musk said that regulations are usually reactive – they try to fix yesterday's problem just in time to prevent a recurrence.

To avert the annihilation of the entire human race, Musk said the first step is for government to get a better understanding of the fast-moving achievements in developing artificial intelligence technology.

We're doomed. They can barely figure out how to unlock their phones, they aren't going to understand this.

If we don't fix it, the future Musk sees is of us doughy sacks of meat being kept as pets by super-intelligent machines.

As long as they are nice to us and feed us three times a day, let us nap when we want and buy us squeaky toys to play with, that actually doesn't sound too bad.

But as we know, owners aren't always that nice to their pets.

We can only hope that the intelligence we create will be nicer than the people that create it.

07.04.18

Thwarting the Will of Some of the People.

The row about the passport printers rumbles on.

The papers are wrapping themselves in the flag and competing with each to show that they love the country more.

About 300,000 on-line Daily Mail readers were persuaded to stop commenting on how fat some celeb photographed on a beach had got, to click an online petition to force the government to change its mind about which company prints our passports.

The paper handed the printout to Downing Street where several Tory MPs who had not gone away for Easter met them for a photo call.

The issue is that a Franco-Dutch firm Gemalto was selected for the contract, rather than British rival with a foreign name - De La Rue.

The Mail thinks this is very serious and its campaign is about British jobs and the security of our travel documents and is not an attempt to boost circulation with a Brexit flag waving campaign, goodness me no, why ever would anyone think that?

It seems likely that if the government had chosen De La Rue in the first place, at an extra cost to the poor tax payer of £120m, the same papers that are whining now would be whining about that, complaining that is £120m that could have gone to the NHS, or on red, white and blue bunting for the royal wedding.

One of the Conservative MPs present, Andrew Rosindell said: 'The British people voted to leave the EU on the understanding we were going to get back control and one of the things we should be controlling is our British passports.

'We should have the gold standard of British passports. As far as I'm concerned, it can't be that unless it's manufactured here in the UK."

That makes sense, after all, Johnny Foreigner doesn't yet know how to print things on paper.

Give them a while, they'll catch up eventually.

This would be a strange fit for the post Brexit, open for business, outward facing, free trading Britain that we have heard so much about.

Being protectionist and awarding a contract based not on price but on whether the company is British seems more to represent a country not confident of itself and anti-competition.

The message would be that if you are a foreign company that can provide a service at a more reasonable rate than a British company, you still won't get the work.

That's not open for business, that's the opposite.

And if it was given to a British company on the basis of security, it would seem perverse given that we are inviting China to build nuclear power stations here, against the advice of our own security agencies.

Rosindell said, 'The Government needs to change this pretty quickly because most people out there don't understand why this has been allowed to happen.'

Really? I would say that the people don't care about where anything gets made as long as it is cheap.

The reason the British clothing industry is no more, apart from a few isolated pockets, no pun intended, is that we do not want British shirts. They cost too much.

We want ones made by child slaves in Chinese sweat shops, because they are three for a tenner and we can throw them away once we've worn them and go out and buy some more to get that shopper's dopamine hit of good-feeling brain juice.

We don't buy British things from the British corner shop because it's not there any more because we buy foreign made things from the foreign owned internet company, delivered by the foreign owned delivery company.

It's a bit late to start getting all misty-eyed and patriotic about where our stuff is made, after we've caused British stores to shut and British manufacturing to close and sold off British infrastructure.

Where were the newspaper led protests about selling off the water and the electric and the gas?

British bidder De La Rue protests that it came out ahead of its foreign rival on quality and was undercut only on price.

But as consumers, that's the only thing we appear to care about.

Conservative MP Nigel Evans said: "I hope the Government will listen to what Daily Mail readers are saying and what the general public are saying."

That's dangerous talk.

If government policy were dictated by simply getting a large number of people to click on a web page to register their support of an issue, then the Tories and their newspapers might not like what they would get.

The Number 10 website hosts petitions that have received as many, or more signatories than the one concocted by the Daily Mail.

There was the one that was for us to accept more asylum seekers and increase support for refugee migrants in the UK.

That got 450,287 people to mark their support.

Another was to make the production, sale and use of cannabis legal. Almost a quarter of a million people signed that one.

Over a million agreed with the petition to prevent Donald Trump from making a state visit to the United Kingdom

And for the petition that read, "We the undersigned call upon HM Government to implement a rule that if the remain or leave vote is less than 60% based on a turnout less than 75% there should be another referendum."

Fully 4,150,260 signed their agreement to that one.

The government ignored all those petitions.

I'm not sure the Mail would have appreciated it if they hadn't.

13.04.18

Seeing red.

Tube drivers have gone on strike in support of a colleague who allegedly ran three red lights.

Someone who drives anything for a living should not be caught going through signals that say stop.

But the lights were not on the roads, that would be bad enough, it was much worse than that. The lights he went through were the ones on the railway lines, the ones that stop one train smashing into another.

London Underground thought that, all things considered, it might be best for the comfort of the passengers if they weren't sent headlong into an oncoming train, so they suggested that the driver might want to do something less taxing for a living.

They didn't fire him, they gave him a less hazardous job, where disobeying commands might not kill so many people.

This was completely unacceptable for the brothers and sisters of the Aslef union, who downed tools and marched off the job in a move reminiscent of the bad old days of perpetual industrial action.

There have been so many rail strikers lately that if they all wore Brutus jeans and orange shirts with collars you could land a plane on, it would seem like the 1970's all over again.

A 24 hour strike of the District Line was organised. If you use that line, your train will have been cancelled for the convenience of a man who doesn't know what the colour red means.

You might have thought the union would have demanded the man be fired. After all, they seem to place customer safety at the top of their priorities when they complain about the reduced role of the train guards.

That concern cannot possibly be fabricated to resist the march of artificial intelligence into the railways can it?

They wouldn't cite safety as an excuse to prevent their jobs being taken by robots would they?

What is not safe would be to allow a driver who sailed through three red stop signals in a four week period to continue to be in charge of thousands of unsuspecting passengers.

They just want to get in a carriage and find a seat that doesn't have too much urine on it and to avoid catching anyone's eye 'till they get home. It would put a kink in their day to have to pick themselves out of the wreckage of a train crash after a hard day at the office.

Transport for London said it was 'simply not safe for this employee to continue in a role as a driver' and that he was offered another role.

Apparently, the driver agreed to this. I bet he couldn't believe his luck that he was still keeping his pay packet.

The union was having none of it though, and the 800,000 passengers who use the District Line every day had to suffer, as rail passengers have suffered so many times before.

London Underground explained this to their customers but announced that the rest of the lines would be operating "normally".

There can be no more dispiriting news for the average rush hour commuter to hear that their lines will be operating as they usually do.

The Aslef union balloted its members over the way the Signals Passed At Danger policy was applied to this member of train crew and accused Transport for London of failing to discuss the issue.

What's to discuss? The driver seems to be dangerous in charge of a moving vehicle that is approximately the same weight as Canterbury Cathedral. He should stop driving immediately. End of discussion.

Nigel Holness, London Underground's director of network operations said, 'No disciplinary action has been taken against the employee and our action is in line with the safety policies agreed with our trade unions.'

That seems supine in the extreme – he passed 3 red signals and they still didn't fire him.

Makes you wonder what you need to do to get fired on the London Underground.

Bring a lion to work?

The belligerence of the unions will be their undoing. You know what wouldn't run a red light?

A driverless train.

14.04.18

Mission accomplished?

Here we go again. Theresa May, Emmanuel Macron and Donald Trump are deterring the Assad regime from indiscriminately killing people, by indiscriminately killing people.

After half a million deaths in the Syrian war, we finally found some that we object to.

We didn't mind when people in Syria were getting their arms and legs blown off and their bodies squashed under the falling ruins of what used to be their homes.

Two years ago, there had been 470,000 people dead due to the Syrian war after which the United Nations stopped counting.

Russia has been bombing the place for years and there was no urgent allied government action, no threats to attack from America or Britain or France.

The Syrian city of Aleppo looks like the film set of a disaster film rather than an actual place where people still live.

Yet while it was being bombed back to the stone age and its people were being exterminated we didn't raise a finger, because those were deaths that we didn't see much on the news – they don't tend to show bits of bodies and mangled torsos on the telly in case they make you turn over.

They have no problem showing people dying with foam coming out of their mouth though, because there's less blood.

That's why governments are clutching their pearls and demanding that something must be done – they saw something that upset them on the telly.

For the people of Syria, they probably don't think it necessarily an improvement in their circumstances to be killed by a bomb to being killed by a gas attack.

The gas might kill them instantly, while a bomb might leave them dying in agony in a pool of their relatives' blood for days leaving their infant babies to starve to death.

It also seems a bit rich for us to rush to occupy the moral high ground while at the same time selling weapons of mass destruction to the Saudis, in the knowledge that they use them to blow up hospitals and schools in Yemen.

If the Prime Minister actually cared about the people of Syria, she might have done something after the first 100,000 deaths, or maybe the first quarter of a million, but the government carried on ignoring them and fretting instead about more important things like what a threat Jeremy Corbyn is to the pound in our pocket, or whether they'll be able to hose the homeless off the streets of Windsor for Hazza and Sparkle's wedding.

If the President of the United States cared so much, wouldn't he have accepted some of those poor homeless Syrians as refugees?

Perhaps, up to now, they were potential terrorists and allowing them in might embolden Mexico to send some more of its "bad hombres".

But show someone foaming at the mouth on Fox News and the president does his nut and starts barking at the TV and threatens to attack Russia with missiles that are "nice and new and smart", in something of a contrast to the man that would OK their use.

If they're so smart, maybe one of those missiles would like to be the leader of the free world?

He actually tweeted "Mission Accomplished!" after the first night's strafing. How tone deaf do you have to be to repeat George W Bush's premature boast about America's adventure in Iraq?

I know that no-one ever learns anything from history but was that long enough ago to count as historical?

Theresa May didn't wait until parliament got back from its Easter holidays before declaring that we were in on the latest western adventure in the Middle East.

She probably didn't want to risk asking parliament to vote on it and hearing the word "no", as her predecessor did.

I wonder if the PM is keen to do whatever Donny wants because he is grumpy and temperamental and we need him to do us a favour on trade.

The World Health Organisation has said it believes 500 people were affected by the apparent attack in Douma on Saturday.

Five hundred die in a certain way on TV and we act – 500,000 die away from the cameras and our attitude seems to have been that we are busy, we've got other things to think about, we'll get to it later, where's Syria, what war?

Now things are different – the allies agreed it is vital that the use of chemical weapons should not go unchallenged, which is instructional to every murderous dictator out there.

The message is that you can do what you want and kill as many people as you like and leave whole towns in rubble and untold lives ruined, just don't use any gas because it makes us feel uncomfortable.

We will get all fighty when you kill a few people like that, while we'll look the other way if you kill hundreds of thousands in any other way.

Or at least the government will get fighty.

The public are not so gung-ho.

A poll taken after the gas attack had 22 per cent saying they are in favour of action and 43 per cent against.

But that can't possibly be, because that would mean that the PM is thwarting the will of the people and we know how she feels about that.

20.4.18

Assailed from all sides.

Vast numbers of doddery, chuntering old geezers coalesced into one giant geriatric fist of fury that dealt the government a biff on the bonce.

It was one of the largest votes that the House of Lords has ever seen and they were there for one purpose. It was to stick up for Britain's interests or to thwart Brexit, depending on your fixed-in-concrete point of view.

The Lords voted by 348 to 225 that the government should have to consider remaining in the EU's Customs Union.

This did not go down well with Theresa May who had personally drawn a red line around that issue.

She seems to have been free with the use of red lines.

The Prime Minister has drawn so many red lines on various negotiation points concerning Brexit that she stands in a swirling maelstrom of them and she might be hard pressed to find an escape.

The Lords also thwacked the government on its disinclination to guarantee the rights of EU citizens once we leave the EU.

Twice stymied in the same week.

But that was not the extent of the Mrs May's troubles.

There was also The Troubles.

Brussels rejected all of Britain's fudging about the border between a brexited Northern Ireland and the rest of the Emerald Isle which will remain in the EU.

European negotiators insist that there cannot be no border between the EU and the UK, but the British insist that there can be no hard border because people might start shooting each other again.

The EU say there must be border controls for tax and standards reasons but the British say that the border must not be in the Irish Sea, or on land.

Meanwhile, Sinn Fein want Northern Ireland to remain in the Customs Union and Single Market but the DUP, on whom the PM relies, want no difference in rules from the rest of the UK.

If we leave the EU completely with a hard Brexit, Sinn Fein will be upset, if Northern Ireland retains some synchronicity with Europe, while the rest of the UK goes its merry way, the DUP will be upset.

If there are no borders, the EU will be upset and if there are borders, the UK will be upset.

Basically, everybody that has a say wants something completely different from everybody else and it's a bit like untangling the Christmas tree lights – you know there must be a way to straighten it all out but you can't quite fathom how.

If European setbacks for the government had ended there this week, it would have been bad enough, but there was more.

A group of ex-pats are attempting to have the entire Brexit process annulled because they have been disenfranchised.

The referendum rule that stated that those Britons living overseas for 15 or more years should not get a say deprived those people of their rights to vote.

If, after Brexit, they will be forced to relocate to these damp isles, after sunning themselves in Spain for years, they will be livid.

Hence the campaign to throw out the whole leaving process.

They have been reduced to second class citizens without a voice on issues that directly affect them.

That's hardly taking back control.

And if that were all that the government had to contend with, on top of the festival of apology over the Windrush scandal, it would have been plenty, but it wasn't all.

A British fishing firm has won the right to appeal the decision by Boris Johnson to award valuable licences to fish British waters near the Falkland Islands to foreign companies.

This is the same Boris Johnson who, before the referendum, exited the Leave battle bus - the one with the lie about £350m a week for the NHS - and declared to the fishermen of Lowestoft that foreign firms were stealing our fish.

Now he has stopped them stealing by giving the fish away instead.

It is an interesting solution to the problem. If that policy were rolled out, the crime numbers would fall in an instant.

It's all a bit of a muddle.

Is this the strong and stable government we were promised by the PM?

It's a good job it's not a coalition of chaos, because that would be embarrassing.

21.04.18

Tressed out.

A ten year old boy was taught a lesson in health and safety that he will never forget. Neither will the man who taught it to him.

The child was at the barbers and was playing with razor. These are particularly sharp, as you know, and are not toys.

To ensure that the lad remembered not to play with sharp objects the barber gave the youngster a "number one".

This is a cut with the clippers set at their most extreme – it's how you used to get your hair cut when joining the army or the skinheads.

The boy was then tasked with sweeping up his own hair, which must have taken all of 30 seconds.

As this occurred in the present day and not in the 1970's, when disruptive boys were thrashed for their disobedience, the boy did not suffer in silence, he called the police.

Naturally, with police numbers so low and resources stretched such that they will not come to your home if it has been burgled, or if your car has been broken into, the police politely declined to intervene.

Just kidding, they appeared as though by magic and spirited the errant barber away to suffer the full weight of the law.

The youngster, who was said to be "proud" of his old hairstyle was laughed at by his peers after it was cut, so his human rights had been compromised.

There was no alternative for the judge than to admonish the barber, express the court's displeasure and impose a small fine.

Once again, I am kidding, the man was sentenced to eight months in jail.

The court heard that he was of good character, admitted his guilt straight away and had no previous convictions but was moved to lock him up anyway because of what the judge called this " most disgusting piece of humiliation".

It is odd how things change. It used to be that the police were there to protect the public from muggers and thieves and murderers.

Humiliation, meanwhile, was dished out in school as often as the dinner ladies made semolina pudding.

Now, the police do not attend break-ins and announce that policy for all to hear. Burglars are going on robbing sprees because the likelihood of being caught is almost non-existent.

Yet the police and the courts have time to send a barber to jail for cutting a boy's hair too short.

By the time they have fitted the convict for his prison issue overalls, the kid's hair will have grown back.

By comparison, in 2009, a 21 year old man from Formby, Merseyside, was sentenced for a "cowardly assault" on pizza delivery man, who suffered two broken bones.

The man had two previous convictions for assault, including punching one police officer between the legs and another in the eye,

He was not sent to jail at all but merely had his ten month sentence suspended.

In 2017, a disqualified scrambler bike rider narrowly missed hitting pedestrians while speeding through Liverpool city centre, shooting through red lights and driving into the path of oncoming traffic.

He had already been banned from the road for drug driving.

He was sentenced for dangerous driving, driving while disqualified and driving without insurance.

He got just six months. That is the same sentence you could receive for taking a selfie in a polling booth.

Justice seems so random.

The barber's name, by the way, is Abdulrahim Omar.

I wonder how this story would have ended if it had been Fred Smith.

27.04.18

Orangutan grooms terrier, regrets it

I don't know what was more vomitous this week – the sight of Donald Trump and Emmanuel Macron holding hands and kissing, or the massed ranks of the toothless flag wavers waiting outside the private hospital where Princess Wotsit went for a hair-do and make-up.

If they are indicative of the royal fan base, it doesn't bode well for the future of the House of Windsor. It looked like a flag shop had thrown up on a freak show.

Was the circus in town?

I wouldn't let that lot within three miles of a baby, royal or otherwise. Most of them looked like they should be in a secure facility.

When the new-born was held for the inspection of the press, writers cooed about how marvellous it was that the mother looked so fantastic after such an ordeal.

It's amazing what having an unlimited amount of money does to the appearance.

The clouds of attendants and stylists and baby wranglers didn't hurt either.

The next day, Wills was pictured falling asleep during a church service. The usual royal hem-sniffers of the commentariat noted that being a new dad, he was probably up all night.

He probably was – up all night choosing the staff that will be doing all the baby stuff.

He won't be able to do it, he has a full schedule, what with all the smiling and the waving.

There was much of that in evidence when the Bromance Across the Atlantic got going in the Whitehouse.

Donald Trump gripped onto Theresa May's hand when she popped over because he is frightened of, among other things, ramps and stairs and had to negotiate a small example of the former without falling over, so he held on to her like a toddler holds his mummy's hand to cross the road.

Why Trump held onto the hand of the French President is less obvious. Maybe because Melania won't let him hold hers and hookers are off the menu for the moment, so he craves the personal touch.

Macron let him do it because he didn't want to make a scene, I assume.

The French President did not appear to enjoy Trump announcing that Macron had a dandruff problem and that the leader of the free world was going to pick it off for him, like a dominant gorilla picks fleas out of a subordinate's fur.

Trump called a press conference for the two, wherein the US President declared that: the Paris climate accord was the worst deal ever and the Iranian nuclear pact was the worst deal ever and there was no collusion and I never paid a porn star hush money I mean do I look like I need to pay of course not I can tell you that and it's a real witch hunt and a disgrace everybody says so.

Or something like that.

Macron addressed the room in what was for him a foreign tongue, and he spoke better English than his host.

Trump tweeted "Busy day planned. Looking forward to watching President Macron of France address a Joint Session of Congress today. This is a great honor and seldom allowed to be done...he will be GREAT!"

Either he lied about looking forward to it, or he had no idea about the publicly expressed beliefs of the man he was promoting.

In his speech, Macron said that we must resist "closing the door to the world" and retreating into nationalism in the face of threats from globalization, terrorism and criminal states.

He said, "I believe facing these challenges requires the opposite of massive deregulation and extreme nationalism. Commercial war is not the right answer".

Macron derided Trump's withdrawal from the Paris Accord, his clinging to old fossil fuel technology and that when it comes to climate change, "there is no Planet B".

He criticised nationalism and isolationism as a temporary remedy to our fears.

Basically, he took the hand that picked the "dandruff" from his jacket, twisted it up behind Trump's back and gave him a spanking. On television.

Trump's Twitter account went strangely silent after the French President had finished speaking.

So that's how you get him to shut up.

28.04.18

Don't look directly at the light.

Walking home on a dark night, on a dark street is something that makes us fearful, with good reason.

Danger lurks in the dark.

Unfortunately, danger also lurks in the light, by which I mean the actual light itself.

Scientists have studied 4,000 people living in various parts of Spain where that new-fangled LED lighting has been installed in street lamps.

Their findings do not make for good reading, especially if you are reading them by the light of one of those lamps.

Light-emitting diode bulbs dramatically increase the chances of developing breast and prostate cancer.

Experts are warning the authorities to stop the roll out of the new street lamps but it might be too late.

A third of the lights on motorways and A roads have been changed to LED's and councils across the land are busy replacing the warm glow of the old orange bulbs with the bright white light of the future.

The problem is that they might look white but in fact they emit a blue light which is like the light of the dawn. This tells our bodies that it is time to wake up, when in fact it is time to sleep.

Our circadian rhythm gets disrupted, our production of the sleep regulating hormone melatonin is decreased and that means our brains don't know whether to pass out or have breakfast.

The resultant disrupted sleep pattern means, according to the study, a doubling of the risk of developing prostate cancer and a 150% higher risk of breast cancer.

All from dodgy street lights.

There are now so many of them that our hormones are completely on the blink.

But it is worse than that because the same blue wake-up light is made by our bestest and most special friends: our smartphones and tablets.

We might be persuaded to venture home in the dark but you would have to take our phones from our cold dead hands.

Staring into them causes our hormones to be in perpetual wakefulness mode.

It is especially bad to stare at them late at night, when millions of us do just that, in case we have missed some vital update about a friend's dinner or an important video of a puppy dog doing something cute.

That light is everywhere now. It is above us in the street and comes from the phone in our hands and the LED bulbs are the ones that are fitted to the front of new cars.

They are installed for safety reasons so that other road users can see the car they are fitted on.

We can see them all right. They are so dazzling that after getting a blast of them in the eyeballs we can't see anything else, rendering the safety aspect somewhat compromised.

LED lights are, however, cheap to run and therefore better for the council's budget.

That might be why they are so keen, despite the health warnings.

And if they take the money they don't spend on electricity and use it to bump up the remuneration of the chief executive, wouldn't that be illuminating, if not completely surprising?

04.05.18

Call it a draw.

It was the week of the very important local council elections that hardly anybody appears to care about.

This seems odd because the local council affects your daily life more than the national government.

They are the people that clear your rubbish away, keep the streets clean, run the library, child care, pensioner services, schools, transport, make planning decisions, manage parks, provide play areas and clean up the doggy-do.

Local councils do not have the glamour or cachet of national government, but they have a greater effect on our lives, just like the weather forecast at the end of the news is usually the only part of the bulletin that affects us personally.

And yet, almost no one could be bothered to vote.

People missed going to the polls because they needed to go to the pub after work, or were in an area where it rained, or they forgot it was voting day or they couldn't remember where the polling station was or they just flat out couldn't be bothered.

The turnout was about 30%. In some areas, they couldn't even reach that.

And what did we learn? Nothing.

The right-wing press (henceforth known as simply "the press") declared it a victory of historic proportions because Labour didn't flatten the Tories

But as the Tories and Labour were absolutely level on 35% of the vote each, it takes a pretty big squint to see that as a major victory for either side.

The main parties are like two old sluggers, collapsing after pounding each other to a standstill.

The problem for Labour was that certain people in their ranks got excited and overestimated what their party could do.

The Conservatives, meanwhile, dampened down expectations.

On the basis of how each side publicly stated they might fare, it looks like Jezza lost and Tezza won.

It was not much of a win for the blues though, after the biggest negative campaign against any politician in memory failed to sink Jeremy Corbyn.

He just won't die. He seems indestructible.

It must be infuriating for the people that run the nation's favourite newspapers who have been gunning for him ever since he declared that he would look into the concentration of ownership of news outlets.

That caused a wailing fit that you could hear from the off-shore tax havens their owners inhabit and they have been after his hide ever since.

The big headlines were that Labour failed to win in Wandsworth and Westminster.

I have lived in Wandsworth and I work in Westminster and if Labour had won either of those two councils it would have been a miracle.

God Herself would have had to engineer such a feat.

The reason that the Tories are never going to lose Wandsworth is that they have one of the lowest council tax rates in the country.

The highest you pay in the biggest house in the area is only £1445

Compare that to Richmond, for instance, another Tory council, and its £3277 – more than double – for the same band.

Wandsworth is a flagship council for the Tories and they have managed to keep the council tax artificially low to hang on to it.

Wandsworth is also about as aspirationally middle class an area as you will ever see. They would be as likely to vote Labour in

Wandsworth as would the audience on the opening night at the Covent Garden Opera.

And did anyone seriously think that Kensington and Chelsea would not vote Conservative, or that Westminster would swing to the left?

The reason the press are calling these Labour failures is that some dopes in Labour said that they might win those councils.

When the inevitable happened it looked like a loss, instead of a draw, which is what happened over the country as a whole...or the 30% of the country that could be bothered to express a preference.

It's a nation divided and there was no clear winner.

One thing that has become clear though, is that UKIP's got no mates.

05.04.18

The doctor will embarrass you now.

In the run-up to the election in November 2016, Donald Trump's personal physician released a letter that stated the presidential candidate would be the healthiest person to ever be elected to the presidency, totally healthy, no one ever saw such health, he's the most healthy of anyone, ever.

Turns out that Donald Trump dictated that letter. Can you believe that? Of course you can.

The physician's name is Dr. Harold Bornstein, and I recommend that you look up a picture of the good doctor on the internet.

If you are feeling depressed, it will cure you immediately. He looks like the man that would get sent over if central casting called for someone that looks like Doc Brown from Back to the Future, but kookier.

In August 2016 he told NBC that he picked up Trump's kind of language and interpreted it on his own to write something that would please him.

He asserted that, "his health is excellent, especially his mental health." Then he laughed.

Now he has changed his story to admit that he didn't write any of it at all and that his client dictated the letter to him, presumably to differentiate himself to Hilary Clinton, who Trump described as not physically up to the task of the top job.

Like almost everyone that has had contact with the president, Dr Bornstein is no longer in Trump's employ, so presumably feels unencumbered in speaking to the press.

The president's ex-physician said his actions took the truth and moved it in a different direction.

Like an "alternative fact".

Bornstein recalled rehearsing the letter with Trump while in the car with his wife in December 2015.

The letter stated: 'If elected, Mr. Trump, I can state unequivocally, will be the healthiest individual ever elected to the presidency.'

He later said 'I like that sentence to be quite honest with you, and all the rest of them are either sick or dead.'

It said that Trump was in 'excellent physical health', that his blood pressure and cholesterol measurements were healthy, as were his EKG, echocardiogram, chest X-ray and blood sugar.

He wrote that Trump weighed 236 pounds and stood six-foot-three inches tall.

He is actually both heavier and shorter than that but if either measurement had been reported accurately, Trump would have been classed as 'obese' and not merely 'overweight', so the figures were massaged.

It failed to mention the cholesterol medication Trump was on and the pills he was taking for Rosacea and hair loss.

Those facts the doctor kept to himself, until recently, after which he says Trump's goons raided his office and took his patient's files away.

I can't imagine which medical problem Trump wanted to keep quiet about – yes I can - it was the hair wasn't it?

Have you ever seen a man put in so much effort to keep secret the fact that over vast swathes of his scalp, he's as bald as a billiard ball?

After Bornstein revealed the extent of Trump's medical regimen, he says Trump's bodyguard led a 'raid' on his office, after which the doctor claims he felt 'raped, frightened and sad'.

Trump keeps picking fights with all the wrong people.

When he was pretending to be a top businessman, he could get away with it, because he'd just shout and threaten and sue, but when you are President of the United States of America, it's probably best not to pick fights with your doctor, who knows you inside and out…literally.

Or, come to think of it, pick a fight with the FBI and the CIA, who together must have a file on Donald Trump as long as he is wide.

He's not that smart

That's another thing the doctor left out of his letter.

11.05.18

Going Down

Have you heard the one about the professor who got into a lift? Well, it's not funny, I can tell you that.

OK, maybe it is a little funny, as in: weird.

Richard Ned Lebow is the 76 year old professor of international political theory at King's College London.

He made a fateful trip to a convention of the International Studies Association (ISA) in San Francisco, last month.

In a packed lift at the event, he found his inner Mrs. Slocombe, and in the manner of Are You Being Served, when asked by the person next to buttons which floor everyone wanted, he asked to get out at the ladies' lingerie department.

You know – "Ground floor perfumery, stationary and leather goods, wigs and haberdashery, kitchenware and food ...going up".

It's not like he made a crack about having to rush home to feed his pussy, yet his life caved in because his comment was overheard and reported by an American Professor Simona Sharoni, who I'm pretty sure was not the inspiration for that song by The Knack.

Simona Sharoni is, however, a professor of women's and gender studies at an institution called Merrimack College in Massachusetts.

The college's website, which states that it is a Catholic organisation, says: "The women's and gender studies program at Merrimack College equips students with the analytic skills to integrate insights from a variety of fields, enabling them to become conversant with a variety of theoretical and methodological approaches and apply these approaches to the study of gender."

That sounds a very worthwhile way to spend the $60,055 per year that its website states the course would cost.

All that learning doesn't appear to equip the professors at the college with a sense of proportion, though.

Simona Sharoni says she was too shocked to confront Richard Lebow at the time of the crime, so she reported him to the ISA ethics committee, who took the complaint very seriously and deemed the comments in the lift "offensive and inappropriate".

Lebow sent an email of apology to Sharoni saying he meant no insult and that this seemed a bit frivolous and would take time from the ethics committee that they could be spending on real offences that trouble them both.

That comment was deemed to be an even more serious transgression than the original joke.

The ISA has instructed Professor Lebow to write a further "unequivocal apology".

He refused to do so. He said it would be an acknowledgement that 'an innocent remark in an elevator is somehow wrong.'

The indicator gauge of what is acceptable was pretty much straining the stops at the wrong end of the dial for decades but to swing this far in the opposite direction does not seem to be a positive development.

If all humour that offends is eliminated, then you can say goodbye to laughing.

Everything that is funny can offend someone, if they try hard enough to be offended.

The only truly funny bit about this story is that Professor Lebow lists conflict management as among his interests.

See, we can still laugh about some things, but only if they are about white middle-class men.

12.05.18

If you go down to the nature park today you're in for a little surprise

West Yorkshire Police have been boasting online about a drugs bust on their patch. It is nice that they have the time to have a social media presence.

Many forces are so short-staffed that they will not turn out for a burglary or car theft, so the people of West Yorkshire are very lucky to have such well-resourced force.

Unfortunately, on-line comments are not always complimentary, which this force found to its cost.

Officers posted a picture of a piece of green vegetable matter that they had confiscated from a person in a car.

It was not the substance itself that gave rise to ridicule, it was the amount that was the source of amusement.

The evidence bag triumphantly pictured on Facebook held about a thumbprint's worth, which lead to much anonymous merriment.

Comments that were posted included, but were not limited to: "You're a clown", "that's put a dent in the war on drugs", "all the crime going on...haven't they got anything better to do" - that sort of thing.

Naturally, being hardened policepersons, that was all water off a duck's back to them.

Just kidding – they were so upset that they threatened to arrest and prosecute anyone that made fun of them.

Police Inspector Martin Moizer's Facebook post read "***Cannabis Seized***", 'PCSO 687 Ian Campbell and PCSO 882 Ben Hughes attended Walton colliery nature park and seized a small quantity of Cannabis from a young man who was parked up alone. Walton Colliery nature park will be firmly on our patrol plan in the future to prevent this behaviour.'

That nature park sounds like a right den of iniquity. Are the pigeons safe?

The inspector subsequently posted this message, 'Unfortunately we have had to ban a number of people from using this page today.

'I would like to remind everyone that this is a police page and whatever your thoughts on one of my officers seizing drugs in the community, being insulting, abusive or offensive can and will result in a prosecution under the Malicious Communications Act 1988.'

That seems a bit thin-skinned. It is the sort of reaction that the right-wing press would call the words of a snowflake, if it had been uttered by a student, for instance.

PCI Moizer said that his officers would 'not overlook the significant harm that illegal drugs cause to our communities.'

I suspect that the harm done by marijuana in the community is because it is illegal, which leads to the stabbings and shootings and gang warfare that we read about on a daily basis which is dealers competing for territory.

It rakes in hundreds of millions of pounds a year, all of which is going to the criminals, apart from the coin sized piece that the West Yorkshire Police got hold of.

That's safe in the evidence room, unless it isn't.

It was so small it could easily get lost.

The same force also suffered internet mockery for posting a photo of two crates of Strongbow cider they seized from youths.

One person wrote on their website: 'Good policing but sure more effort should be focusing on searching for knives and offensive weapons rather than a few kids with some cider!'

That amounts to a hate crime against the force for which they could be prosecuted.

Your right to free speech is trumped by other people's right to not be offended.

Apparently, it's the law.

19.05.18

The Firm's new recruit

It was a great day, as though the Queen's silversmith had personally buffed Windsor to a sparkle for Meghan Markle.

No doubt about it, the sunshine, the dresses, hats, flowers, stars, horses, carriages and regalia looked fantastic. It was a terrific show.

You could have put on a show like for your wedding, if you too weren't paying for it.

At home we peered to see who got the best seats. The Clooneys appeared to be the tip toppermost stars there and were sat up the front.

The Queen managed to bag the best spot, despite arriving just in the nick of time, as usual. How does she manage it?

The bride arrived in a dress so huge it looked like she had got her foot caught in a marquee and was dragging it behind her.

Why do brides have to dress like that, as though they have no purpose other than to look good as an arm adornment for a man?

The groom was kitted out in some form-fitting and ergonomically correct gear in which, if necessary, he could have changed the tyre on the car that brought him there.

The bride was swathed in diaphanous meringue clouds so awkward she needed the assistance of at least two page persons to help her up the stairs.

Plus – white. Really?

The strains of a female chorister faded into echo and the religious bit began.

It was God this and God that, as though the Almighty didn't have enough on Her plate what with all the strife happening on this planet, let alone all the other planets in Her purview.

Archbishop Justin Welby hoved into view in an outfit that was so bright it was hard to look at him.

He appeared to have been caught in indecision in a gay jewellers and decided to wear the lot.

At least he was commendably brief.

The same can not be said of the American religionist that took over from him. It was like James Brown had walked on stage at an Enya concert.

He went on and on and on as if he was auditioning for his own TV show.

Did anyone actually vet that speech, or was he just making it up off the top of his head?

It seemed as though at any moment he would punt for donations for your own personal prayer – have your credit card ready and call the number on your screens and you shall be saved, praise the Lord.

He droned on so long I forgot what we were there for.

If ever there was a need to reinstate the vaudeville comedy sheep hook for acts that outstayed their welcome, it was then.

After what seemed and age, he climbed down from his religious fervour to address the happy couple, saying that he was going to sit down now as "we've got to get you married", after which he continued to speak as though he hadn't heard himself.

A brief wave of hope that he might be finished was extinguished as he traced the history of Man from the Stone Age to the Bronze Age, the Industrial Revolution and the rise of the internet, all the while burbling about love, love, love.

Donald Trump makes more sense. At one point he actually asked those present to nod if they came by car. Heads were nodding all right, but not in agreement.

There followed the sweet relief of some music. A gospel choir sang a Ben E. King song, which was nice but oddly loose-limbed in such stiff surroundings.

It seemed like an attempt to wrest some modern multiculturalism out of a conventional and very old-fashioned ritual.

Formality was resumed by the reappearance of Welby, at which point there followed more God stuff.

The union was being overseen by God and the promises of faithfulness were expressed under God's watchful eye, and God was expecting a lot judging by the number of mentions God got.

The trouble is, God has heard all that before. Almost half of all the marriages that God has witnessed end in divorce.

All those declarations of "'till death us do part" don't mean much.

They are just something people feel expected to say, and they certainly don't believe in God or they would be fearful of being caught lying to Him.

Meghan Markle promised God she would be faithful for ever and ever but she presumably promised the same thing the last time she got married.

If people are so unafraid of God that they casually lie openly to Him in His own house, perhaps they should stop the pretence and take God out of the equation.

I don't know much about religion but I am fairly sure that God wouldn't appreciate all the shallow assurances of people that wrap themselves in the bits of the religion they like – the pomp and ceremony, but don't actually believe in it enough to carry out their solemn undertakings.

The cellist was nice and the carriage procession, with mounted military, kit gleaming, horses bouncing, crowd waving, was a tremendous sight.

Those watching in the rest of the world should know that it is not always picture perfect weather here – the throng got lucky.

Meghan looked like she fitted right in to the old Firm.

She is an actress after all – looking comfortable in weird surroundings is what she does for a living.

She has probably not experienced anything quite as odd or unforgiving as her new family, though.

If those in the royal orbit, who have inherited money and have never needed to work, call the mother of Prince William's wife ""Doors to manual" because she was once so low as to have an actual job as an air hostess, can you imagine what they will call a mixed-race foreign actress from a poor broken home?

20.05.18

Versailles comes to Windsor

At the risk of coming over all "enemy of the people", it seems that the more I think about it, the worse it gets.

Twenty four hours removed from the event, which was very enjoyable, the reality of it has sunk in.

The generally agreed cost of Hazza and Sparkle's wedding is about £32m, for an advert for the royal family that lasted just over one hour.

That seems quite a lot for what is actually a personal event dressed up as a national occasion

In fact is seems like a dizzyingly large amount of money to splurge on anything that doesn't float or have walls.

The detail of the spending is frankly astonishing.

The cost of the silver plated trumpets, bought specially for the occasion was £90,000. I don't know what the personally engraved harp cost but I am sure they don't come cheap either.

A wedding planning company estimated the cost of the little things that made the day special.

The cake cost £50,000. That is, a sponge and cream creation with frosting on the top that would be gone that night was the same price as a new BMW with all the options ticked on the order form.

Those lovely flowers that adorned the doorway to the chapel would have been about £110,000. You can buy a house in some areas of Her Majesty's realm for less than that.

A glass marquee for the evening reception for the extra special guests with the right invite would have come in at £300,000.

Outside the world's largest occupied castle that has around a thousand rooms, the largest of which is 55m long, they felt the need to add an extra room, for one night only, at the cost of a year's salary for fifteen nurses.

The dress for the glowing bride would have been about £400,000, apparently.

How you can spend even half that much on a white dress that will only ever be worn once for a period of a few hours is unfathomable.

The sausage roll and a cup of tea that were provided for those 2,640 people specially selected to be near the ceremony, but not actually a part of it, were £10 each.

Twenty-six grand on snacks.

The big expense was the security.

We are told the bill for that, which was presented in its entirety to the taxpayer, was over £30m.

Police officers had their leave cancelled and were bussed in from neighbouring forces to supplement those stationed nearby.

There were uniformed police and plain clothed ones and armed response specialists and snipers and all the rest of it. No measure was left untaken to protect the happy couple.

Think of that when you have your home burgled, or your car stolen, or you are mugged or assaulted and the police are reluctant to attend because they don't have the staff due to the massive cuts in their budgets since the policy of austerity began.

Cressida Dick, the Metropolitan Police Commissioner says she needs an extra 600 officers urgently. The Met has lost £600m of funding since 2011 but there was no such worries about a lack of funds for the grand event.

If you are a criminal, and you could bear to miss the show, it would have been a fantastic time to do a bit of robbing in the south east of England.

Thirty million pounds for security seems a bit steep, but that's not the half of it.

That doesn't include the ceremonial security - the ones on horseback with the gleaming chest plates and bouncy hair helmets.

I do not know how much it costs to run a horse, but I am sure they don't come cheap and neither do the stables they keep them in.

Add to that the non-combatant uniforms and shiny accessories that only ever come out for the royals and the bill must be in the hundreds of millions.

Some of the money was apparently paid from the royals' own pockets.

Let's leave aside that they only have that money because their ancestors took land from the people and gave it to themselves, let's forget that on top of that there is the vast yearly income that we gift them - £82m to the Queen last year alone.

It is not really relevant that the Queen paid for the flowers or that Meghan might have paid for the dress, or that the royals laid on the champagne and the langoustines wrapped in smoked salmon and the grilled asparagus and the quails' eggs for themselves and their friends and celebs.

What is relevant is that while Her Majesty's subjects sleep in doorways, while the NHS is so underfunded that even cancer patients have to wait a year for treatment, while the use of food banks is at an all-time high, while even the middle class find they are only just getting by and after years of lower government spending on essentials like care for people suffering, the family of our head of state is behaving like Marie Antoinette.

Except it is worse than that.

We are not invited to eat cake, we are invited watch THEM eat cake.

26.05.18

Peace man attacks.

The committee can relax. They can put the Nobel Peace Prize back in the cupboard.

There will be a short interval before the embarrassment of Donald Trump accepting it, as the historic meeting between him and the North Korean leader is on hold.

I have no doubt he will get it. He seems to able to get anything he wants. He wanted to be rich and have sex with supermodels, and despite his chronic inability as a deal maker and businessman and his obvious and vast physical impediments, he has done exactly that.

He wanted to be able to wander unimpeded through the changing rooms at the Miss Universe contest, he wanted to have sex with his friend's wives and he wanted to be the world's most powerful man to wreak vengeance on anyone that has crossed him, and he got all that too.

Who would bet on him not getting the Nobel Peace Prize that his gap-toothed, hollering fans are chanting for him to receive?

He said: It will be the biggest Nobel Prize ever, in gold with diamonds, better than anyone else's Nobel Prize I can tell you that, a lot of people say I should get it and I could take that big beautiful peace prize and smash Kim Jong-un over the head with it to Make America Great Again.

Or something like that.

At the moment though, that is on hold as the President has had a change of heart.

He changes his mind as often as he changes TV channels.

North Korea is furious. They said that, with great respect, America should get back to them once they elect a leader who is not a clueless tubby ball of lard with a bad haircut.

Donald Trump replied that he has a huge weapon, it's the biggest and hardest weapon anyone has ever seen and he hopes he doesn't have to use it.

The problem started when the American Vice President, that lukewarm glass of milk and the world's whitest person, Mike Pence went on television and stated that the outcome of the meeting that the Trump government was looking at for North Korea, unless it got everything it wanted, was the Libyan model.

This reiterated the thought expressed by the current, though no doubt soon to be fired, extravagantly moustachioed National Security Advisor John Bolton, who said that the US was seeking the Libyan model in its efforts to denuclearise the Democratic People's Republic of Korea.

The Libyan model, for those with short memories, or who can not be bothered to look it up, started with a US led invasion and ended with the Libyan leader tortured, mutilated and dead.

The reason Kim Jong-un built those nuclear weapons in the first place was to avoid exactly that scenario, so it looks very much like the Americans deliberately torpedoed the summit.

Why would they do that, after the DPRK had been making nice?

There might be two reasons. The first is that the meaning of the word 'denuclearisation' might be as difficult to define as it is to say.

The Americans think it means getting rid of all of Kim's nuclear weapons.

The Koreans think it means that they will not test any more nuclear weapons. They blew up their testing facility to show good faith.

To be fair to the US, that is not much of a concession – how many times do you need to test a bomb? You press a button and it goes bang.

You can't test all the bombs, as they will all explode and you will have no more bombs. At some point, even a country that is run by a madman will have to say that those weapons have been tested enough.

The second reason for the Americans blowing up the peace process might be that powerful forces in the administration, and possibly even the great deal maker himself, realise that the last thing that Donald Trump is prepared for is meeting the head of a nuclear state, one on one, with only an interpreter as company, as it might not have the best outcome.

Trump is a man whose idea of negotiation is to fall to the floor and scream and whine 'till he gets his way.

This works if the other party is a grown-up. When two toddlers go at it, it could rapidly escalate to a shouting match and the world would be a charred cinder by the time the tea arrives.

Maybe Trump recognises his limitations and holed the meeting under the waterline to get out of going through with something he knows he is incapable of pulling off.

Just kidding – he thinks he is the most fabulous and effective leader any country ever had, so perhaps he crashed the summit by accident.

It does not really matter to him though, peace is not something that Trump's fans will respond to.

Trump's whole routine is to stoke fear in his supporters – Mexicans will rape you, Hillary will take your guns, the deep state is spying on you, the security services are against you, the liberals want to take your freedom.

A successful peace accord doesn't really fit into his act.

His fans don't want peace, they want war. Any war will do, it doesn't really matter who with, just as long as they get to watch some "bad hombres" getting killed on the news.

The human race seems to have taken a wrong turn.

We were going pretty well for a while there, but if aliens from space landed and asked to be taken to our leader, after some prevarication, we would be forced to introduce them to Nobel Peace Prize contender Donald Trump.

How embarrassing is that?

26.05.18

For whom the bell won't toll.

Today, number 87 in a never ending series of wonderment called: What Do They Do All Day?

In this episode, Andrea Leadsom obsesses about bongs.

Brexiteers have been told by the Commons authorities that Big Ben will not ring out to mark Britain's departure from the EU.

They are furious, but then fury is the emotion that seems to define the Brexiteer Ultras.

The only way some of them can tell they are still alive is if they are exhibiting signs of fury.

Conservative MP Andrea Leadsom took time out of her busy schedule to argue that the bell in the big tower should 'absolutely' peal in 'celebration' of the historic event, the moment that we rid ourselves of the European straitjacket that has plunged the country into austerity, ruined the NHS and caused potholes to remain unmended in the roads.

It must be the EU's fault, it can't be the government's fault, goodness me no, why would anyone think that?

When Ms Leadsom and her Tory colleagues were told the bad bell news they were sore upset.

That they were told that news by their current bête noir, the Speaker of the House of Commons John Bercow, just made it all the harder to take.

They announced, through their sodden hankies, that Remainers were in denial about leaving the EU.

Nothing will please them. They won the referendum but will remain unsatisfied 'till the entire nation unites behind them in glorying our departure with smiles and song and calls of hallelujah.

Haven't these people got anything better to do than play silly games about what bell rings when?

The reason the clock bell has not been heard since the New Year is that it is shrouded in scaffolding while undergoing what we are told are necessary repairs alongside the rest of the Palace of Westminster at a cost of everything we've got that's not being spent titivating Buckingham Palace.

These handsomely rewarded politicians might better spend their time wondering why we have an unlimited budget to tart up palaces but can not find the money to operate on tax payers' knees, hips and eyes.

That would be more a more useful way to while away the hours between lunch and dinner but wouldn't give them the opportunity to wrap themselves in the flag and score points in a game of who's the most patriotic.

Speaking as someone who once read the back cover of a psychology text book, I think these leaver MPs have got a screw loose. In campanology terms, they are one ring short of a peal.

Perhaps the leavers in Westminster are so touchy because they sense that, even now, they are in the minority.

The MP leavers numbered 156 on the day before the referendum, on 22 June 2016, the remainers were 425, the rest may have been too drunk to understand the question.

That nagging doubt that they might not have the support they need to get what they want might explain their determination to ring in the changes.

Celebratory Brexit bells would drown out all dissent.

Ms Leadsom is disappointed. Fellow Tory MP Nigel Evans said he was hugely disappointed.

Comedy top hatter Jacob Rees-Mogg expressed his disdain in that clenched, supercilious manner of an old Etonian from a bygone age.

Perspective was introduced by Eloise Todd of the pro-EU Best for Britain group who said: 'First it was stamps, then a bank holiday, then a new Brexit Britannia, then a plane and now Big Ben's bongs.

If these MPs actually concentrated on Brexit rather than rubbish like this then maybe we wouldn't be in this car-crash situation.'

Spot on Ms Todd.

The massed buffoonish ranks of the Brexiteer Ultras do not seem like serious people, but they have serious jobs.

Andrea Leadsom's website boasts that she is the Leader of the House of Commons and Lord President of the Council.

I assume these are ceremonial positions, as she is also an MP supposedly representing the interest of her constituents of South Northamptonshire, not to be confused with North Southamptonshire, which is east-west of there.

That's three jobs and yet she still has time to devote to fretting about the soundtrack of the glorious escape from our European overlords.

What dedication!

01.06.18

Hell is other people on holiday

Shane Richie has experienced his worst nightmare.

In case you don't have a television, or you have an aversion to ugly people shouting at each other in your living room, I should explain that Shane Richie is one of the stars of the long running misery-fest that is East Enders.

His worst nightmare come true was a "holiday from hell" that he paid good money for in a place called the Moon Palace Resort in the tourist hotspot of Mexico's sunny Cancun.

The holiday was so bad that Mr Richie is reportedly suing the travel firm that was so lax as to send him there.

He explained to the press that he decided to take his in-laws on a 17 day break, and I know what you are thinking – taking the in-laws on a 17 day holiday to anywhere sounds like the holiday from hell. What did he expect?

Well, the in-laws were not the problem, they were fine, the problem was everything else.

In the interests of research and journalistic integrity, I looked up Mexico's five star Moon Palace Resort to see what his hell-hole looks like.

It says right there on the front page of its website that it is an all-inclusive resort which they say means "kick back and relax, the check is covered."

"With the Palace all-inclusive experience," it says, "your only responsibility is to sue us afterwards".

I made that up, it did not say that. It actually says "your only responsibility is to enjoy unparalleled service, signature amenities and luxurious accommodations, 24 hours room service, and world class dining."

You can see from the pictures on its own website that it looks absolutely terrible, if your idea of terrible is an almost completely empty, spotlessly clean, fabulous sun trap which appears to have only a few gorgeous models as guests.

Maybe that was Shane Richie's problem - in that beautiful company he stuck out like a sore thumb.

No, that wasn't it either.

Mr Richie claimed, and this is a direct quote: 'loads of things happened'.

If those loads of things that happened were confined to a quiz night and a mariachi band in the bar, it might have been OK but apparently those loads of things included, but were not limited to, loud drum and bass music blaring out around the pool at 10.30am.

I'm with Shane Richie.

No one should have to put up with that.

And by "that", I mean you shouldn't have to listen to any music that was made after you turned 30.

Young people have always seemed determined to listen to music their parents can't stand.

My generation offended the ears of grown-ups with punk rock. The teenagers of today listen to a racket called drum and bass, which is OK if they are doing so in a sound-proof room, in the basement of an abandoned building on a deserted island.

It is not OK if they are playing it by the pool of a five-star luxury resort at 10.30 in the morning, in the presence of a television personality.

He said, "It was my worst nightmare. It was 'f*****g horrendous. I got spanked by them."

That word "spanked" must be East-ender slang denoting disappointment, and not some sort of service he bought on the spa menu.

The travel agents who are the subject of potential litigation are also disappointed.

A spokesperson said, "We are disappointed"

They said, "We did everything we could to help in the resort, including complimentary upgrades and an offer to move to the premium hotel next door."

I have been disappointed by a hotel experience and yet I have never been offered a complimentary upgrade or an offer of a better hotel next door.

In fact, the most I was offered was the opportunity to get lost, but that might be because I had not taken the precaution of becoming a TV star.

The Mail reports that a source close to the travel agency said: "Shane complained about holidaymakers taking pictures of him, having to get up at 5.30am to put towels on sunbeds, loud music by the pool and queuing to get eggs in the morning."

I have a solution to those problems:

a) don't take holidays among the general public if you are famous and like your privacy,

b) don't bother putting your towel on a sun lounger at 5.30 in the morning – you're on holiday for Pete's sake, lie in, relax, you deserve it,

c) if you follow solution b, you won't have a lounger, so you won't be by the pool and you won't hear that music.

Unfortunately I have no solution to the last problem.

Those pesky eggs won't queue for themselves you know, even in a five star, luxury, all-inclusive, unparalleled, world class resort.

02.06.18

All that bleeping is making you itch.

The thing you have in your pocket is a giant distraction machine.

Steady on there, I'm talking about your phone.

Every time your phone beeps or bleeps or buzzes or pings, it sends a shot of cortisone around your brain that makes you anxious.

It's that old FOMO: fear of missing out.

The constant calls for attention mean that you cannot give whatever you are supposed to be doing your full consideration. It's like an infant, always making a noise, insisting on being heeded.

Teenagers are particularly susceptible - brain scans show teenagers who have become hooked on their phones are more depressed, anxious and impulsive.

And if there's one group of people that don't need to be more depressed, anxious and impulsive, it's teenagers.

On grown-ups, it makes you miss deadlines, fail to be productive and appear as though you lack diligence.

Your smart phone is making you stupid. I have to admit that's a bit of relief – I thought it was just the way I am, turns out my phone is making a dummy out of me.

It's worse than that though because even if you switch your phone off, the computer on your desk is at it as well.

The bings and bongs from that are constantly demanding your time as well, so you cannot do the work you would have been doing if you hadn't been interrupted.

Scientists have even put a number on it – if you let your mind be perpetually disturbed by the persistent alarms of arriving communications, your productivity can go down by 40%.

It's a wonder we achieve anything at all.

If you get to the end of the working week and look back and reflect on what you have not been able to get done, don't despair – it's not that you are lazy, it's the internet's fault.

Doesn't it feel better to have something to blame?

Unfortunately, having an excuse for a lack of accomplishment does not mitigate the harmful effects of being placed always on edge by the vibrations and alarms of incoming messages.

All that cortisol running about your brain is usually to aid a flight-or-fight response.

It gears the body up for explosive action, it sits the mind on the edge of its seat, so to speak.

When no such action is forthcoming, when you do not spring out of your office chair and sprint down the corridor, the mind and body do not know quite what to do with all those danger chemicals.

The heart rate goes up, the muscles tighten but there is no release.

The effects build up to leave us in an almost constant state of fear. Every alert from your connected device means that supply of cortisol is topped up and eventually, we seek it out as a high.

It is the reason that people go on roller-coasters and see scary films – it is a little thrill without the associated dangers of doing something really perilous.

As long as it is infrequent, those activities add to the pleasure of life. If they are constant, on the other hand, they start to make you ill.

Imagine what life would be like if you had to travel everywhere by roller-coaster.

The result is more or less the same if you have your phone sound the arrival of every update, news story and message. You feel anxious until you can look at what that sound relates to.

We have become addicted to it, which is exactly what the tech giants want.

It didn't happen by accident, they planned it that way.

How the makers of other goods would love to get us addicted to their product.

There are laws about that though, especially if they have an effect on the brain.

Recreational drugs are illegal for that very reason.

Happily for the phone manufacturers and the social media companies, their products do not make you high, they only make you ill, so as far as Her Majesty's government is concerned, that's all right then.

09.06.18

Get out your bearskin party hats.

Rejoice! It is Her Majesty's birthday. Not the real one, the extra one she gets as a bonus for excellence in waving.

What do you get for the woman who has everything? A fantastically expensive and completely pointless nostalgia trip involving thousands of soldiers, musicians, horses, bands and carriages.

They stand in straight lines for ages, then twirl their rifles and march up and down to the accompaniment of quite a lot of shouting, which is the only thing that keeps much of those watching awake.

Her Majesty can see this ruinously expensive spectacle because she was lucky enough to jump straight to the front of the queue for cataract surgery, while her subjects idle on waiting lists 'till they go blind.

It is the Household Division, her personal soldiery, which provides the troops – more than 2,000 of them, all got up in costumes that must cost thousands and are totally useless for anything other than standing bolt upright, or perching on horseback while clip-clopping along at a stately pace.

The breathless television commentary told us that these men would be delighted that the Duke of York was leading them onto the parade ground.

I had to look up who the Duke of York is. It's Airmiles Andy! I'm sure the hardened men of that fighting force are over the moon.

Not only do they have him as their leader, the job they do was described as one of the worst jobs in the British Army.

The Daily Telegraph reported in 2005 that the troops who protect the royal palaces and the Tower of London are forced to live in "atrocious" conditions and have to undertake a variety of tasks that senior officers described as "onerous, debilitating, repetitive and unattractive" and that constitute "real and unique pain".

If you have ever stopped to gawp at one of them stood still for hours on end outside one of the many palaces at the royal family's disposal, you might have wondered how they do it. The boredom and discomfort that must come with remaining stationary under all that kit in the blazing sun, or the pouring rain, looks excruciating.

They do it because of the severe punishment that is doled out if they fail.

Still, as long as the Queen's happy.

Those poor soldiers, at least some of whom must have signed up because they believed the ads on the telly about hanging out in bars with your mates, impressing girls and going to exciting places to shoot people, are instead spending most of their day polishing silly bits of antiquated uniform that seem designed to collect dirt and repel a shine.

And what kit they have got! Each and every one of those men and women parading up and down must be stood up in thousands of pounds worth of uniform, knee-high boots and hats made of dead bears.

The horses don't come cheap either – you can't just park one and forget it 'till the next time a royal personage requires an escort from another age.

Then there's the cost of the barracks in prime central London and the assorted trainers and handlers and all the tailors, hatters and cobblers.

If there are over a thousand officers, two hundred horses and more than 200 musicians with all their instruments and regalia, shall we say that it must cost easily five million pounds a year to maintain those that put on the birthday parade?

This, at a time when the Prime Minister's former Chief of Staff Nick Timothy said senior military figures have told him that government cuts have left them with their worst equipment shortfall in decades.

There are barely enough tanks, artillery pieces, radios and body armour to properly equip 40,000 soldiers – less than half of the army's 82,000 standing strength.

We don't have the money to protect our soldiers in battle, but we do for an RAF fly-past and the cost of closing much of London and all the attendant police security.

It's not as though the police couldn't be better spending their time. The incidence of violent crime has increased by 100% in the last ten years in the capital. The murder rate went up 44% last year alone.

Yet there they were, making sure that no passing member of the public got too near the show they were paying for.

They could probably hear the national anthem from behind the barricades, even though they won't have been able to see the person it was being played to.

That funereal tune is all about the leader of the family who happens to be in the big chair when it is played. The winner of the game of thrones is the one who our country's own song is about.

The hymn of praise doesn't mention us lot at all, apart from the bit about us being pleased to pour on her our "choicest gifts".

So that's what you give to the woman who has everything, on her second birthday of the year.

10.06.18

Cancelled for our convenience.

You may have to travel to work on one of our (third) world-class train lines. The man to thank for the conditions on your commute is Mark Carne, who is Chief Executive of Network Rail.

If you want to thank him though, you will have to hurry, as he is leaving the job that he has held for four years.

And what years they have been.

It might be that long since you were able to find a seat on the 8.05 to Waterloo.

As he departs his exalted position to go home, he can reflect on the impact that he has had on the essential transport infrastructure of the nation.

He'll probably take a cab.

He can afford it. For the job of stewarding the railways to its current level of efficiency and exactitude, he was paid £820,000 last year.

You will recall that in 2014, he oversaw the Boxing Day misery that left tens of thousands of travellers stranded or delayed and refused to cut short his holiday to sort it out.

When questioned over whether it was appropriate for him to accept a bonus on top of his vast salary, he laughed and said it was only going to be a maximum of £135,000 and he thought we had "more important things to talk about" than his finances.

That's the way to ingratiate yourself with the poor, penurious public who fork out through the nose to use a transport system that fails them on a daily basis.

It's that tact and diplomacy that got him to the top.

He was berated in the press and after ridiculing the suggestion that he should forego the bonus, he relented just 24 hours later.

More recently there has been the debacle of the new improved timetable.

It would not have been an improvement if it had replaced no service at all.

Calculating the number of cancellations, delays and slow running trains would have taxed Microsoft.

Over the past month, if you were going for a train, you simply assumed it would not arrive, so as to avoid disappointment.

Passengers have been blown across station forecourts by the volume of apologies coursing from the loudspeakers of rail companies.

They were sorry for the cancellation of the train that replaced the train that didn't arrive because of scheduling difficulties. They apologised for the inconvenience and hoped that the non-arrival of the "service" did not delay our journey.

WELL OF COURSE IT BLOOMIN' WELL DID!

It has got so bad that we have strayed into realm of old jokes.

Did you hear the one about the driver of an empty bus who sailed past queues of people waiting at the stops because if he had halted to let them on, he wouldn't have been able to keep to the timetable?

Well, that's exactly what is being planned to ease the overcrowding on the trains – just don't let passengers on.

I am not making that up.

The government's proposal, penned by the geniuses at the Department of Transport proposes that some trains are not listed on the timetable or the station departures board.

These ghost trains would appear as though by magic and would let passengers off but not allow them to board. That way it cuts down on the crush.

The report titled "CrossCountry Passenger Rail Franchise public consultation" would affect cities like Leeds, Sheffield, Newcastle, Glasgow, Bristol and Birmingham.

If you happen to live in any of those fine places, your train might be arriving shortly, we really can't say when, it's a secret.

Network Rail is the company that controls the tracks and the stations, and you will be pleased to know that as it has presided over cancellations and delays, while punctuality has fallen, as it has missed public performance targets and as less than half their customers think they are getting value for money, their profits have surged.

The more people complain about the delays and the toilets on board and not being able to find a seat, the company that is responsible is doing better than ever.

And profits means bumper prizes for those in the offices on the top floor.

Oh, and the Chief Executive Mark Carney was just awarded a CBE.

He is now a Commander of the British Empire for services to the rail industry.

That's one of those jokes that isn't funny.

15.06.18

Making frenemies

While the President of the United States of America cosies up to dictators and calls them smart, European officials are still upset over their treatment at the hands of the demented orange whirlwind.

The French Foreign Minister Jean-Yves Le Drian hit the nail *sur la tête* when he said, "In the space of just a day you see President Trump attacking Canadian leader Mr. Trudeau, who is an historic ally...and the next day practically hugged a dictator born into a communist dictatorship, which just a few days ago he said he was completely opposed to,"

Donald Trump changes his mind more than most people change their underwear.

First, the meeting with the North Korean leader was never going to happen - "waste of time", then it was all infantile insults about "little rocket man", which he repeated so often that he must have thought it was among the most amusing witticisms that humankind has ever created – best insult ever, everybody says so, I can tell you that, totally great insult, I know the best insults, no-one knows better insults than me...

This was followed by the summit being on, then off, then on again.

Who would doubt Trump's word, apart from anyone that has ever had any dealings with him?

At the meeting, he cosied up to L'il Fat Kim so much that Melania must have got jealous...or probably relieved that her husband has a new love interest.

132

Trump claims that the "deal" he made with Kim was all due to "my touch, my feel, it's what I do", as many former Miss World's can attest.

Of course, the "deal" was all worked out ahead of time, before Trump even landed in Singapore. He reportedly became bored and grumpy on arrival on Sunday and demanded that the meeting be moved from Tuesday to Monday.

This is understandable, as the whole thing was just a photo-opportunity, no real deal making was entered into.

He was persuaded to keep to the timetable as it was explained to him that, had the meeting taken place on Monday, it would have been late at night on Sunday in America, and he would not have received the wall-to-wall TV coverage he craves so very much.

When asked by a reporter how he knew that Kim would keep his word, Trump replied in that self-aggrandising way that is his trademark and announced that he had an unparalleled ability to read people.

Pressed on what might happen if the North Koreans acted as they had in the past and agreed to things they never had any intention of delivering, Trump slipped up in his Tourettes stream of lies and said something true.

He said, "I may stand before you in six months and say, 'Hey, I was wrong."

Then he caught himself and added: "I don't know that I'll ever admit that, but I'll find some kind of an excuse."

And there you have the political philosophy of the US President: take all the credit, unless it is something bad, and then it will be someone else's fault...probably Hilary's.

Those in the West are trying to understand what motivates Trump to appease dictators and pick fights with America's traditional friends.

Donald Trump never met a murderous, tyrannical dictator he didn't like. That weasel who runs Canada on the other hand...

He says the mass-murdering psychopath Rodrigo Duterte of the Philippines is "doing an unbelievable job on the drug problem", a "job" that has seen executions in the thousands and cash rewards for those that kill anyone either dealing or taking drugs.

Duterte said "I don't care about human rights, believe me". It looks like he has a soul mate in the Whitehouse.

Trump called Chinese President for life Xi Jinping a "good guy", Vladimir Putin is "very smart", yet America's closest ally, Canada, is run by a man who is "very dishonest and weak".

Trump falls over himself to appease dictators and cosy up to every strong man ruler he can find, while showing how tough he is by starting fights with allies.

This just shows how needy and weak a person Trump is.

He doesn't want war, he ran for office on the promise to bring back troops from abroad not send more out, so he appeases America's enemies to avoid conflict with strong adversaries.

He knows that Britain or France, Canada or Germany will not attack under any provocation, especially desperate-for-a-trade-deal Britain, so he treats allies like dirt, knowing he can get away with it.

It makes him appear tough, and his presidency is all about appearances.

That piece of paper he signed in Singapore, with that big-boy angry squiggle, guaranteed absolutely nothing and contained weaker promises than those previously given by North Korea that they subsequently broke.

On his arrival back home, Trump tweeted that "There is no longer a Nuclear Threat from North Korea."

The most optimistic scenario you can think of is that he doesn't actually believe what he tweets – that he knows he is lying and just says anything to make himself look good at any time.

That would be OK if he was still just the host of that stupid Your Fired game on the telly but, embarrassingly for the human race, he's our default leader.

There seems a fault with our default leader.

16.06.18

Here we go, here we go, here we go (again)

It's that time again, when the nation lines up behind our boys and fails to dampen their expectations that this time we're going to go all the way.

Previous experience tells us that this will not come to pass. Knowledge of the ability possessed of the Germans or the Brazilians counts for nothing.

The new manager knows his stuff and Kane, Alli, Rashford, Vardy et al are all top players, right up 'till their first disappointing performance when they will instantly morph into donkeys, dopes, has-beens and never-weres.

In the period up to the start of the World Cup, the lack of expectation was palpable. Unconcern was in the air.

Now it's begun, the emotions take over, the nation demands that the lads will do their duty, the beers are bought and the flags are out.

Except they aren't. Not the flags anyway – against council rules, you see.

Taxi drivers in Barrow-in-Furness have been told they could be punished by the council's licensing committee for displaying England flags on their cars.

To be fair, this also applies to other nation's flags but that was lost on one cabbie who said it was political correctness gone mad.

In truth, I don't know if anyone has actually said that, but it's a fair bet.

Graham Barker is Barrow Borough Council's Public Protection Manager, a position I am not making up, and he said the flags were banned because: 'We don't want taxis with clip-on flags or internal flags. It's not allowed. It may well distract drivers of other vehicles.'

He's right, but then they could also be distracted by those beads and crosses and car fresheners and other assorted nick-nacks that people hang off their rear-view mirrors.

Roadside adverts that look like giant TV screens, constantly changing, they're quite distracting…that's their purpose.

The radio is distracting too, especially when a talk-show host such as myself says something stupid that causes the driver to shout at their dashboard.

A car's passengers can be detrimental to concentration, as can wasps and totally hot babes of all three sexes on the footpath.

Ogling causes accidents.

Fortunately, there are no hot babes in Barrow-in-Furness, or so I have heard.

There are footie fans, though, and many would appreciate the opportunity to visibly take part in the nation's imminent disappointment by displaying this country's emblem.

The National Private Hire Association spokesperson said that the only way for drivers to get around a ban would be to take the council to court.

But really, what's the point, we won't be in the tournament long. Legal proceedings seem like so much effort.

The NPHA person explained their opposition to the ban by saying that 'The public aren't going to stand in the middle of the road and get knocked down.'

Unfortunately, that's not true, they do – they walk into the road gawping at their phones, or they walk in front of traffic and assume that if they are tough, that traffic will stop for them…but a 2 ton car driven by a wimp usually beats a doughy human pedestrian with an attitude.

This is lost on them 'till they are flung through the air into a bus stop by an apologetic driver.

The flag ruling is not restricted to just Barrow - the Royal Mail banned its 125,000 walking, cycling and van delivery workers from displaying flags and stickers to support England for health and safety reasons.

Bosses claimed the flags and stickers could blow off and become hazards.

Is it that, or are we still somewhat embarrassed by the England flag?

We are alone in the world as people who have given up ownership of our own national emblem because some ultra-right-wingers once used it.

We seem to have said, well, that's not fit for polite society any more and gifted the flag of the nation to extremists.

The Japanese wouldn't let that happen and neither would Australia, Iceland, Portugal or Peru.

And yet we share one great similarity with all those countries.

They aren't going to get to the final either.

23.06.18

Trump gets a cage

On the subject of taking babies from their parents and putting them in cages, Donald Trump is letting his wife's wardrobe do the talking.

Melania doesn't care and he doesn't care.

And anyway, those babies aren't the best and the finest.

When Mexico sends its babies, they're not sending their best...they're sending babies that have lots of problems...they're bringing drugs, they're bringing crime, they're rapists...and some, I assume, are good babies.

The whole world was aghast at this fresh hell that came out of the Trump administration this week.

Even some of his fans stopped cheering him at the sight and sound of children crying in cages.

Foreign governments expressed their dismay and Time magazine placed on its cover a smug Trump lowering over a crying child,

Trump likes Time magazine a lot.

He preened when they made him their Person of the Year, assuming that it was a celebration of his great orange awesomeness and not simply a reflection of him being the most newsworthy person of the previous twelve months.

He likes featuring on the cover so much that he lies about how many occasions that he has featured on it and even had a fake cover made, arms crossed, heavily made up, with a headline boasting about his ratings on the Apprentice TV show that he had framed and hung in his golf clubs.

Time wanted that one taken down and Trump didn't want to see its latest one at all, as it showed him in an unflattering light as a cruel and unusual man so desperately needy that he would pick on children to get his way.

That cover might have been the final push he needed to rescind his policy on separating families which he thought would force the Democrats to fund his big beautiful wall on the border.

The state broadcaster, Fox News, maintained its line that everything Trump does smells of roses and blamed Hilary, or the Democrats, or the Fake News Media for the splitting apart of families.

Trump couldn't do anything to help, they said, it was the law, you see, and God insists that the law is good – says so right there in the Bible, so that's all right then, Jesus is OK with it.

His wife, Melania, went to see the crying children for herself wearing that "I really don't care, do you?" jacket.

That was a middle finger raised to the world, a doubling down from the Trumps, a massive trolling that eclipsed even her husband's worst Twitter outpourings.

There followed more outrage than even Trump could withstand and it forced him to reverse his policy.

With a flourish of his big-boy squiggle on what looked like a restaurant menu, he casts edicts out like a boy throws away a burger wrapper and his minions run around trying to work out how to adapt to this new direction.

The right wing press was already on-side. They praised Trump for his kind-hearted leadership.

The BS is piling up so fast you need wings to stay above it.

This is the man that we are desperate to ingratiate ourselves with to get a trade deal after we leave the Evil European Empire.

That's not in the least shameful or embarrassing – why would anyone think that?

Our government's attitude to Trump appears to be that we will stick by him no matter what he does, aside from a little light scolding that I am sure is telegraphed to him ahead of time, so as not to make him grumpy.

When it comes to how we make money, it seems that we don't care either.

24.06.18

A special relationship

Donald Trump's right hand man and emissary to these shores says that the special relationship is still as strong as ever.

Robert Johnson is a close friend of the President and has coincidentally been gifted the prime position of US Ambassador to Britain.

The Ambassador is not a relative of Robert Johnson, the blues singer – he is the talcum-powder white heir to Robert Johnson of the Johnson and Johnson baby products fortune.

He didn't make that fortune, he was just fortunate enough to be born into it, and now he is using his position to tell us Brits how to go about our business.

He told us to be less pessimistic and have faith.

On the first count, he doesn't know us very well – pessimism is how we like to approach life, it defines us and might be down to the weather – constantly grey and depressing.

We positively wallow in pessimism, so asking us to drop that emotion is like asking us to whoop during an orchestral recital.

On the "faith" issue, we have turned the corner on that, thank you very much and we no longer subscribe.

Two thirds of Britons described themselves as having no religion in 2015, and we have shown no desire to return to the pews.

Mr Johnson is particularly baffled by our lack of faith and pessimism over Brexit.

He said, 'How can a country with this great a history, this great a language, this great a legal system and this great a presence not be successful?'

Well, in the same way that a company that has a great history and a great advertising and legal system and presence on the high street can fail.

Things that were great fail all the time, it's called Darwinism.

Those entities that used to be fit for their environment can wither when their environment changes – just ask the dinosaurs.

Ask those other former giants brought low by circumstance and mismanagement like the Roman Empire, ask Woolworths, ask newspapers, ask Venezuela, ask the USSR.

Johnson explained that we should be running our country like Donny runs his, by giving out tax cuts.

Those US corporation tax cuts were announced with great fanfare as a way to Make America Great Again and some companies immediately proposed wage increases for their workers to give that notion credence and maximum publicity.

What they did not say was that only about 5% of the tax cut was redistributed in higher wages for the workers, 95% of it was shared out among those few occupiers of the executive suites and the already spectacularly wealthy stock holders.

Remember, 80% of the world's stocks are owned by the richest 10% of families.

By an amazingly lucky break, the tax cuts that Trump has put in place have also benefited the family of one Donald Trump.

He has about 500 separate businesses, which pass money to the Trump family, an income that used to be taxed at about 40%.

The new tax regime places a cap on that tax rate of what is called pass-through income of just 25%.

When he passed the tax law, Trump said to a private meeting of fellow billionaires at his Mar-a-Lago golf resort: "you all just got a lot richer", and so did he.

The 5% for the workers received a lot more publicity from the Whitehouse than the vast increase in wealth it afforded the rich.

When put like that, it does seem like the sort of the policy that the Conservatives would be eager to follow.

Their main source of funding is a few rich individuals and corporations who would be delighted to be able to keep even more of their money than their armies of clever accountants currently allow.

In that regard, we're playing follow the leader just like we always have.

That's the nature of our special relationship and it remains as strong as it ever was.

29.06.18

Titfer Stat.

Britain's economy grew faster than expected in the first three months of the year.

The hard times are over. It's a Brexit miracle!

Finally the Remoaner nay-sayers will have to eat their words. Project fear is vanquished. Jacob Rees-Mogg for Prime Minister...no..make that Queen.

The man who sounds like he's straining his vowels through a linen handkerchief he keeps his monocle in should be made Head of State with immediate effect.

Sorry Prince Charles, you get passed by – you're not remotely posh enough.

Onwards Albion, onwards and upwards!

Just one thing – we may be outdoing the growth figures the Office for National Statistics predicted for the first quarter of 2018, but that doesn't mean we are doing well.

It just means we are doing less badly than originally thought.

The ONS, the nation's foremost producer of official statistics and probably its least fun place to work, announced that in spite of its earlier pronouncements, the UK's income did not grow by 0.1% between January and March.

They got that wrong. They must have had pizza smears on the inside of their spectacles when they came up with that figure. I mean, it's preposterous...who would believe that fast-forward, open-for-business Brexit Britain would produce such a risible result?

No, our national growth figure was not 0.1%, it was a heady 0.2%.

Hallelujah, austerity is over, the economy is right on track, we're a force to be reckoned with, the EU need us more than we need them, stick that in your pipe Monsieur Barnier!

But how did we achieve this world beating outcome?

Well, it was the construction industry what done it.

The business that produces all those charmless towers of luxury flatlets for foreign investors that decorate the London skyline, and the tiny houselets with tiny rooms and tiny windows for us Brits, have done very well.

Or rather, they have done less badly than previously thought.

The reason the ONS had to revise its figures on our national growth is that the construction industry did not retract by 1.7%, as previously thought, it only fell back by 0.8%.

Let the bells ring out; it's bad but not as bad as we thought.

And that's good news for Britain, or it is less terrible news than expected, which counts as a stellar result if you are trying to convince the public that we are profiting from our exit from the Evil Undemocratic European Socialist Superstate.

If only there were figures for how our major competitor nations fared over the first quarter of the year, we might be able to contrast our stellar performance with their languid affairs.

Happily, I happen to have those figures to hand.

The Organisation for Economic Co-operation and Development publish the figures for growth of all the countries on Earth.

I shall omit the ones for places that I can't point to on a map and concentrate on our main competitors.

The OECD disagrees with the ONS about our growth rate – they insist that it is 0.1% for the quarter, but let us assume they are wrong and our own ONS are right.

That still leaves us trailing...well, almost everyone.

Here is a full list of the countries that did worse than us: Saudi Arabia, Ireland, Estonia, Japan and South Africa.

Absolutely everywhere else in the first world, and much of the second, fared better than us.

Belgium made a 0.32% increase in its income, Norway scored 0.63% growth, Spain's economy improved by 0.7%, Sweden scored 0.72%, Poland's finances improved by 1.64%.

The EU as a group averaged 0.4%, which is either two or four times our result, depending on the statisticians you believe.

I know that's a lot of figures, and that no-one is interested in facts any more, but the upshot is that if those numbers indicate that we are profiting from Brexit already, I'll eat Jacob Rees-Mogg's monogrammed eye-glass polisher.

30.06.18

All aboard the gravy plane!

Their royal highnesses Prince Charles and the Duchess of Cornwall took a modest government plane on a two-week holiday last year.

When I say holiday, I do of course mean that they were on official business that entailed being entertained, wined and dined and had their every conceivable need and whim catered for.

It might seem like a holiday to us but that is because we do not see the very hard work they do while they are on such sojourns, to wit: smiling, shaking hands and engaging in chit-chat.

They took in Singapore, Brunei, Malaysia and India last autumn and the transport that got them there was indeed a government plane but it was modest only in that it was coloured grey.

They took a lavishly converted Airbus A330, a plane that is so large you could race horses in it, and the cost to us poor dopes who pay taxes was a princely £362,149.

It was the most expensive trip taken by a member of the Royal Family last year but that does not mean the others were what you might call economical.

The usual royal hem-sniffers were sent out to explain that this expense was right and proper and the future king could not possibly be seen arriving in the third world on anything as low grade as First Class on an ordinary plane.

Imagine the embarrassment!

They further insist that the Royal Family understand how the finances of the nation are suffering, as when William and Kate went to India and Bhutan the previous year, they flew by a lowly commercial airline at a cost of only £35,372, after which they had their people hire a private jet to travel between the two countries for just £62,331, totalling about £100,000.

See? It can be done on a budget! Only a £100,000 charge to the public for the flights for a brief trip to the sun.

Truly the Windsors understand the constrained finances of Austerity Britain.

It is a good job they do, as while Charles and Camilla were working their socks off in Brunei, his brother Prince Edward and his wife Sophie went there to, by scheduled airline, at a cost of £21,534.

They couldn't have gone on the same empty plane, from the same country to the same destination?

I suppose we should be grateful that they only cost us 21 grand.

Still, that does seem a lot for two people to go to a place that is not in outer space.

Palace apologists claim that the royals do not chose where to go on official overseas tours, they are requested to go by the Foreign Office, by a mode of transport chosen by the Royal Travel Office.

And that may be true, but would you be entirely surprised if the Palace called up the Foreign Office and said: Charles would like to go to meet his billionaire friends in Brunei and he'd like to go by a really big plane so he doesn't lose face in such rich company and would you be so kind as to officially ask him to go so that he doesn't have to pay for any of it?

I mean, they don't call up and send him off to somewhere he doesn't want to go, like he's a child going to boarding school.

Those plane trips aren't the half of it, though.

There's the royal train.

If ever there was a train that takes the strain out of travel, it's this one.

It costs us £20,000 every time Charles gets on board. He did that seven times last year. One hundred and forty thousand pounds for seven trips to the countryside.

It runs on rails - he could have got any other train that runs on those rails and paid for the whole of first class so he didn't have to slum it with the proles and he would still have easily saved a hundred grand, but what does he care?

He isn't paying for it. Us poor dopes who pay taxes are doing that.

We are like a one arm bandit that pays out every time a Windsor walks by.

The authorities say the bill for the royals just getting about the place was £4.7m last year. That is probably just a top line figure and doesn't include preparations for their majesties' arrivals and departures, policing, the plumping of royal cushions and all the rest of it.

When the royal travel expenses figures are released every year, their staff then have to furrow their brows and try to sell this as value for money to a public that has had its operation cancelled by the NHS for lack of money.

Security concerns are always a winner.

Nothing to do with us, they say...government security advice..couldn't take an ordinary plane...much too risky for their majesties.

If that doesn't wash, they pull out the "it's for your own good" excuse: well, of course his royal highness must arrive on the most wildly extravagant mode of transport...sends out the right message while we're after trade agreements, you see?

If they are really pushed into a corner, they will produce their trump card which is to take a low estimate of the cost of the royal family, ignoring the bulk of the expenditure which is on things like security and the tarting up of places they visit, and say how much it costs us individually.

Instead of conjuring excuses, I would have thought it would be appropriate for the family of the head of state of a country that can't afford to investigate crimes or fund the health service to be seen to be doing their bit by reigning it in, but I suppose that's traitor talk

It's not like they can't afford to pay their own way.

The Prince of Wales income from the Duchy of Cornwall rose by 4.9 per cent to £21.7million last year, and he also got £1.2million from the Sovereign Grant from the Government.

He paid £4.8million in tax, which he does voluntarily,

Wouldn't that be nice, to be able to pay whatever amount of tax you want on a purely voluntary basis?

Charles' mother isn't short of a bob or two either.

If he thinks times are tight on only £30m a year – he could ask for a loan from the bank of mum and dad.

The Queen's income also rose last year, as you would expect. It went up to £45.7million, and next year it will be £82m.

Right on cue, a spokesman tasked with placating any sceptical members of the public said the cost of the royals broke down to 69p per man, woman and child in the UK.

You know someone is trying to hide an unpalatable truth when they break a number down into 66 millionths.

06.07.18

What the public likes, the public gets

Shock news just in: people like what's bad for them.

A survey is taken twice yearly to gauge the public's favourite company for customer satisfaction.

Drug dealers and brothels are ineligible, so the list is made up of what used to be called high street names, before the high street had more empty spaces in it than a tramp's teeth.

The tip topper-most name on the list is probably John Lewis, you might suppose.

They run an employee-owned partnership that shares its profits with its staff, rather than exclusively among the people in the boardroom.

They have that "never knowingly undersold" slogan they have stood by for 92 years and hot and cold running assistants to attend to your every question, curiosity, problem and need.

In one of John Lewis' 48 stores, the customer can finger the goods, stroke them, touch them, smell them and fondle them, see how they might fit in their home and check them for quality.

They have a marvellous returns policy and it is a shining example of what a retail outlet can achieve when all its staff are valued and rewarded and given bonuses, not just the people who run it.

The bosses are rewarded well, of course, but not so well that their other car is a spaceship.

The 30,000 partners that work in John Lewis did not win this survey, however, little rocket man Jeff Bezos did.

Amazon, the disruptive goliath with the scorched earth policy, the global mega-corporation that has decimated once thriving town centres is Britain's best company for consumer satisfaction.

Customers are apparently happy with the death of their high street and the disappearance of all those jobs and businesses.

They must be happy with the collapse of their local book shops, electronics stores, clothes boutiques, toy marts, kitchen emporia and baby chains.

A few low paid, menial jobs in warehouses have replaced the multitude of life-affirming ones lost by people that used to run their own stores or who dealt with the public face-to-face.

Those workers now pull things off a shelf in some dystopian mega-shed, as ordered by a computer, and the public is fine with that.

They are happy with one company becoming so vast that it can have entire cities competing with each other to give it tax breaks to host one of its facilities there and they're happy that its owner Jeff Bezos is now worth about $120bn and is the richest person who ever lived and spends his money on rocket ships and leather jackets, rather than redistribute some of the profits to his minimum wage workers.

The British customer is also happy, or couldn't care less, that their favourite company also doesn't appear to pay what a reasonable person might call their fair share in tax.

In Europe as a whole, Amazon paid £15m in tax last year, which is a lot of money, but not as much as £19.5 billion, which is the amount they booked in revenue through their tax efficient office in Luxembourg.

In the same year, Amazon halved its payment to Her Majesty's Revenue and Customs to just £7.4m, despite the fact that its income from the small amount that it actually declares in the UK doubled.

Think of that – its income went up 50% and its tax payment went down by 50%, and the British public couldn't be happier.

I suppose it could be worse – we could owe THEM money. In other news, HMRC handed Amazon a £1.3m tax credit in 2017, despite its British sales surging to £7bn.

Oxfam's head of inequality, Ana Arendar, said multinationals like Amazon "are able to exploit flaws in global tax laws and use tax havens to avoid paying their fair share".

Amazon trotted out the usual line which is utilised by every giant corporation that wishes to swat away such complaints, saying Amazon pays "all taxes required in the UK and every country where we operate".

Six years ago, the then head of John Lewis said Amazon's tax avoidance 'will drive UK companies out of business'.

That they have done.

All the tax that used to flow virtuously thorough the economy, from customer to bricks-and-mortar shops, to managers and assistants and suppliers, who paid their taxes in full because they had to because they lived and worked here and didn't have armies of accountants and lawyers to minimise their obligations – that's all gone.

The money has been drained out of the economy like water down the pug hole of a bath.

The money we once used to fund the NHS, build and maintain the roads, pay the police, keep the lights on and collect the rubbish, now sits unused, as a number on a screen in an empty office located on a moon circling Jupiter for tax reasons.

It looks very much like we poor dopes who pay taxes are subsidising the richest man who ever lived by stumping up for the health of his workers, the highways he delivers his goods on, the protection afforded his business interests by a keeping a law abiding society and cleaning up the place.

The British people have declared that they are happy with all that because they saved ten pence and had someone bring them the thing they didn't need, that they bought with money they didn't have, rather than put on their clothes and step out of the house to go to the shops that they complain aren't there any more.

07.07.18

What are you like, grandad?

A new study has found that the older people get, the more racist they become.

Isn't that an astonishing finding? Aren't you absolutely stunned?

Not everyone, of course. If you are a senior citizen reading this, I am sure that you are the very model of acceptance and inclusivity.

I'm talking about other, older, less "woke" people than your good self.

This discovery comes from the branch of social science I took at university, which I know as the study of the bloomin' obvious.

Psychologists have three suggestions as to why people become more racist as they age.

Firstly, they claim that they become more prejudiced with the passing years because they feel increasingly insecure and anxious about death.

Some scientists say that hating an easily identifiable group can bring a sense of belonging and identity, and discussing their boiling hatred with others helps deal with facing their imminent demise.

Like a box of chocolates, prejudice is good to share.

It gives them a sense of enormous well-being to swap their poison about those that are different from them, with those that are the same as them.

It almost makes life worth clinging on to.

This is all according to Dr Steve, a psychologist at Leeds Beckett University, which is an actual institution of learning, and not something I just made up.

He thinks that the fear of death is countered by clinging to identity, to try and gain a sense of belonging, to be part of a gang, which helps engender a sense of protection.

By demonising other groups we deal with the anxiety of our own mortality by establishing our own identity.

Sorry to disagree Dr Steve, but I don't think that's it.

An alternative view was expressed by psychotherapist Dr Allison, who thinks that rather than a need to belong, it is the insecurities caused by ageing that propels the aged into prejudice.

Her conjecture is that the myriad quirks of advancing years – ill health, the drooping, sagging and malfunction of our bodies makes us project onto others our own self-loathing.

If you don't like yourself, how can you like others? Low self-esteem leads to the externally expressed hatred of others, because the alternative is to project that hatred inwards, and we would rather hate others than hate ourselves.

I'm not sure about that one either.

The third explanation is that their brains are on the fritz.

Research from the University of Queensland, Australia, showed that as we age, the part of our brain that regulates emotional outbursts gets smaller.

The thing that is involved with controlling our thoughts is the frontal lobe, which is not as rude as it sounds.

As it shrinks, the elderly lose that voice in their heads that tells them to tone a notion down a bit before expressing it out loud.

What results is that they lose the ability to censor their views, and then they are filmed ranting at a passenger on a train and they achieve fame late in life when the video goes viral on YouTube.

While that is persuasive, I don't much like that explanation either.

I would suggest, based on no knowledge of anything whatsoever, that people do not get more racist as they get older, they were always that racist.

After stifling their darkest thoughts and bottling them up for fear of public castigation during the politically correct decades since the 1980's, they get to an age when they just don't care what people think any more and all that contained bile just starts spewing out.

Society finds it in its heart to forgive or ignore them because they are old.

I think people appear to get more racist as they age because they get a free pass for bad behaviour when they get a free pass for bus travel.

13.07.18

A hugely, tremendously, most special relationship.

The news this week, as it has been ever since the Screaming MeMe became the leader of the free world, was dominated by Donald Trump.

The wide-eyed awe and kid-in-a-sweet-shop delight that the press approach the permanent news-gasm that is the President of the United States of America meant that even the rescued boys from the Thai cave and the victims of the Russian poisoning in Salisbury were shunted off the front page as The Donald made an all-out assault on America's longest suffering ally.

Since taking office, he has made it his focus of attention, when he is not picking Twitter fights with celebrities, to destabilise all of America's traditional friends, while lavishing praise on their historical enemies.

He attacks Germany because it is a strong country in a powerful block. The EU is the only trading entity that comes close to the heft of the United States. It is practically their economic equal.

Trump's, and coincidentally Putin's goal is to split the EU up in order that their respective countries would be stronger by comparison.

Divide and conquer – it's the oldest trick in the book.

It is why Trump is urging Britain and France to split from the Europe completely, in order that he can negotiate with much weaker entities than would be the case if we were still part of the EU.

In that scenario, we would simply take what we are given and be grateful, rather than bog the President down in the tedious negotiating of trade deals that are not his forte.

He doesn't do detail. He prefers to issue edicts off the top of his head and have his minions run around trying to translate them into policy.

The berserk attacks on America's friends, like Canada for instance, should be sending warning bells ringing through Whitehall that he is not a man to be trusted, let alone depended upon for the future wealth of the nation.

We are leaving the security of the EU gang, to bet our future on the whims of an inveterate liar who has shown himself time and again to be a vain, narcissistic bully, only interested in how any action can benefit him personally, and who changes his mind about an issue in the same breath.

What could possibly go wrong?

His bizarre genuflecting before dictators can be explained through the prism of his preening self-interest.

When arriving at a friendly country like ours, he lobs a diplomatic hand grenade out of the plane before he touches down, to unsteady his hosts which has the result of making him appear stronger, in his mind.

It also places him in the spotlight, without which he may well wither like the melting Wicked Witch of the West.

The furore he creates plays well with the yokels in the Make America White Again hats back home. He's a tough guy, doing tough-guy stuff.

This is all in stark contrast to his behaviour towards dictators.

His ingratiation with Kim Jong-un and the boasting of peace in our time was in direct contrast to the North Korean leader's pronouncements and that country's actions after their bizarre "summit".

The Donald left tweeting that the world was a safer place and that he had worked his special orange magic on the roly-poly despot who had agreed to abandon all his nuclear weapons.

The Kim eventually said: oh no I didn't, but by then Trump has issued a mountain of other lies and the fact checkers of the fourth estate were left in a swirling eddy of misinformation that is the modus operandi of the occupier of the Whitehouse.

He says so many self aggrandising lies that it is impossible to respond in real time. The press scurry after him issuing corrections but by the time they have gone to print, they are hopelessly behind and buried under another volley of mendacity.

It must be like trying to crawl out of quicksand – the more you attempt to keep above ground, the more you sink into the mire.

What is obviously not "fake noos" is that Trump's special friend is, of course, Vladimir Putin.

As far back as Oct. 7, 2016, the Department of Homeland Security and Office of the Director of National Intelligence issued a joint statement on behalf of the agencies of the U.S. Intelligence Community – all 17 of them - that stated that the Russian Government "directed the recent compromises of e-mails from US persons and institutions, including from US political organizations...intended to interfere with the US election process."

The Robert Mueller investigation into Russian interference in the US election has so far led to the indictment of 25 Russians and three Russian companies and five guilty pleas from those that worked on Trump's campaign.

But Donny says he asked Vlad if he did it and Putin said *nyet*, so that's good enough for him, case closed, nothing to see here.

He is going to pay his respects to the Russian leader this week.

I will eat Jacob Rees-Mogg's top hat if he issues one word of disrespect to the leader of that nation, as he has done to the leaders of countries that have traditionally stood by America and acted with them against its perceived enemies.

He will do as he did when they last met – perch on the edge of his seat and blab about how tremendous a leader "Pootin" is and how well their talks have gone, while Putin sits back, motionless and silent, commanding the room, as his visitor fills the air with noise like a toddler on a sugar rush.

The contrast to how he treats the leaders of real democracies could not be more stark.

If we really are in a special relationship, it seems like an abusive one.

If our two countries were people, we would either be in counselling or the neighbours would have called the police by now.

14.07.18

He loves her, he loves her not.

Donald Trump is cross. He's grumpy like an infant that hasn't been burped.

The reason for his orange ire is the press. As usual reporters have written down what he said and put it in their newspapers, which is very unkind of them, BAD!

This time it is that they misrepresented the huge numbers of people marching through central London on Friday by reporting that they were rallying against him and not for him.

Their support could clearly be seen by the writing on the cards they were holding, which included but were not limited to :

"Feed him to the corgis", "We shall over-comb", "Without immigrants, Trump would have no wives", "In England, Trump means fart", a baby holding a sign that read "I'm less of a baby" and "Super callous fragile ego Trump you are atrocious", all of which were clearly marks of respect but the failing news media didn't report it that way, SAD!!

In order to make clear his position on our country, Trump sat down with a journalist from The Sun newspaper.

During the encounter, he criticised Theresa May's leadership, the way she was dealing with Brexit, declared that her nemesis Boris Johnson would make a great Prime Minister, threatened to kill any prospective trade deal with the UK because she didn't handle Brexit the way he told her to and furthermore, he didn't like her shoes.

Apart from that last one, which I made up, his words were transcribed and relayed into print at which point his aids must have run around like they had a cattle prod up their nethers to try and reduce the harm caused by insulting and undermining the host of the country which had gone out of its way to make his trip extra-special.

In trying to row back on his recorded position, Trump fell back on his special power of declaring that he had not said what he had just said.

Trump addressed The Sun's interview on Friday saying: "Unfortunately, there was a story that was done which was, you know, generally fine, but it didn't put in what I said about the prime minister, and I said tremendous things, and fortunately we tend to record stories now, so we have it for your enjoyment if you'd like it, but we record when we deal with reporters. It's called fake news."

No such recording was made available by the Trump administration.

The Sun's response read: "We stand by our reporting and the quotes we used – including those where the president was positive about the prime minister, in both the paper and in our audio – and we're delighted that the president essentially retracted his original charge against the paper later in the press conference.

"To say the president called us 'fake news' with any serious intent is, well … fake news."

Just wait 'till someone tells Trump that the owner of The Sun is the same Rupert Murdoch that owns Fox News, which is his main defender in America, to the point that it is practically the state broadcaster.

For the purpose of providing accuracy, this is an unedited transcript of the interview, which I have just made up:

"Theresa may is a disaster, she's weak and school-marmish and her hands are tiny – my hands are huge compared to hers, everybody says so I can tell you that.

I have the greatest respect for Theresa May, she is inspiring, she's doing a fantastic job,

She's terrible, she is so bad, it's really terrible for her country.

I like her, our relationship is special, it's the most special relationship of all time, even better than the relationship between me and my hot daughter…have you seen her…you know if I wasn't her father…well, I can tell you she's like Theresa May who is a great beauty, she is strong and a true leader.

She's hopeless, she's weak, and not that great looking, I have to tell you.

She is tremendous, I want to say that, Theresa is a great friend of mine.

I hate her, I would rather Boris Johnson was Prime Minister, he would do a lot better job.

I certainly would never say that anyone should be Prime Minister of another country, I never said that but I would say that Brexit is a catastrophe.

It's going very well.

It's exactly what the people voted for.

It's not what the people wanted at all.

And I haven't seen demonstrations, everybody in Britain loves me and I won't come again because of all the demonstrations that I have seen, which is not nice and totally wrong to insult a leader of such huge stature as Donald Trump who loves Theresa May very much.

We have a special relationship of great specialness.

I'd like to punch her in the face.

And anyone who says otherwise is fake news."

20.07.18

Maybe Vald made him an offer he couldn't refuse

During his hallucinatory press conference with the Russian President, Putin slouched in his chair and Donny perched on the edge of his, filling the air with noise, while Vlad made no attempt to look anything other than bored.

He didn't even acknowledge the flattery love-bombs that Trump was lobbing his way.

It seemed like we were intruding on a couple's relationship therapy session, where one partner was yearning for affection, while the other was mentally packing his suitcase and leaving a note on the mantelpiece.

If Donald Trump really is in the pocket of the Russian Premier, this is what it would look like.

A compromised US leader would side with the Russians over his own security community and would warm to the idea that Russia be allowed to interrogate accused Russian agents, on behalf of America, in order to assess whether they were guilty of spying on the US.

In return the Russians would get to interrogate American officials they deemed unfriendly.

Trump was impressed by what he called this "incredible offer".

Great idea, really tremendous, very generous, thank you.

Immediately after that press conference, even ordinarily spineless Republicans said damning things about their man, so Trump informed the press that he had got it wrong and apologised.

Just kidding, he blamed the media for writing down what he had said verbatim and printing it in their papers.

He wheeled out the hits that he repeats when he is at one of his safe-space rallies:

'The Fake News Media is going Crazy! They make up stories without any backup, sources or proof. Many of the stories written about me, and the good people surrounding me, are total fiction. Problem is, when you complain you just give them more publicity. But I'll complain anyway!', he wrote on Twitter.

Maybe it's his genius for misdirection, or maybe he's just flailing his arms in frustration that he can't just have journalists silenced like Putin does, but for a man who lies on record at an average of ten times a day, and who always quotes unnamed sources to back up his lies, that's a bit rich.

How many times have you heard him say something like – "a lot of people are saying...", or "everybody thinks that...", in order to back up some bizarre assertion?

It's ALL unnamed sources with him, because he just makes it up and then hushes people when they question him on detail.

This is another tweet - 'The Fake News Media wants so badly to see a major confrontation with Russia, even a confrontation that could lead to war. They are pushing so recklessly hard and hate the fact that I'll probably have a good relationship with Putin. We are doing MUCH better than any other country!'

What does that mean, "We are doing better than any other country"?

Better in what way, where's the proof, where's the source, what's he talking about?

And the idea that the media would prefer World War III rather than write something positive about Trump's relationship with the man who is trying to destabilise the US demonstrates a vaunting narcissism and a wide streak of victimhood.

Psychiatrists could have a field day. They'd need a bigger couch.

He also tweeted - 'The Summit with Russia was a great success, except with the real enemy of the people, the Fake News Media. I look forward to our second meeting so that we can start implementing some of the many things discussed, including stopping terrorism, security for Israel, nuclear........'.

The "enemy of the people" line, is lesson one in dictator school.

As for the meeting - we have no idea what they talked about because on Trump's insistence, no one else was present except the translator.

No records, no recordings, no notes.

What's suspicious about that?

At the press conference and photo call, they resembled two Mafia Dons – Don Vladimir "Snake-eyes" Putin and Don Donny "Wide-boy" Trump.

Between them it looked like they were carving up the world for themselves, in secret.

It also looked like Putin was Michael Corleone, the boss of bosses, and Donny was the dim-witted thug that runs the poor end of town and is careful not to step on Snake-eyes' territory for fear of being rowed out to the middle of a lake, like Fredo.

In that classic scene from The Godfather, Fredo famously insisted – "I'm smart. Not like everybody says, like dumb."

Ring any bells?

21.07.18

Offensive language

As part of Theresa May's strategy to win hearts and minds in Europe, she has had her people translate her finely moulded Chequers White Paper called 'Things the Cabinet Pretended to Agree on to Make Sure They Got a Car Home'.

Unfortunately, as you would expect if you have been following her travails, things did not go as smoothly as they might.

Firstly, the document was translated in its entirety from English into only one other language.

You might assume that would be French, which is historically the international lexicon of diplomacy, and you would be wrong.

German perhaps? Nope - Welsh.

The paper that is our offer to our European Union friends was provided in full in a language that is not recognised by the EU.

Welsh was chosen because...well, it makes as much sense as anything else that's been happening lately.

If we were to pick just one language, it might have been appropriate to produce it in Irish. The border question is a major sticking point after all, and it would have been a conciliatory gesture for having put them through so much stress.

When Donald Tusk, the President of the European Council, travelled to Dublin he made a point of addressing reporters in Irish, which they liked very much.

Shows respect, you see.

Our British exit offering was eventually produced in Irish as though it was an afterthought, in much the same way as our officials considered the Brexit consequences of the Irish border itself.

You can rest assured that the executive summary of the 100 page document was, of course, sent out in all of the twenty-two languages of the European Union.

They were translated badly, with the competence and accuracy that have become the hallmarks of this government, and released to expectant diplomats who received them with bemusement.

This is normal for Britons. When abroad, we do not bother ourselves with the minutia of our host's speech.

Instead, we address Johnny Foreigner in our own tongue and do so VERY LOUDLY, to aid comprehension.

If we don't make an effort when communicating face to face, why on earth should we do so on paper?

We leave that to the Europeans, who really do try hard at this sort of thing, which seems a bit like cheating to us.

Our diplomats' error-strewn translations of the executive summary into the European vocabularies did not go down well, thus somewhat ruining the gesture.

Among a vast kaleidoscope of errors, the German version invented verbs that the Germans had failed to come up with themselves, despite centuries of Teutonic effort.

The Dutch version was described in a leading newspaper as reading like something put through the "cheapest available" translation software.

The Estonian and Finnish versions misspelt "Estonia" and "Finland", if you can believe that, and the French version translated the phrase "principled Brexit" into a French phrase that means Brexit is a moral good.

Take that Frenchie!

Would you blame them if their collective response was a finely wrought paragraph of epithets and accurately written Anglo-Saxon expletives?

27.07.18

Everything you need to know

Sometimes, a shared adversity can tell you everything you need to know about a country's people.

For the past few months, Britons have been suffering through the longest spell of nice weather since 1976.

They have been the sort of conditions that we board planes to get to. On our holidays, we revel in not having to take out our hat, coat, scarf and gloves on a typical summer's day.

We leave our hotel in our shorts and T-shirts knowing that it will still be pleasantly balmy come nightfall when we return.

Britons spend an enormous amount of money going to places that are guaranteed to give us the sort of temperatures that we have been moaning about constantly since June.

To be fair, on holiday we don't have to get up at seven on the morning and squeeze ourselves onto a hot train or bus and arrive at work drenched with sweat, only some of which will be our own.

Rather than make a scene, some travellers have invested in thermometers to record just how hot was their commute, so as to post it on social media.

This tells you everything you need to know about us modern Brits. We're still loathe to make a scene but now we quietly broadcast our stoicism to the world.

On London's Central Line, one clip showed that it was almost 100 degrees Fahrenheit, which in Celsius is VERY HOT INDEED.

As you would expect in an open-for-business, fast-forward, go-getter place like modern Britain, our state-of-the-art infrastructure coped with the temperature perfectly well.

Just kidding – the entire country swooned and crashed to the floor like a spurned woman in a Victorian novel.

Trains were cancelled during rush hour, somewhat inconveniencing passengers who had to squash themselves into extra-full coaches in order to get out of the sweltering city.

The trains that did run went very slowly so as not to jump the buckling tracks. This allowed the commuters extra time on-board to really savour the experience.

Air-conditioning units on carriages broke down, presumably because they had not been manufactured to work in the heat.

One rail operator cancelled people's tickets so as to give them a better service by not serving them at all.

This tells you everything you need to know about the railways.

Outside of the transport system, other organisations were also caught out by what most of the world would call a run of pleasant weather.

Hospitals cancelled non-urgent operations due to the influx of people who had neglected to apply sunscreen because they thought that their personal toughness would protect them from burning.

But as hospitals routinely cancel non-urgent operations, this was not deemed very newsworthy, which tells you everything you need to know about the state of our health service.

What did get a lot of coverage in the press was that people locked their pets in cars in the blazing sun and then went shopping for hours only to come back to an almost dead dog and a person filming their stupidity for YouTube.

Dog shows were called off because the Dogs Trust were concerned about the effect of exertion in the heat, presumably for the dogs and their panting owners.

Horse trials were cancelled because the ground was so rock-hard that anyone falling off might not get back up again.

The Fire Brigade advised against barbecues in parks and Highways England warned against throwing rubbish out of car windows in case glass started fires on verges.

Apparently, people need specific instructions not to throw stuff that they are finished with out of their windows, like they are medieval.

What do they do when caught short in their living rooms – pee in the corner?

Even the constipated, buttoned-up cricket world felt the heat.

The MCC, the custodian of the game's rules and regulations announced that gentlemen would be allowed to move around the pavilion at Lords without their jackets.

Indeed, for the first time in its history, members would be permitted to arrive at the hallowed ground without even bringing a jacket with them.

And if that doesn't tell you everything you need to know about cricket, I don't know what does.

28.07.18

The equation of happiness

There is a famous Dickens quote that I can recall perfectly off the top of my head by simply looking it up on the internet.

It is from David Copperfield, which I am almost certain is a book.

The character Wilkins Micawber states that, "Annual income twenty pounds, annual expenditure nineteen [pounds] nineteen [shillings] and six [pence], result happiness. Annual income twenty pounds, annual expenditure twenty pounds ought and six, result misery." "

If that is true, then this entire country is currently in misery, but as it is Great Britain I am talking about, that's not such a surprise, as misery is one of our defining characteristics.

And so is living beyond our means.

Households in Britain spent about £900 more than they made last year. That doesn't sound a great deal but it adds up to £25bn that we spent that we didn't have.

This gets added to the vast, expanding bubble of consumer debt that currently amounts to over £300bn, according to PwC, who get paid to know about this sort of thing.

Experts say that this level of unsecured debt, on top of the amount we owe on mortgages, is unsustainable. In other words: bubbles pop.

When this one pops, we will be showered with something more dangerous than glitter and confetti.

I am not saying that Brexit has anything to do with it, but those members of the Evil European Superstate that are our nearest competitors are doing much better than we are.

The government's researchers at the Office for National Statistics state that the French made more than they spent, to the tune of 2.7% of their Gross Domestic Product.

The perfect Germans fared even better, recording a surplus equivalent to 5.1% of their GDP.

In spend spend spend Britain, we have a deficit among households of 1.2% of the money we make as a country.

The report from the ONS was titled "Making ends meet: are households living beyond their means?"

Yes. Yes they are.

And it is getting worse. We are taking out loans to make up the shortfall - £80bn worth of loans in 2017 alone.

This money is used to buy things we don't need with money we haven't got. Things like cars. We buy cars like people from other less splurging countries buy shoes.

When there is a new model out, we can't stand being in last year's version, so we borrow a year's wages and spend it on an asset that halves in value as soon as we drive it out of the shop.

There is also our addiction to buying stuff we don't need on the internet. Every day can be like Christmas when the postman comes knocking with a parcel of things we had forgotten we purchased while drunk the night before.

The reason why Amazon's Jeff Bezos has tired of buying leather jackets and RayBans and is now into rocket ships is because we have thrown all our money into the bottomless pit that is his bank account.

As you would expect, the rich are suffering the most.

Of course, I am joking.

It is the millions on low incomes that are falling deepest in to the debt trap.

The ONS say that the poorest 10% of households spent 2.5 times their disposable income last year. You can't do that without borrowing on the sort of interest rates that will keep the amount owed constantly creeping up, beyond their ability to pay it off. Ever.

The richest 10% spent about half their income in the same period, which is why they look better than the poor - less stress.

There's nothing that will improve your appearance more than waking up laughing.

Unfortunately, income for the poorest third of us is going down, not up. The post-crash financial recovery has not touched those who need the money the most.

And what is the caring, forward together, meritocratic government doing to help?

They have waved us all bye-bye and gone on holiday for seven weeks.

They will tell us that they are hard at work and I bet they are – working hard at trying to figure out how to put the cost of it on expenses.

And if they can, result: happiness.

03.08.18

How come his pants aren't on fire?

The investigation into Trump's Russia ties must be, for him, like sitting in a room with the walls closing in.

His defence against the charges of colluding with the Russians to swing the vote his way has morphed from...I don't know any

Russians, to: I had no contact with Russians even though I did know some, to: OK, we met them a few times but it was about adopting children, to: all right, there might have been some information offered but I didn't take it, to: OK, maybe I colluded but so what, colluding with a foreign state to influence an American election isn't even a crime!

Even he must know that's a bit of a stretch, legally speaking, so Ancient Orange got grumpy and had to scramble off to his safe space, which is on-stage at one of his demented rallies.

These are the unhinged events in Republican strongholds, where he rambles on about whatever generates applause, which he laps up like he's impersonating Mussolini – chin up, chest out, inflated like a balloon.

He doles out his phoney I'm-one-of-you rhetoric like he throws out those Make America Great Again hats, which are the only Trump products that are actually made in America.

He yodels on about how tremendous he is and how unfairly he is treated to the white conspiracy nuts and the gullible yeeha's who came to hear the hits: it was the greatest win of any president ever, I beat Hillary, there were millions of illegal votes, huge inauguration crowd, lock her up, dictators are great people, the media are the enemies of the people, tax cuts for the rich, Vladimir Putin is a close personal stranger, Mexicans are rapists, gonna build a wall.

As well as repeating the content of all his previous rallies, this time, he went on about meeting the Queen - he told the rally in Pennsylvania that his first official trip last month was a 'beautiful, beautiful visit'.

He said, 'I have great respect for the UK - the United Kingdom. Great respect. People call it "Britain", they call it "Great Britain". They used to call it "England", different parts. But the UK - great respect.'

I have quoted him verbatim, which he would deem very unfair, totally not fair, SAD!

He said, "So, I go to England, which is in London, not a lot of people know that and I'm there for the Queen OK...so what?...she's nothing special...and she's very nice, awful person, very small, and I'd say about a "three", not hot like my daughter...have you seen Ivanka? You know, if I wasn't her father... And so I say to the Queen, what do you think of Donald Trump? And she says he's late, which is fake news, so I'm looking at the men with the big hats, kind of stupid if you ask me, they all wore the same hats, like it's a parade or something...and we're racing and she gets left behind because I'm very athletic, not like the Queen who is a very low energy person, and I totally won that race and then we had a meeting which was a great meeting and a huge meeting, a lot of people tell me that it was the greatest meeting anyone ever had with the Queen of London and I say where's the King? Donald Trump wants to meet the man of the castle, why is Donald Trump getting parked with the wife? And she didn't get it, I mean, she's not that smart, trust me, and I said do you know Scotlandland, which I own, and she'd never even heard of it, which is frankly embarrassing for her country, so I won that meeting and all the people cheered, they said "booo", which is how they greet important people in London, which is very nice by the way, worst city ever, I hated it, we launch missiles at noon."

OK, I made that up – he didn't say that, but I can't confirm that he didn't think it, so that makes it true.

Trump actually did say that the 'fake, fake, disgusting news' was responsible for lying about his meeting with the Queen by saying that he kept her waiting, whereas , it was the Queen who kept HIM waiting.

He said: "I landed, I'm on the ground and I'm waiting with the King's and the Queen's guards, wonderful people. I'm waiting. I was about 15 minutes early and I'm waiting with my wife and that's fine. Hey, it's the Queen, right? We can wait. But I'm a little early.'

'So here was the story by the fake news: The president was 15 minutes late for the Queen. Wrong.'

He has high standards when it comes to reporting the facts, so let's examine what we know from the live television coverage of the event.

Trump's helicopter landed in the castle grounds at about 4:50, for a royal meeting at 5 o'clock.

It takes about five minutes for him to unstrap himself from his seat, make his way down the very scary steps, without Theresa May there to hold his hand, and lumber over to his car.

Then another five minutes to be driven at walking pace to where the Queen was waiting which takes it to exactly 5 o'clock when he got out of the car and greeted Her Majesty at 5.01.

There was no 15 minute wait, he lied about that, and by his own exacting standards, that makes HIM fake, fake, disgusting news, but at least that's not a crime.

He's guilty of lying, but that won't send him to jail.

Not that particular lie, anyway.

04.08.18

The very junior doctor will see you now.

Here's a Brexit bonus you weren't expecting: Health Minister Stephen Barclay has suggested that in order to address the shortage of medical staff after we leave the Evil Overlords of the Unelected

Socialist Superstate, we should allow people to become doctors with less training.

That sounds a little alarming, so Stephen Barclay, who voted Leave, did not put it quite like that. He said that what he was proposing was that we should adopt "bespoke British regulations".

"Bespoke" sounds like a good thing...luxurious, even, like a hand made suit.

But when it is used to mean that the person seeing to you in hospital will have had less training, it does not sound like something you would buy in Savile Row, and more like an old rag lurking in the remainder bin at a charity shop.

Mr Barclay fleshed out his wizard notion by claiming that one element of a British doctor's training that we can do without, is the year of on-the-job experience that hospital staff undergo between completing medical school and qualifying as a doctor.

He said that bringing forward the point at which medics can officially qualify to practice could save millions of pounds.

I thought that the idea of leaving the EU was that the NHS would be getting *more* money, not having to scrabble around desperately trying to find ways to make up a shortfall. Maybe I read that sign on the bus wrong. My eyes may be failing me. Perhaps I need to see a doctor.

In this quote to Her Majesty's Daily Telegraph, which I am not making up, Health Minister Stephen Barclay said: "There are opportunities that come with Brexit - not to lower regulatory standards we want to maintain standards - to look at how we make things more bespoke to UK needs.'

He said. 'At the moment you don't qualify as a doctor when you leave medical school - you have to do a further year and that brings with it some additional costs.'

Too right it does.

I say we should go one step further – to really save money we should simply ask anyone passing a hospital if they know anything about medicine, and if they say: "well, I take a lot of drugs", hire them on the spot, give them a white coat and let them get on with the sawing.

If you as a patient declare that you would prefer to be seen to by a medical professional with experience, well I am sorry but that is just typical defeatist, unpatriotic Remoaner talk.

I hate to lecture someone with the medical expertise that must come with being a Health Minister but junior doctors are already much less experienced than they used to be.

They used to do 100 hour weeks, now thanks to the EU directive on working hours, they are doing about half that but still graduating at the same time, which means much less time on the job.

That's not the fault of the EU, it was a completely sensible precaution on their part against doing a job when over-tired.

If you are making a cake on your 100th hour of work that week, then screwing it up is not that serious, but if you are trying to save someone's life and you haven't slept for days, then errors are a little bit more important.

That doctors are still graduating in the same time frame is the fault of the people that run this surprisingly broke country.

That we haven't extended the time it takes to become a doctor to fit in with the sensible hours is entirely down to us.

Now this bloke wants to reduce the time on the job by a whole year on top!

And what of his history in the field of health? What experience has he brought to bear in coming to this notion?

Well, Stephen Barclay read history at uni, became a solicitor and worked for a bank that bears his name.

Ideal material to be Minister of State for Health and Social Care. What he doesn't know about medicine, you could write on the back of a prescription pad with a paint roller.

Sarah Wollaston, on the other hand, understands very little about the medical profession, as she was only an actual GP and never worked for Barclays.

She is in charge of the Commons Health Committee. In a delightfully pithy response to the idea put forward by Stephen Barclay she said, "'It's not a Brexit dividend to have worse training for doctors fgs. What planet are these straw clutchers on?"

I think it's a planet called Private Medical Insurance, on which you can select the doctor of your choice from a range of those with enormous experience.

For those of us who reside on planet NHS, under pesky, interfering EU rules, medical students are required to have at least five years of medical education before they are registered.

Our glorious Brexit means that graduates who do four year medical degrees could be trying their best on you straight away.

If that's our bespoke solution, don't wait 'till we get our country back, you'd better get ill now.

10.08.18

Boris prepares to take his punishment.

Theresa May has doubled her lead over Jeremy Corbyn in the latest poll.

That sounds good if you just run through it quickly and don't turn back but you have to remember that it's Jeremy Corbyn she's being compared to, not the Labour Party

The way that Uncle Jezza has been getting it in the neck lately, I wouldn't be surprised if the boss of Southern Rail hasn't doubled his lead over him – I wouldn't be shocked if the Yorkshire Ripper was ahead of him in the polls.

The latest YouGov survey for The Times newspaper shows that 36 percent of those asked said they think Mrs M makes the best PM - up from 32 percent a week ago.

Over the same period, the survey found Jeremy Corbyn's ratings slid from 25 to 22 points.

However, before Mrs May's camp puts out the bunting, the candidate that is the most popular is "Don't know" which got 39% - a clear lead.

Those numbers again for who would make the best PM – Mrs M 36, Jezza 22, don't know 39, which is 97% ...so 3% didn't even know enough to say "don't know"!

The same poll says the Tories have overtaken Labour and now lead by four points despite the Boris Johnson burqa row.

Or more likely *because* of the Boris Johnson burqa row.

In case you have been in a coma this past week, Boris declared that burqas make their wearers resemble letter boxes and bank robbers.

He couched those old gags in a column that was superficially against the banning of them, as has happened in many countries, Denmark most recently.

He covered his back by making the thrust of the article about being tolerant, while also making the kind of old joke that will rub people's fur up the wrong way.

He can say, look, the thrust of the piece is that I am totally OK with it – I'm on your side, while the whole point of the article was to lob in an incendiary device and then scarper off on holiday while his minions defend him from those meanies on the left.

Talk about having your cake and eating it.

It's a classic move – say something that is bad enough to make the lefties drop their falafel nut-burgers, then the right-wingers shout 'over reaction' and coalesce around the person that's doing the baiting.

Boris Johnson represents the Donald Trump-isation of British politics - it looks like a pretty naked move to position himself as the plain-talking man of the people to take over the Tory party.

(I apologise for putting the words 'naked move' and Boris Johnson in same sentence.)

The truth is that burqas make most British people uncomfortable.

It's not in our culture to not be able to see someone's face, just like it would make us feel uncomfortable if we were in the presence of a stranger in a mask.

It is bad enough when you're talking to someone wearing mirrored sunglasses.

So I suspect that Boris didn't accidentally drop a gaffe when he wrote about letter boxes and bank robbers, it was calculated to offend those that are keen to be offended.

He knew they'd make a big fuss and that the rest of the country would have the opportunity to agree with him, and feel relief that someone was talking their language.

Boris Johnson will be seen as the defender of British Britishness, become a folk hero and ride on a wave of ecstasy right through the door of number 10 Downing Street.

If that was the plan, then it is going very well. The nation has spoken of little else for five days straight.

What's not been mentioned much is how a man who has just stopped being Foreign Secretary and is currently still the full-time member for Uxbridge and South Ruislip can walk straight into a £275,000 job as comedy columnist for the Daily Telegraph?

It looks to an ignorant outsider such as myself as though it's one of those revolving doors into the private sector we've heard so much about.

Would the Telegraph have been as keen on securing his services if he hadn't been an MP, let alone such a high ranking member of the government?

Under the ministerial code, ex-ministers must apply to the Advisory Committee on Business Appointments and wait three months before they can take up a new job.

But Mr Johnson did not seek permission before agreeing to sign on with the Telegraph.

Presumably, that three month rule is to avoid any sense of impropriety if, for instance, some higher-up in the MOD waves through an order worth billions from a defence company and then magically is appointed to the board of that same company the moment they leave office.

They are supposed to wait 90 days so as to avoid all charges of corruption.

If that satisfies the public that nothing untoward may have occurred, then we are stupider than I look.

And what of the punishment that can be doled out if an ex-minister, like Boris, chooses to ignore this gossamer-thin cover of rectitude and integrity?

Well, nothing at all. There is no punishment of any kind for ignoring the rules.

That'll teach him!

11.08.18

A sense of proportion

This week, an air strike killed dozens of children on a school bus. It happened in Yemen. This sort of thing seems to be happening there a lot.

The Saudi Arabians have been fighting a war in Yemen for some time.

When explaining why they had bombed a school bus, the Saudis said they were attacking a legitimate target. So that's all right then.

The Red Cross said, "Body parts were scattered all over the area, and the sounds of moaning and crying were everywhere. The school bus was totally burned and destroyed."

Which sounds less like a legitimate target and more like a war crime.

It was another incident of that conflict that did not get much attention over here, just like when the Saudis bombed a funeral.

In October of 2016, a Saudi air-strike hit a funeral hall in the Yemeni capital. It killed 140 people and injured hundreds more.

And I know what you are thinking – you are thinking what on earth does that have to do with Boris Johnson?

All week long, this country has been obsessed with Boris. Barely a breath has been expelled that did not carry his name upon it.

He wrote a column in the Daily Telegraph that concerned the issue of women wearing burqas; Denmark is the latest country to ban them.

Boris claimed he did not think that forbidding them was necessary...oh, and by the way, they look like letter boxes and bank robbers.

He lobbed those old jokes in to the column he once famously said that he dashed off in half an hour and scarpered off on holiday to Europe while the entire country engaged in pitch battle between those that clutched their pearls to their chests and had an exaggerated fainting fit, and those that were delighted that someone had publicly announced what they had always thought but were too cowed to say out loud.

It seems like pretty small beer when you think about it outside of the bubble of perpetual fury that are the airwaves and the newspaper columns.

It rather pales into insignificance when put alongside a bombed out school bus. Witnesses to that tragedy said some bodies of the children were burned beyond recognition, others were riddled with shrapnel.

Yet we heard not one word of it through the fog of approval and recrimination swirling round the absent ex-Foreign Secretary.

But what does that school bus have to do with him?

Well, the same Boris Johnson that offends and amuses in equal measure, that affects a carefully dishevelled appearance so as to leave the impression that he is less wily and ambitious than he is, that dons the look of a naughty but loveable school boy, was the same Boris Johnson that stepped in to ensure that Saudi Arabia got its weapons from us.

After the funeral bombing, the UK Trade Secretary at the time, Liam Fox, delayed the signing of export licences of military hardware to Saudi Arabia.

Officials were instructed to suspend sales of weaponry to the Gulf state.

Documents obtained by the Guardian show that the Foreign Secretary at the time personally intervened to ensure the sales continued.

That official was one Boris Johnson.

In the six months that followed, £283m of arms sales were made to the Saudis, including £4m of bombs and missiles.

That was on top of the £1 billion of bombs and missiles that we had sold them in three short months in the summer of 2015.

If we can assume that those bombs were not used exclusively for peaceful purposes, then it seems that Boris Johnson has some more serious charges to answer than whether he offended a few people in a silly newspaper column.

17.08.18

Darwinism goes into reverse.

It's official – the human race has peaked. Look around...this is as good as we'll get.

The problem started with the invention of the internet. That was the beginning of the end for reading.

Thanks a lot Tim Berners-Lee!

Things got a lot worse when smart phones came along. That was the fault of Steve Jobs.

We should have known not to trust anything sold to us by a man in a turtle-neck.

Those phones are not that smart – they don't seem to learn anything for a start.

They are still stunned when we leave the house to go to work at the same time every day and are completely unprepared to offer us any advice on, say, the cancellation of the train we always get.

We have to look it up manually. If they are so smart, they should alert us that we'll have to leave the house early, but they never do.

What is worse is the effect they are having on us.

Smart phones do not make smarter people. In fact the opposite seems to be true.

Take pictures, for instance.

Whenever someone lifts a phone in front of you, looking like they are taking a snap of you and intruding on your day, rest assured that they are not. They are, in fact, taking a picture of themselves.

Everyone has their camera permanently on selfie-mode.

In "the good old days", people used to take images of the places they visited and then replayed the results in slide shows to their bored friends.

"Here is the Eiffel Tower", they would say..."and here is the Grand Canyon....and that's the Hanging Gardens of Babylon".

Not any more – if anyone under the age of 50 were to narrate a showing of their holiday images they would say, "here's a picture of me, and here's a picture of me, and here's a picture of me...and oh look – it's a picture of me!"

If you think that is the apex of the superficiality of the Me Generation, then prepare yourself – it gets a lot worse than that.

Apparently, actual grown-ups are buying clothes on the internet, uploading images of themselves wearing them to Instagram and then sending the clobber back for a refund.

They do this to "keep up" with the internet "stars" who parade an Outfit of the Day for their "fans".

If you are fabulously rich, then you might be able to afford to buy 365 outfits a year, but "ordinary people" can't. So to emulate the ones that can, and show off online, people order kit they can't afford, record themselves wearing it and then pop it back in the post to get their money back.

In all your life, have you ever heard of anything so stupid?

Following the posts of some airhead fashion blogger is bad enough; there are only so many hours in a life, but there surely is something more vital they could be doing than scouring the internet for something they might look good in and then take 100 pics of themselves to get that special shot and then upload it to social media in order to get "likes" from strangers.

What's worse is that this is no isolated occurrence. There are approximately 200 million Outfits of the Day posts on Instagram alone.

Research by a credit card company suggests who is most guilty of doing this.

The study says it's not young women, it's 35-44 year olds and - here's a bigger surprise - mostly men!

If that's true, I'm a yellow beret.

There's no way that middle-aged men are behind this stupid waste of time.

Men do not buy clothes off the internet to make it look like they've got a different fashionable outfit for every day of the year.

Men pick up whatever is the least dirty thing on their bedroom floor and wear that, don't they?

Unless I am ageist, sexist and mistaken, it must be the daughters of middle aged men using their dad's credit cards.

Or the researchers were drunk when they wrote their report.

Either way, it doesn't really matter. A large enough number of people are doing it to help make up the £7bn worth of kit we send back each year.

One in ten on-line shoppers admit to ordering things they don't want just to kid on to strangers on social media that they have such a fabulous life that they can afford them.

One of the most stated reasons is that they don't want to be seen in the same outfit twice.

Not including socks and underwear, I have been wearing the same dozen things for at least the last ten years, and five of them are T-shirts.

The shame!

You know, pretty soon there won't be any space left on the internet because everyone on earth will be putting up endless pictures of themselves pouting and making gormless goo-goo eyes.

Millions will be leaving their jobs in order to spend more time with their significant other – their phones.

They won't have any money coming in but at least they won't have to buy anything – they'll just try everything for the day and then send it back for a refund.

I bet people start doing it with food.

18.08.18

Trickle up economics.

As we approach the end of the month, we peek at our bank balance and wonder where all our money went.

If you are anything like me, some of it went on the take-away you knew you shouldn't have had but you ordered anyway, some went on the alcohol that sent you over the recommended maximum for the week and some went on assisting rich people to buy houses.

A scheme, funded by you, designed to help first-time buyers get on the housing ladder is being used instead by families earning over £100,000 a year.

If you are one of the people in this country that earns that amount, you might not think that it qualifies as being rich, but as it puts you in the top 4% of earners, you are richer than most, so stop whining.

According to the government's own figures, more than 6,700 households with incomes over £100,000 have bought homes using Help to Buy.

Under this scheme, the Government gives borrowers a loan of up to 20 per cent of the value of a new-build home or 40 per cent in London.

This is to aid people seeking a mortgage but who can't afford the deposit, or at least that was the stated aim.

The problem needed addressing because house prices have risen so much that the home that used to cost a year's wages when your parents or grandparents bought theirs, now costs ten years' wages because we haven't built enough over the years.

The government enacted this plan to supposedly plug that gap between earnings and the cost of buying a roof over your head.

But instead of helping those in desperate need, about one in 20 households who have taken out these loans, provided by you, have six-figure incomes.

Families with incomes of £50,000 or more have now received 40 per cent of those loans,

This makes the scheme seem less like supporting struggling families and more like welfare for the giant building companies.

They are building a small number of expensive homes, which people can't afford, so they got the government to bung some cash at the potential purchasers so that they'll be able to buy one.

The result is that house prices are kept high because there's an artificial demand for expensive properties that would otherwise not be affordable.

Banks win too by lending out ever more stupendous sums to people that can't afford it, which is exactly what caused the last financial crash.

The problem is a lack of supply, and that's partly due to the building companies themselves who have huge areas of land that they own but aren't doing anything with, in order to keep up prices.

Help to Buy is the same kind of idea that fuelled the asset boom and takeover frenzy after quantitative easing, wherein the government took your money, flooded the market with it, the rich helped themselves and instead of trickling that wealth down, as they were supposed to, they bought wine and gold and classic cars and other companies and shares in their own companies, which raised the stock price which kicked in their bonuses, all the while inflating bubbles in the prices of everything.

You could call that unintended consequences. That would be the kindest reading of what happened.

A less rosy view would be that the result was exactly as intended – a massive transfer of wealth from the masses to the rich, and particularly from the young to the old

This is the first time in history that the young will be poorer at every age than their predecessors.

There was an increase in household wealth since 2006, right enough, but it's been completely driven by pension wealth – household wealth held outside of pensions has actually decreased on average, and the amount of wealth concentrated among those at the top has become more concentrated, according the Institute for Fiscal Studies, who get paid the big money to know these things.

If that wasn't the actual plan of the wealthiest, who were the ones making the decisions about the response to the financial crash and the lack of housing, then it seems to have coincidentally worked out very well for them.

Funny that.

There's further evidence that backs up the notion that Help to Buy is really help for builders: it only applies to new-build homes.

You don't get tax payers' money to buy an old home, of which there are millions, you only get a government bung if you are buying a newly built one.

So the builders can put up any old rubbish, knowing that the government will step in and throw money at them and that people will want one because they're desperate to get on the housing ladder.

That's why houses all look the same wherever they're built – no architect would ever admit to designing those things.

They're made on the basis of how cheap they are to construct, not how nice they might be to live in.

That is why windows are so tiny on new houses - because bricks are cheaper than glass.

And there's no room in them which is why so many storage companies have sprung up all over the place, for people to store all the stuff they used to put in cupboards, when houses were built with such things.

The other type of homes these companies build are, of course, charmless towers of tiny executive flatlets to sell to people in Malaysia who aren't going to live in them and to the international criminal super rich who want a safe way to launder all the money they nicked.

The result in both cases is that the nation is blighted by eyesores at ground level and scraping the sky and is also why there's a chronic lack of cash in your bank account come the end of the month.

24.08.18

Who do you think you are kidding Mr Putin?

Russia has lost a nuclear missile.

On hearing that, Harrison Ford usually enters screen left and saves the day in two hours of nail-biting tension and stunts performed in a surprisingly agile way for a man of his age.

This is not the films though, this is real life.

Vlad has been putting it about that, even though the world is gripped by the unravelling of the US President and whatever Brexit has become, he's still there, still bent on world domination.

Back in March, Rootin' Tootin' Pootin boasted about the size of his new missiles and how advanced and super-dooper they were. He said they could hit any time, any place, anywhere, like a Martini.

To be fair, he did not say it could hit anywhere specific, just that they could hit anywhere.

And that is exactly what happened when the tested them four times – they went anywhere. They were so unpredictable that they have now actually lost one.

Scientists are concerned that the nuclear material on-board could actually start harming the ocean. You know it has to be serious when a whole ocean in is danger.

Fortunately, we have Gavin Williamson to protect us. He is our Defence Secretary.

He is reported to be out of his mind - not with worry - people are saying that he is actually out of his mind.

It is not because he famously keeps a tarantula spider in his office, about 30 years after most small boys would have given theirs up.

The reason that sources within the Ministry of Defence have called into question his mental stability is that he keeps coming out with daft ideas to protect the nation.

In a school class, the notion that there are no stupid questions is used to encourage learning.

When the 42 year-old Secretary of State for Defence asks if we can make up the shortfall in the defence budget by fitting "really expensive guns" to tractors, then perhaps there ARE stupid questions after all.

He also asked MOD officials if they could disguise missile defence systems in Coca-Cola lorries.

I'll go one better – we could get Jones the butcher to cut some holes for rifles in the roof of his delivery van, so the stout menfolk of Walmington-on-Sea could 'have at' the Luftwaffe as they pass overhead.

They don't like it up 'em, you know.

Her Majesty's Defence Chief also suggested turning old ferries into beach assault craft, which could morph into mega robots with lasers in their eyes that could fly and become invisible.

I made some of that up – not the beach assault craft part.

He was coming out with all this desperate Dad's Army stuff because his budget has been slashed by £20bn, so all the shiny new kit he had his eye on is now not in our price range.

Instead, we're going to have to weaponise Lilos and trampolines.

We could mount rockets on the backs of cows. How about exploding cupcakes?

You are probably keen to know just what kind of experience of military matters would lead a man to suggest such things.

According to the internet, he once worked in a pottery firm and is a patron of the World Owl Trust.

We're in good hands.

Let's hope Putin doesn't get his rocket back.

25.08.18

Animal Tragic

Let's check in with the world of animals before climate change renders their habitats unlivable or Donald Trump's sons shoot them all.

Those people who graze the internet looking for things to be upset about were sent into what the papers call "a frenzy" when they read about a restaurant that was serving cow.

Don't worry, the cow was dead. That was not what caused the furore. It was the trolling before it died that did it.

At the centre of this tale is a restaurant in Cardiff, which shall remain nameless, because it didn't bother to give itself one and simply goes by its address: 29 Park Place.

Actually, it has spelled out the numbers, so it is really called Twenty Nine Park Place, because that's classier.

They have a special offer on beef and alerted Twitter to that fact by posting a picture of a cow, minding its own business, with the caption 'Daisy is a little bit worried! Why? It's steak night!'

As you can imagine, the internet went into what the papers call "meltdown" because people presumably imagined that steak is created in Styrofoam trays at the supermarket, and no animal is harmed in its production.

Comments on Twitter included but were not limited to: 'Oh my god, this is dreadful' and 'So cruel and immoral', which is, of course, nonsense.

If God didn't want us to eat cows, he wouldn't have made them out of meat.

And besides, cows can't read.

This did not stop the restaurant from prostrating itself before the internet and begging its forgiveness.

This seems to happen a lot – people on the net taking offence on someone else's behalf.

It is the first time I have heard of them taking offence on someTHING else's behalf.

The restaurant shouldn't have bothered with the prostration as the Twittershpere had already moved on and was weighing in on the plight of another defenceless animal.

And by defenceless, I mean it is equipped with the deadliest poison of any living thing.

A black widow spider was found in a crate which had been shipped to Scotland from America.

In their homeland, black widows live for about two years, which is approximately two years too long.

Workers at a business park in Aberdeenshire discovered the spider in the crate, noted its distinctive black and red makings and said (and this is a direct quote): "AAAARRRGGGHHHH!!!"

They called the Scottish animal welfare charity, the SPCA.

Their website is littered with pictures of cute puppy dogs and pussy cats and absolutely no deadly spiders at all, so they announced that they were not very interested in trying to re-house it.

There's not much call for something that looks like a prop from a horror film and could kill all of your other pets and you too, if it felt like it.

So, much to the displeasure of those on the internet, the Scottish charity that exists to protect animals suggested that the spider be "put to sleep".

This sounds like it might involve singing it a lullaby while gently rocking it to and fro, but as one bite could put you in a coma, I think that it was code for bashing it flat with a rolled up copy of The Scotsman newspaper or the underside of a Scotsman's slipper.

If Donald Trump's sons tire of blasting at lions with assault weapons and they want to shoot at black widows before another one finds its way here, then that is OK by me.

Just between us though, I might be secretly rooting for the spider.

31.08.18

Incoming!

A new report says Britain remains the number one destination in Europe for foreign investment.

Put out the bunting – Global Britain wins again.

Despite warnings that a leave vote would deter foreign investors, from what Uncle Nige would call the whingers, the whiners and the moaners, the report says London remains the number one city globally for foreign direct investment (FDI).

Dr Liam Fox, the International Trade Secretary, said this proves the economy will remain competitive whatever the outcome of the Brexit talks.

Great news...except that it doesn't prove anything of the kind, unless the report comes with a crystal ball as a paperweight.

How does Dr Fox know what will happen, regardless of the Brexit deal?

What's he a doctor in - divinity?

Did he hear it from God?

Regardless of what happens down the road, in the here and now, The Department for International Trade estimates foreign investors are holding a record £1.2trillion of assets in the UK in relation to FDI projects.

Isn't that fantastic? No, not necessarily.

How many times have you read in a paper that some totally British company that wraps itself in the flag and trumpets its British Britishness is actually owned by Indians, or Americans or Aby – bloomin-syrians?

We don't own anything any more and this FDI is the reason - people comin' over here, buying up our stuff.

If The Will of the People is to get our country back, I have bad news: we've already sold it to the Saudis.

That's what foreign direct investment is – companies abroad buying up British companies, running them from Qatar or wherever, and booking the profits in an office on a moon circling Jupiter for tax reasons.

Think of it, if we are doing so well out of all this foreign investment, how come wages are going down in real terms – where's the benefit for us poor dopes who pay taxes?

If we're doing so well out of flogging everything we own to some medieval petro state dictatorship or evil American hedge fund, how come we can't afford anything?

We can't afford to treat the sight of pensioners that are going blind, we can't afford to fix their hips and knees either, we can't afford to fix the potholes in the roads that are actually killing people, we can't afford to equip our soldiers with the kit they need to do their jobs and we can't afford to put police persons on the beat to keep us all safe from getting stabbed and shot and burgled.

When you actually look at our crumbling infrastructure, when you try to remember the last time you got a seat on a train to work, when you see how long it takes to get an appointment with your GP, assuming you still have one in your area, and you try and fail to think of a single company that displays its British heritage that is actually still British, you have to wonder if FDI is actually a synonym for selling the country down the river for a quick profit.

A profit which is, of course, shared exclusively among the already super-rich.

Foreign direct investment is mergers and acquisitions – when that American company bought Cadbury's – that was foreign direct investment.

When the private equity firm bought Boots the chemist – that was foreign direct investment.

When the Germans and the French and the Australians bought our water and electricity and gas – that was foreign direct investment too.

When we sold off ICI and P&O and Jaguar and our steel and glass and airports – that was all foreign direct investment.

Last year, foreign companies spent £35billion acquiring 254 UK companies - gone, no longer British.

We shouldn't be celebrating this, we should be curtailing it.

Foreign direct investment is vital for third world countries to grow – they don't have the money to invest in their own businesses to compete on the world stage – but for first world countries, it is often just profiteering.

Small British businesses are being bought up by fewer and fewer companies which use their might to crush the outfits that they haven't acquired.

The result is that everything you buy is on one web site and the all food you eat is made by just five enormous companies and the power you use is provided by a small handful of mega-corporations.

People are losing good jobs working in actual shops, dealing with actual people, earning decent money and paying taxes and they find themselves working for peanuts in some hell-hole warehouse picking things off shelves for minimum wage while all the money that used to use to make the country go round ends up in the pocket of some offshore megalomaniac who spends it on space ships.

But please Dr Fox, do tell us some more about how fantastic this all is.

01.09.18

Cooking up another one.

You know what there aren't enough of on television? Programmes about cooking.

The BBC are reportedly working on yet another cooking show to rival The Great British Bake Off, a programme that answered the question: what would people who don't like cooking like to watch while they're eating baked beans straight out of the can with a spoon?

Two previous series starring Mary Berry and Nadiya Hussain failed to find an audience, so instead of coming up with an idea for a programme that has a hint of originality to it, the vastly paid and highly regarded experts in telly-land have decided to do the exact same thing again, to see if that works.

That is just what we need in this country right now – more programmes encouraging people to eat sugar.

We haven't reached peak fat yet, so grab your elastic waisted sweat pants because we're going extra-large.

According to The Sun, BBC bosses are casting around for competitors to appear in a programme that they have called Celebration.

Guess what it is going to be. That's right, a competition between cooks to see which of them will connect with an audience enough to be granted a book deal.

It will have two teams of rival bakers and cooks tasked with...oh I can't be bothered to explain, you know exactly what it will look like because it has been done a thousand times before.

Does anyone have an original thought in television?

If it isn't cooking, it is dancing, or dancing on ice, or dancing while diving into a swimming pool off a ski jump.

If one TV channel has a hit, every other channel wants a piece of the...er...pie. That's why everything is replicated endlessly until all life is squeezed out of a format and only then will the executives forlornly search around for something new.

It is an exercise in covering themselves against blame. If a new show in a tested format fails, it is the fault of the presenter. If a brand new format fails, it is the fault of the executive that suggested it.

That is also why the same people are on everything.

If a programme featuring Stephen Fry is not a hit, it is Stephen Fry's fault. If a programme that does not feature Stephen Fry fails, it is the fault of the person that did not hire Stephen Fry.

The weirdly successful show about making cakes called the Great British Bake Off moved to Channel 4 in 2016 losing its judge Mary Berry and presenters Mel and Sue.

Channel 4 searched and searched and by some miracle they found someone just as unfunny as Mel and Sue, a man who looks like he is a dead member of the 1970's glam band The Sweet.

Even with him on board, it still failed to achieve the boffo ratings of its predecessor, and neither did anything the BBC put on against it, so now we will get another show about fiddling with ingredients to join the 53 million other shows about cooking on the BBC.

Is that what we really want from a state broadcaster that is supported by a tax that you will go to jail for not paying?

This new show will be added to the ones with star names on the marquee that are already on and being repeated endlessly like Keith Floyd Gets Drunk and Grills Something, Nigella Pouts, Two Fat Ladies Drink Cream, Gordon Ramsey Swears Too Much For It Not To Be Put On and Paul Hollywood Has Blue Eyes.

Added to that, there are a myriad of no-name competition shows and celebrity versions of all of the above.

When they're not on, it's Jamie bloomin' Oliver on every channel, every minute of every day.

And we STILL don't cook anything from scratch, we just ring for a pizza and stuff our fat faces while we watch that lot do it.

07.09.18

Britain gets tough.

Vlad's really gone and done it now.

We did not blink when he annexed Crimea and we said nothing when he helped bomb Aleppo back to the Stone Age and we did not demur when anyone that criticised him seem to feel rather dead the next day but when he sent his grinning henchmen to kill people in the sleepy cathedral city of Salisbury, a stern response was required..

As Russia is demonstrating its ability to go to war, with a military exercise in its Eastern territory, including but not limited to: 36,000 tanks, 80 ships, 1,000 planes and 300,000 troops, our government has wisely decided to engage in cold financial warfare rather than the hot alternative.

If you have a home in what estate agents call prime central London, then sell, sell, sell because the Oligarchs are in the sights of our National Crime Agency and when the Russian money leaves those gilded palaces in South West London, there goes the property prices of Kensington and Chelsea.

All those empty, unlit, bolt-holes may all be sold at once, and with them will go the sky-high prices at the tip-top of the market.

The government is finally asking itself how an ordinary Russian man, scratching a living out of selling shower curtains in a Moscow flea market can, in the blink of an eye, have made enough money to buy a yacht the size of a Mediterranean island.

How have all those Oligarchs come by their unbelievably vast sums, and why do they all seem to be close personal friends of the Russian Premier? Could the two be in any way connected?

Dozens of these people that have bought their way into this country could have their assets seized in the wake of the Salisbury poisoning.

If it had not been for that, we would not have made a peep about all that dodgy money flowing through the country.

Those ten million pound penthouses on the tops of those charmless high-rise blocks of executive flatlets that crowd the London skyline are quite often just safe assets in which to park giant wealth.

There's hardly ever anyone living in places like that. Just look up you will see the lack of lights on the upper floors of those towers. There's no one home. They are bank vaults with a view.

Whitehall suggests that The National Crime Agency could target more than 100 foreigners with 'unexplained wealth orders' in the coming months, mostly Russian.

That word "could" is the most important one in that sentence.

I very much doubt they will because washing money clean is what we do for a living – all those shiny buildings of accountants and lawyers and upscale estate agents - that's what they're for.

We sell ourselves as a place that oligarchs and drug barons and kleptocrats can park their stolen money, away from the tax man and the law.

When the government trumpeted recently that London is the top city in Europe for foreign direct investment, that's partly why.

Billions and billions of pounds of hookey money comes pouring in, and now we are up against it with Brexit, it seems a little doubtful that the government is going to acquire some principles and wave bye-bye to all that cash, stolen or not.

But don't take my word for it – British police were given new powers at the start of this year to go after foreigners in the UK that they think are as dodgy as three rouble note.

If they cannot show a legal source for all that cash they use to buy the parts of Knightsbridge that haven't already been scooped up by the Qataris, then the authorities can confiscate their cash – snatch it out of their hands like a toddler's lollipop.

In the first six months of having such powers, the government used them just three times. That's how keen they are to frighten the money away.

Security Minister Ben Wallace said of that dismal record: 'Watch this space.'

At least he didn't say to Putin 'go away and shut up' like the very un-scary defence secretary Gavin Williamson.

Downing Street responded to the failure to do anything meaningful by saying that Russian oligarchs linked to Vladimir Putin might suffer searches of their private flights.

That implies that up 'till now, private flights haven't been searched much.

If you are poor enough to have to fly in cattle class you will have an intimate body search on your way through Heathrow, even if all you have on you is a bottle of water and a boarding card.

If, on the other hand, you can afford your own plane, then the authorities avert their eyes because Britain is open for shady business.

So don't hold your breath for a crackdown. They've got a lot of money and our ethical foreign policy is to do whatever those with the most money say we should do.

Arms sales to dictators who blow up schools and hospitals with the bombs that we flog them - certainly sir, how many would you like?

Tax havens for ill-gotten wealth...of course sir, which off-shore British dependency did you have in mind?

Want to sue some journalist for telling the truth about your vaunting criminality? Come right this way, we have the best laws in the world to protect those that can afford them.

Just try not to kill anyone while you are parking all that money you stole, because then we might go as far as to say that something should be done.

08.09.18

Saving the planet one bag at a time

The supermarket chain Asda has had to replenish its supply of shopping baskets. Don't worry, they can afford it. It is owned by the Walton family of America. They are the richest family in the richest country on earth.

On top of that, Asda is merging with Sainsburys, whose major shareholder is the Qatari Wealth Fund, the current owners of most of the west of London.

So, they have the cash to buy all the shopping baskets they need, that's not the problem. The problem is that the Earth might not be able to afford it.

You see, the reason that the stores are having to re-stock their receptacle collection is that people are taking them home, instead of buying a 9p bag to put their groceries in.

Let's assume that a person that does that won't bring it back the next time they visit to buy more beige, fried food in boxes, they will just chuck them in a convenient canal, or hedgerow and be done with it.

The only reason that Asda charges for bags is that, after dragging their feet for years, the government decided that we really should use less plastic, by which I mean: throw less plastic away.

The five pence charge for a thin plastic bag was introduced after much humming and hawing and after waiting an age after Ireland led the way.

This was because timid British politicians (T. May) were too scared of any backlash from a furious public to bring in the charge before it had been thoroughly road tested by another, nearby country.

Ireland's experiment was judged a success and after two short years, our government got up the courage to do the same here.

Mountains of poisonous plastic were saved and the world became a better place. For a while.

The charge for forgetting to bring your bags with you was increased from 5p to 9p by Asda but the quality of the bag they offered also increased significantly.

That extra four pence bought you a bag for life – a sturdy offering that could hold your goods all the way home and not fall apart and scatter your treats all over the pavement and under a bus.

Unfortunately, it was that extra 4p that broke the will of Asda shoppers to do the right thing.

At the checkout, they baulked at having to fork out a whole nine pence for something that was not covered in chocolate and so they simply took home the thing that they had carried their food to the tills in.

This makes perfect sense if you are the sort of person that the rest of us should keelhaul, for the benefit of society.

Talk about not rowing in the same direction – what can you buy for nine pence? You can't even spend a penny for nine pence.

It fair boggles the mind how anyone can be so selfish as to take home a shopping basket. Shopping trolleys cost stores over £100 each, so a basket can't be cheap either.

The cost of these conveniences are, of course, added to everyone's bill. You are paying for a stolen basket, whether you took one or not.

Come on people, we're trying to save the planet here.

The bag charge has had a great effect – 13 billion bags were taken out of circulation in the past two years. Of course, it would have been many more billions had not the government dragged its feet for fear of doing something controversial, but let's not get bogged down in "what ifs".

Let's look at the way forward, because while 13 billion bags is a lot, it's not a dent in the Everest sized mounds of plastic that we take home covering our food and then throw straight away.

Nor does it come close to the country-sized craters that we will need to put all the cardboard that is wrapped round those things we buy off the internet that we don't need, with money we haven't got.

Having scored a significant success though, pretty soon the government will increase the price of a basic supermarket carry-all from 5p to 10p.

That's even more than Asda currently charges.

They are going to need a lot more baskets.

Perhaps we should help those that help only themselves by furnishing them with a plastic bag of our own.

We concerned citizens could take an extra one to the shops in case we see someone who has come without theirs and is not keen on adding a whole ten pence to their bill.

We could put it over their heads and secure it with a bungee cord around their necks, so they don't lose it.

14.09.18

Clearing up a few loose ends.

This week, two Kremlin-sponsored Novichok assassins were ridiculed after claiming to have been ordinary tourists,

or…

two completely innocent metrosexuals have been caught up in an international storm after going on holiday together – why can't two men simply enjoy each other's company in their private rented bedroom without everyone calling their sexuality into question?

The men, Ruslan Boshirov and Alexander Petrov claimed to have had nothing to do with the poisoning and were instead victims of a "fantastical fatal coincidence".

They said of Salisbury, "Our friends had been suggesting for a long time that we visit this wonderful town."

Then, giving a little bit too much information, added: "There's the famous Salisbury cathedral. It's famous not only in Europe, but in the whole world. It's famous for its 123 metre-spire. It's famous for its clock, one of the first ever created in the world that's still working,"

That is an impressively factual account that, coincidentally, closely resembles the Wikipedia entry about Salisbury.

Despite being so keen on Salisbury, and visiting it twice, they declined to actually stay there but rented a hotel room over a hundred miles away in East London.

They also did not take any pictures of that wonderful city or cathedral, as tourists might have done, preferring to commit it to memory.

They also claimed that they tried but failed to get to nearby Stonehenge, even though a bus was running to there from outside the railway station they arrived at.

The men also claimed they had to cut short their trip because the snow was up to their knees in Salisbury, but while it had indeed been snowing there in the days before they arrived, the pavements were clear by the time they got there.

Intrigue piled on confusion when it was revealed the pair had booked two alternative return flights from London to Moscow, giving them the option of leaving on Sunday or Monday, and when they finally departed, they did so without the luggage that they had arrived in the country with.

There are many unanswered questions regarding the two men's behaviour, so to help clear matters up, I am pleased to provide a transcript of Ruslan and Alexander's televised interview with Russia Today (RT) which they willingly agreed to do, when they were told that Vladimir Putin insisted on it.

RT: What about the Novichok found in your hotel room?

R&A: Oh that – that was not Novichok, that was new scent for men who like take holidays with each other from favourite western designer ...is called Poison...not actual poison, is just a name...smell very nice...manly, like President Putin

RT: Why did you decide to stay in East London to visit Salisbury?

R&A: Ah that's easy - Russian satnav. Is big problem getting anywhere in Russia – nobody knows where they are or how to get to where they're not.

RT: You complained about the snow but there did not seem to be any when you were there.

R&A: That's easy too – we were not complaining about the snow in Sal-is-bury, we were complaining is not enough snow. We Russian, we like snow, hate warm weather - warm weather make you weak and fat like your Boris bike person

RT: It is said that you were filmed travelling in the wrong direction for visiting the cathedral and that you did not actually go there.

R&A: Once again, is Russian satnav failure – I swear, I will kill person who invented it – not actual kill of course but pretend – we having fun yes?

RT: You said you wanted to visit Stonehenge, saying the bus tours were cancelled but they were not cancelled that day.

R&A: Well, is good thing we did not go because is just some stones, who cares?

RT: What about the two return flights and the missing luggage?

R&A: Well, is always best to have multiple exit possibilities from Sal-is-bury because is quite boring and as for no luggage on way home – well, we used all the Novichok so we left empty case – simple – now can we go please? This whole area probably contaminated.

15.09.17

The saviour of the poor.

Boris Johnson has set out his vision for Government, at a black tie gala in Washington.

The ex-Bozo of the FO said his top priority as PM would be social mobility.

He said that with a straight face while wearing a bow-tie and a dinner jacket.

Those poor people need social mobility, he announced – they need to get more mobile, they need to stop standing there and get a lick on and bring over the champagne, this glass is empty.

Asked for his top priority for Britain, Mr Johnson said: 'Social mobility. If you think back to the great achievements of the Thatcher era, it was about helping people to seize control of their own destiny.

'It was about buying shares or buying their own homes ... We need to recover that momentum.

'One of the reasons people voted to Leave was because they felt they were not getting a fair suck of the sauce bottle, as they say. People are stuck in entry-level jobs and they're not progressing. We're not focusing on those issues, we're not helping people enough.

'People are not being made to feel needed enough. And it's a serious problem.'

Boris Johnson, class warrior – a millionaire of aristocratic stock who thinks that £250,000 a year for one 1,000 word newspaper column a week, that he dashes off in half an hour, is "chicken feed", a man who was a member of the most superior club in the most superior school in the land has found, late in life, a passion for equality.

Has he expressed this burning desire before, or did it come to him during dinner?

As for Margaret Thatcher allowing people to seize control of their destiny, the Institute for Fiscal Studies, in their 'Two Decades of Income Inequality in Britain: The Role of Wages, Household Earnings and Redistribution' said that after increasing sharply through the 1980s, income inequality in Britain has fallen across most of the distribution over the past two decades, although incomes towards the very top have continued to pull away.

In other words, the 1980's saw a massive increase in income inequality, when a certain M Thatcher was in charge.

In the 1980's the income of the top 1% grew massively against everyone else's income and the bottom 99% flat lined – all the increased income created by the work of the 100% went to the top 1%.

Wealth inequality is far worse than income inequality, of course. The richest 1% have vastly more of the wealth of the country than they do the income of the country.

The same study says, coincidentally, that there was a period of relatively "inclusive" growth from 1997-2004, which happened to coincide with the prime ministership of one Tony Blair.

The only other period of relatively evenly spread out growth in the past 20 years happened during the great recession, when almost everyone took a hit.

It may be coincidence, but in the past 40 years, relatively inclusive growth only happened under the watch of Labour leader Tony Blair and during a catastrophe for the entire economy.

Under a Conservative government, outside of an all encompassing economic crash, the only people that did well since the 1980's were the top 1% - and that's not me saying that, it's the Institute for Fiscal Studies, who are not known for their tree-hugging, hippy communist principles.

So beware Boris Johnson.

Beware the man with the artfully distressed hair-don't. Beware the man who checks the mirror before he leaves the house to make sure he isn't smart.

Beware the man who wants a return to Thatcherism because he and everyone he knows are likely to be the ones that benefit.

The rest of us will be left wondering how we work harder for less money, while those that are rolling in it will be donning their bow-ties, pulling on their dinner jackets and telling us it's the best time of our lives.

21.09.18

Under a cloud

Emmanuel Macron said that the giant swirl of desperate confusion and uncertainty caused by Brexit will teach Britons not to listen to 'liars'.

That elicited fury from from the usual Brexiteer Ultras.

To be fair, the French president would have faced fury from them if he had read out the weather forecast.

Fury is their defining characteristic.

The EU leaders met in Salzburg round a massive table that you would have to shout to get heard across, underneath an enormous chandelier, which seemed to be made of pixie dust.

It was like a giant shimmering, gossamer cloud of magic. Who's decorating these places...Liberace?

It looked like a gay War Room.

Underneath that star-spangled heavenly mist, Monsieur Macron said that the tortuous Brexit negotiations were showing that voters should not heed politicians who say 'you can do easily without Europe'.

He spoke of false promises of easy money, pushed by certain people who 'predicted easy solutions'.

Who can he be thinking of?

He said, 'Brexit has shown us one thing - it has demonstrated that those who said you can easily do without Europe, that it will all go very well, that it is easy and there will be lots of money, are liars.

Those very people are the cause of this problem, he said, those who got us into the Brexit situation and who now tell us that Europe is going from crisis to crisis.'

From the sinking wreckage of our little dinghy, we see the good ship Europa sailing majestically by and we're shouting that THEY are in trouble.

The meeting of EU leaders threw out Mrs M.'s Chequers plan, which demands free trade without free movement of people.

It is the same thing she has been demanding for two years now and every time she draws a red line and hands in her proposition, the answer is always the same – no, non, nein.

The failure of this latest 'take it or leave it' gambit led to the PM threatening (again) to walk away without a deal.

It is a pretty odd way to conduct a negotiation - if you don't give me everything I want...I'll kill myself...then you'll be sorry!

It's like a child threatening to throw herself on the floor and have a tantrum at the supermarket because you won't buy her any sweets.

One of the many problems dogging Mrs M and her attempts to wrench success from the jaws of defeat is the Irish border question.

This is an issue so complex and rife with so many dangers that it is amazing that no one thought of it before the referendum.

Either it dawned on our leaders afterwards, or they knew it would be hard to work around, so they ignored it, in the hope that it would go away.

Transport Secretary Chris Grayling said 'No UK government...could possibly accept any border in the Irish sea, between Northern Ireland and the rest of the UK.'

Which doesn't leave anywhere to have a border between the UK and the EU, while demanding that there is a border because we are leaving.

There can't be a border because apparently that will force some old men to start shooting each other again, which makes as much sense as anything else that's happened lately.

Then it got weirder – the president of the European Commission, Jean-Claude Juncker likened the EU and Britain to 'two loving hedgehogs'.

He said 'When two hedgehogs hug each other, you have to be careful that there will be no scratches.'

Poor Theresa May. I am starting to feel sorry for her.

She was gifted a giant turd sandwich by her predecessor and is trying to wrest something positive from a near impossible predicament, being buffeted by forces from within her party and ridiculed by the very people she is trying to negotiate with.

As she climbed up the political greasy pole for all those years, can she have imagined that this is what it would be like in the top job – sitting under a diaphanous cloud of fairy dust, being lectured to by a man from Luxembourg on hedgehog sex?

29.09.18

A gun fight in Beds.

The little hamlet of Beeston in Bedfordshire is near Biggleswade. If you are not from these parts, you may never have heard of a place called Biggleswade.

You probably think it is so unlikely, so comically British a name that no such place could exist – it must have been dreamed up as part of a sketch in Monty Python: Biggleswade, near to Jinglewood, just down the road from Fartknockering, about ten minutes as the crow flies, or two minutes as the cretin drives.

The modern world, in the form of speeding has come to Biggleswade and intruded on this green and quiet idyll.

But there is a man who is bent on doing something about it – to restore the peace of this old mill town.

A local 72 year old grandfather called Mike Lacey took matters into his own hands after enduring some riotous driving on the A1, which passes directly in front of his house.

He once bought a speed gun, with which he clocked cars going at 90 miles per hour on a stretch of road that is legally limited to 50.

Of course, knowing what speed a vehicle shoots past does not prevent the crime, it merely records it having happened.

Deterrent is the key and to that end, Mr Lacey purchased some wood and pipes and bright yellow paint and fashioned himself a contraption that resembles one of those average speed cameras, especially when seen at some velocity.

The authorities are delighted that someone has taken charge of a dangerous situation to protect the public and increase road safety.

Just kidding, they're furious.

Mr Lacey had tried and failed to get something done through the proper channels and, in taking unilateral action incensed those very same channels.

So annoyed are the authorities that they have formed an alliance. Both the Bedfordshire County Council and Highways England have said the device must go.

The council objects because he has no planning permission, Highways England believe it is a distraction.

Aren't they supposed to be distracting? Isn't that the point?

If they were not designed to be noticed, then why are they signposted before they appear and painted a luminous lemon colour that burns the retina if stared at too long?

The whole point of a speed camera is that drivers' eyes will be drawn to them and be encouraged to moderate their pace, under threat of a fine.

If they weren't supposed to be diverting, why colour them in a hue so violent that they could stop a stampede? Those things could only blend into their surroundings at a funfair.

How can the same Highways England sign off on billboards by the side of the roads? They are intended to be distracting; that is the reason for their existence.

And as though posters weren't bad enough, they are being replaced with huge signs that light up and move like a giant television, constantly changing and flashing.

They couldn't be more distracting if people were having sex on them.

Of all the stuff that lines our roads, average speed cameras, that Mr Lacey's resemble, are the only things that actually calm drivers.

People slow down and speed up round static cameras but when monitored over a stretch of road, they are as good as gold, sticking to exactly the speed posted and not one mile an hour more or less.

Mr Lacey says he will not remove his fake speed camera until the authorities make the A1 safer.

The authorities say the A1 will become safer if he just takes his fake camera down.

It's a Mexican stand-off, in the badlands of Biggleswade.

It's a good job this didn't happen in Fartknockering, because then it would have sounded silly.

30.09.18

Freed red handed.

David Beckham has been sporting a new 'do. His hair has changed. This would normally be about as remarkable as the sun setting in the west but the press are agog because he seems to have gone to a specialist called Mr Loophole, which sounds like his technique is to loop new strands and place them in a hole created in the scalp.

Either that, or he has been seeing the well known legal beagle Nick Freeman, who is also known as Mr Loophole for his uncanny ability to find one that allows his clients to waltz out of court unscathed by the law.

David Beckham had been going so fast in central London that his hair may have been on fire.

Somehow, he managed to get up to 59 miles per hour in Paddington during the evening rush hour, when most drivers would count themselves fortunate to be doing 5.

The posted speed limit is a generous 30mph, and he was captured by a roadside camera whizzing by in a Bentley of such vast proportions that if it had a chimney, it would have been a house.

He was bang to rights, as they used to say on The Sweeney and admitted so, which might have disturbed a lawyer less able than Mr Freeman, who was undeterred by his client's admission of guilt.

The reported £20,000 that secures his legal services is not for nothing. So many stars have swerved neatly round the spirit of the law by nit-picking the letter of the law by using Mr Freeman's expertise that the lawyer has reached the same level of fame as his clients.

The case was heard in court. David Beckham did not attend because he was too busy posting pictures of himself relaxing somewhere else to show up in person.

The lawyer declared that his client admitted that he was guilty and the evidence of the speed camera underlined that he was indeed a guilty man.

The judge took this on board and carefully deliberated over the incontrovertible facts that were brought before the court before announcing, "Not guilty!"

The case hinged on of those loopholes that are only visible to those versed in the fine details of the law.

The Bentley dealership that loaned him the car received the letter that alerted David Beckham to the fact that he was to be punished for transgressing the rules of the road.

This is supposed to be within two weeks of the offence.

Sadly, the 'notice of intended prosecution' is claimed to have arrived just past that deadline, despite having been sent by post four days before the allotted time ran out.

Apparently, that is all you need to get off a speeding fine – declare that you received the letter over a fortnight after being caught. Although, if you try that without the help of a twenty grand-a-time lawyer in your corner, you might not be treated with the same courtesy that Beckham enjoyed.

And that's the problem. Mr Freeman said of his ability to dance round the attentions of a court, 'I realise that may cause some disquiet but that's a matter for Parliament. This is a statutory issue. If the law needs to be changed, so be it.'

Which sounds like the exact same thing that companies like Amazon and Google say when they are asked why the only paid 32 pence in tax on 10 billion pounds profit – 'we always pay all the legally required tax in every jurisdiction in which we do business'.

Companies like that have their people utter that exact phrase so often it is as though they are taunting us.

If you can afford to have a building full of lawyers comb through the legislation, there's always a loophole for the rich.

It is almost as though those loopholes are put there deliberately so that the wealthy can avoid what the poor are destined to suffer.

Beckham celebrated his win by bombing off to France in a private jet to post a picture of the wine he ordered with his meal – a bottle of Louis Latour Grands Echezeaux Grand Cru, which retails at about £1300 a bottle if bought in a (very fancy) off licence.

What it must cost in a restaurant is anyone's guess – almost certainly double that...or about as much as the fine that he would have been slapped with if he hadn't shelled out twenty grand on a clever lawyer.

To the untutored eye, that seemed a bit like rubbing it in, to the poor penurious public who have to make up all the taxes and fines avoided by the rich.

There is no magic money tree, as Theresa May rightly said – the money has to come from somewhere to keep the country running and if the rich would prefer not to pay, then it is down to us.

Maybe it wasn't gloating on his part, perhaps he suffers from a Tourettes-like affliction to post images of his every waking minute.

There are so many pictures of Beckham's tattoos, hairstyles, kids, clothes, houses, meals, cars, planes and holidays that the internet has barely enough room for anything else.

His good-boy image has helped make him one of the richest people on the planet. He never made as much money playing football than he has earned not playing it.

He fronts ads for clothes, cars, watches, food, perfume, razors, soft drinks, hard drinks...you name it, his face is on it.

225

The public's approval has made him the second richest retired sportsman in history. Only Michael 'Air' Jordan is better off.

What he has done to skip round the punishment for an offence that he admitted he was guilty of - the second time in as many days that he had been caught speeding - might make the public think again about buying the underwear or whiskey or cologne with is name on.

That would wipe the smile off his face.

There's no lawyer in the world that can get round the disapproval of the court of public opinion.

07.10.18

Peddling stolen goods.

When someone steals something of yours and you have their name, address, phone number, a picture of the stolen item at their house and an online listing of said item for sale on Gumtree, you would have thought that the police would have been round quick-sharp to feel some miscreant's collar.

But this is not the 1950's, the police are not stationed in Dock Green and Dixon has retired.

In July of this year, Sharron Jenson parked her bike on Kingston High Street, to avail herself of all that the town centre can offer.

Unfortunately, leaving her bike unattended was a big mistake, as any dedicated follower of criminal fashion could have told her.

You can cycle anywhere you like, just as long as you don't slow to a stop, or it is likely that your velocipede will be nicked from underneath you.

After Sharron's bike was stolen, by chance she spotted it for sale on the website Gumtree.

Delighted that the case was solved and that she would shortly be reunited with her transport she alerted the police who arrived in an instant.

Just kidding, they advised her to contact the seller to see if she could get her bike back.

Our intrepid hero did more than that.

In ascertaining the whereabouts of the bike seller, she managed to get all of his personal details. Not even Google knows more about him than Sharron managed to find out.

On presenting these details to the coppers, the balloon of her triumph was deflated somewhat when they told her that she should not go there unaccompanied, which is rich, as Sharon had rather hoped that it would be the police that would do the accompanying.

They were too busy, apparently, so she took off on a perilous mission to recapture her stolen bicycle.

In scenes that would make for a great film, starring Jodie Foster, perhaps, in the main roll, Sharron contacted the seller only for him to go quiet and remove the bike from the website when he became suspicious.

A week later, when the bike reappeared online, Sharon bought a cheap SIM card, so as to disguise her identity and made contact posing as someone else.

She cleverly adopted an air of insouciance and started to negotiate on price, shaving £60 off the asking price.

What Sharon had in mind, however, was to take 100% off the asking price, and here's where it gets exciting.

A meeting was arranged and our hero steeled herself to re-take her prized wheels.

Terrified for her life, she went alone to meet him, parking a few streets away so that she might make her escape and come back for her car later.

The man at the address asked her to go into the house. An odd request considering the bike was outside.

If this were a film, the audience would be on the edge of their seats shouting, "Don't go in the house Sharron!", in the knowledge that she surely would.

I know how this ends and I'm terrified myself – don't do it Sharron...it ain't worth it!

In the real life version, Sharon wisely refused to go inside and instead asked for a test ride and as collateral she handed the man her handbag, to reassure him that she would return.

Unbeknownst to him, the bag was empty, something he would discover when Sharon did not come back. She was pelting away at full speed, thinking that at any minute she would be caught.

When safely far enough away, she called the police with the perpetrator's name, address, phone number, picture, mother's maiden name, waist size and favourite colour.

Armed with this treasure trove of information, the constabulary rushed to her aid an apprehended the villain.

Again, I am just kidding, they said, and this is a direct quote: " All information was reviewed and it was decided that there was insufficient information to proceed with an investigation." and closed the case.

Some while later, the thief rang Sharron and threatened HER with the police if she did not return the bike.

He hung up when she told him that was actually her own, but would you have been remotely surprised if the police had arrested Sharon?

A thief could show up at the cop shop in a face mask, a stripey shirt and a bag marked 'swag' over his shoulder and the police would send him on his way and tell him not to waste their time.

When Sharon explained to the thief that the bike had been stolen back by its owner, he laughed and hung up.

And that seems to be the way that criminals treat the law – they think its funny – they think it doesn't affect them, because actually, it doesn't.

18.10.18

What's at issue?

After we learned that the world is doomed if we don't change the way we live with great speed, and that the changes needed are on a scale that is unheard of in human history, and the dangers of not changing our ways and of not keeping the warming of the earth below a very small amount are so catastrophic that it might be the end of life as we know it.

And after no less a giant mind than that of Stephen Hawking warned of a race of wealthy super-humans that could manipulate their own evolution and leave the rest of us behind, and after we have been warned that artificial intelligence could take over the planet and render us as its slaves...the thing that everybody is talking about with great concern and that urgently needs attention is whether the makers of paper toiletries should call their products "man sized" tissues.

The small parts of the news sites that aren't obsessed about whether Meghan Sparkles has a baby bump is pulling what's left of its hair out about whether Kleenex is sexist.

It seems that by its own admission, Kleenex WAS sexist as they changed the name of their "man sized" tissues to "extra large".

This was after people, who had presumably solved all the other grave matters concerning their lives, found the time to complain about the names of tissues on the internet.

They whined, Kleenex listened, problem solved, nothing to see here.

The troglodytes who inhabit comment sections of news sites and the denizens of the dark places of un-social media can now bank that win and move along to the next issue of no significance that they can get all het-up about.

One small problem, however: "extra large" sounds suspiciously sizeist to me – what about the people who are minding their own business and simply want a non-proportion specific sneeze shield?

Kleenex caved in just after Waitrose decided to change the name of its Gentleman's Smoked Chicken Caesar Roll, which they had named after Gentleman's Relish, which is part of the ingredients.

Delicate customers had spied this product on the shelves and immediately went into what the tabloids call "a meltdown" because lunch should not be discriminatory to those that don't identify as gentlemen, or as male, or as human.

It fell to Her Majesty's Marks and Spencer to stand up to the storm of snowflakes and LGBTQRSTU'ness and say: No, we will NOT change the name of our Mansize tissues...and any woman who doesn't like it will just have to grow a pair.

I'm kidding – that's not what they said – they said we are not currently planning on making any changes, unlike those weak-kneed Man Size Kleenex people who caved in after a mother tweeted that her four year old son had been confused by its name.

The whole world's gone insane.

Next in the firing line – Top Man, which causes outrage on two levels – not only does it specify a gender but also claims some sort of hierarchy.

It will henceforth be known as 'Average Person', assuming we are OK with implying that other species aren't welcome.

In other developments, Mothercare, which discriminates against guardians of a non-female sexual identity and excludes those who are not that bothered about parenting, will now be called 'Guardian Who May or May Not Care' and Hertz will henceforth be known as Shertz.

15 10 18

Strewth.

In a shock to the whole process of Brexit, a grumpy old rich man has said that we should get out of Europe.

That's right - the papers have managed to find a pensioner that voted for Brexit – hold the front page.

It wasn't any old pensioner though, it was 84 year old Michael Caine, who said he still believed in Brexit and said it was better for us to be poorer but in charge of our own future.

You might think that preferring poverty to being part of the EU is easy to say for someone worth £57m and you would be right - he's not likely to be worried about the cost of of his weekly shop at Tescos, whatever the outcome.

Michael Caine said quitting Europe was more important than being better off in the bloc.

And he was cheered to the rafters by the red faced old duffers who would have had a cow that you could have seen from space if he had said the opposite.

If Michael Caine had said we would be better off IN Europe, Brexiteers would have said things like, "bloomin' snowflake luvvie...what does he know about politics?...Bloomin' actors, sticking their noses in, why doesn't he go back to pretending to be someone he isn't and repeating lines that someone else wrote?..It's all he's good for."

And they would have trawled through his filmography to further pile ridicule upon him.

They would have said, 'why do we need to be lectured to by a man who was in Jaws the Revenge?'

But he didn't say we should be better off IN the EU, he said we should be better off OUT, so he is a hero of the age.

Finally, a man with gravitas has spoken, Harry Brown is armed and dangerous and coming for YOU Monsieur Barnier.

Michael Caine, said: "People say 'Oh, you'll be poor, you'll be this, you'll be that. I say I'd rather be a poor master of my fate than having someone I don't know making me rich by running it."

One small point Michael: THAT'S BECAUSE YOU'RE ALREADY RICH!

I would be less worried about the consequences of our leaving the EU if all the most ardent supporters of Brexit weren't so fabulously wealthy.

Are there any of the leading Brexiteers that don't have millions of pounds to cushion their fall?

And besides – is that the same Michael Caine who said that if the tax rate went up just 1% to 51% he would back in America because he didn't want to have to support 3.5m layabouts on welfare?

That was in 2009, the low point after the start of the great recession.

Those 'layabouts' were British citizens who had been turfed out of a job because of the bankers' greed and stupidity, not their own idleness.

Is it the same Michael Caine that joined an aggressive tax avoidance scheme in 2014 that generated huge artificial losses offshore to reduce tax bills, a scheme that sheltered £1.2bn from the tax man.

Is he the same fellow who said that, basically, he is a socialist?

I'm going to get a dictionary. I will have to look up the word 'socialist'. It can't mean what I think it means.

Michael Caine is, basically, everything that would make your average patriotic Brexiteer Ultra boil with rage, except that he IS a Brexiteer, so that's all right then.

27.10.18

It weren't me – I'm a (tremendously) good boy, I am

The press have dubbed him the MAGAbomber after the MAGA hat slogan that Trump took from that other highly successful populist political party, the Nazis, whose leader was keen on repeating to his rallies that he would Make Germany Great Again.

Trump used to keep a volume of Hitler's speeches by his bedside according to a Vanity Fair article from 1990, so he would have had time to flip through it while waiting for his then current wife Ivana to gird herself for what was to come.

The MAGAbomber drove a van round Florida plastered in a collage of President Trump's favourite targets: Hilary Clinton, George Soros, the media in general, CNN in particular, foreigners and so on.

There were so many pictures of the 'enemies of the people' with cross-hairs superimposed on the windows of that van that it was surprising he could see out to drive.

He allegedly sent pipe bombs to Hilary, CNN, Soros, ex-president Obak Arama, Robert de Niro and other frequent targets of Trump's unhinged tweeting and on-stage pronouncements at his Make America White Again rallies.

The President of the United States of America saw this unfold on the TV news, was presumably fully briefed on the incidents by some 'really tremendous people, everybody says so, I can tell you that', and came to the conclusion that it had nothing to do with the barrage of his constant aggression, even though the address list of the bomber was the exact same names as the attack list in his speeches.

It was not Donald's fault, said Donald, it was the media's fault for being so mean to him.

There does not seem to be any limit to how low he can go.

Trump said in a tweet: 'A very big part of the Anger we see today in our society is caused by the purposely false and inaccurate reporting of the Mainstream Media that I refer to as Fake News. It has gotten so bad and hateful that it is beyond description. Mainstream Media must clean up its act, FAST!'

Is there any other way to read that than: you had better start writing nice things about me or you're going to get it?

Sarah Sanders, the dead-eyed White House press secretary, said 'The president's condemned violence in all forms, has done that since day one, will continue to do that, but certainly feels that everyone has a role to play.'

Is she talking about the same Donald Trump who urged his fans to beat up protesters at his rallies, who said he would cover the court costs of anyone doing so, who said 'I'd like to punch him in the face' when someone spoke up against him, and who praised a Republican law maker who body-slammed a journalist?

According to the White House, the President is not responsible for the political climate that he has engineered – why would anyone think that?

When Trump had his next safe-space rally, he actually toned down the rhetoric for a short while and boasted to the crowd about how respectful and nice he was being in the circumstance of all of his enemies having been sent a bomb in the post.

That was like watching a four year old demanding an ice-cream for sitting up straight at the dinner table.

He wants credit for acting presidential. That seems like the least you could expect of someone who is, you know, the president.

John Brennan, the former CIA director told Trump in a tweet, 'Stop blaming others. Look in the mirror. Your inflammatory rhetoric, insults, lies, & encouragement of physical violence are disgraceful. Clean up your act....try to act Presidential. The American people deserve much better. BTW, your critics will not be intimidated into silence.'

Donny would not have liked that. There wasn't much praise in that missive.

The president of CNN, Jeff Zucker said, 'There is a total and complete lack of understanding at the White House about the seriousness of their continued attacks on the media. The President, and especially the White House Press Secretary, should understand their words matter. Thus far, they have shown no comprehension of that.'

I think they comprehend full well what they are doing – stoking fear and fury to win elections. It seems to work quite well.

In the history of the human race, it usually has.

The New York Times used to keep a list of Trump's insults but their computer must have broken under the strain in July this year, so here is a heavily edited list of some of the ones they logged in just one month

Hillary Clinton:

"Crooked"

CNN:

"Fake News"

James Comey, former FBI director:

"Slippery James Comey"

Jeff Flake United States senator:

"doesn't have a clue", "he's a Flake!"

The "mainstream" media:

"Fake News", "so unfair, and vicious", "Fake", "Fake News is really bad!"

Peter Strzok An FBI agent involved in the Mueller investigation:

"incompetent & corrupt"

Justin Trudeau Prime Minister of Canada:

"so indignant", "acted so meek and mild", "Very dishonest & weak"

WEEK OF JUNE 10, 2018

Hillary Clinton:

"Crooked Hillary"

James Comey Former FBI director:

"the worst leader, by far, in the history of the FBI"

Democrats:

"forcing the breakup of families at the Border with their horrible and cruel legislative agenda"

Robert De Niro:

"a very Low IQ individual", "has received too many shots to the head by real boxers in movies", "I watched him last night and truly believe he may be 'punch-drunk'", "Wake up Punchy!"

Eric Schneiderman Former Attorney General of New York:

"sleazy"

Tim Kaine Democratic vice-presidential nominee:

"a total stiff"

The "mainstream" media:

"Fake News", "Our Country's biggest enemy", "Fake News!", "Fake News", "Fake News", "only shows the bad photos", "Fake News"

Claire McCaskill United States Senator:

"so phony!"

New York Democrats:

"sleazy"

North Atlantic Treaty Organization (NATO):

"countries that rip us off"

Justin Trudeau Prime Minister of Canada:

"acts hurt when called out!"

WEEK OF JUNE 17, 2018

ABC News:

"Fake ABC News"

Hillary Clinton:

"Crooked"

James Comey Former FBI Director:

"Slippery"

Democrats:

"weak and ineffective", "Democrats don't care about crime and want illegal immigrants, no matter how bad they may be, to pour into and infest our Country"

Conor Lamb United States Congressman:

"LambTheSham"

The "mainstream" media:

"Fake News", "Fake News", "the enemy of the people", "Fake News", " truth doesn't matter to them!", "Fake News", "Fake News", "Fake News", "Total corruption", "Fake Media"

Refugees in Germany:

"millions of people in who have so strongly and violently changed their culture!"

Allegations of collusion between Russia and members of the Trump campaign:

"WITCH HUNT!", "phony", "Double Standard!", "Crooked Hillary", "Witch Hunt!", "A really sick deal", "Witch Hunt!", "A Rigged Witch Hunt!", "Witch Hunt", "a scam!", "Witch Hunt", "Democrat inspired and paid for Russian Witch Hunt", "A total scam and excuse for the Dems losing the Election!", "Witch Hunt", "Rigged!"

Chuck Schumer United States Senator:

"Cryin' Chuck", "wants to protect illegal immigrants far more than the citizens of our country"

The Washington Post:

"I think a really long strike would be a great idea. Employees would get more money and we would get rid of Fake News for an extended period of time!"

WEEK OF JUNE 24, 2018

Hillary Clinton:

"Crooked Hillary"

Democrats:

"want Open Borders and Unlimited Crime"

Jimmy Fallon Host, "the Tonight Show":

"whimpering ", "Be a man Jimmy!"

The "mainstream" media:

"Fake News is working overtime!"

Members of Robert Mueller's team:

"13 Angry Democrats"

Nancy Pelosi U.S. House Minority Leader:

"will Make America Weak Again!"

Allegations of collusion between Russia and members of the Trump campaign:

"Witch Hunt", "disgrace", "a total sham!", "Rigged!", "Rigged Witch Hunt", "A disgraceful situation!"

Chuck Schumer United States Senator:

"Cryin' Chuck"

Peter Strzok An F.B.I. agent involved in the Mueller investigation:

"a hating fraud", "the leader of the Rigged Witch Hunt"

Mark Warner United States Senator:

" drunk"

Maxine Waters United States Congresswoman:

"an extraordinarily low IQ person", "unhinged", "will Make America Weak Again!"

WEEK OF JULY 01, 2018

Democrats:

"declaring war on Law & Order"

The "mainstream" media:

"Fake News"

Allegations of collusion between Russia and members of the Trump campaign:

"Witch Hunt"

U.S. immigration policies:

"insane"

The U.S. National Security Agency:

"Such a disgrace"

The Washington Post:

"a disgrace to journalism", "constantly quoting anonymous sources that do not exist"

Maxine Waters, United States Congresswoman:

"Crazy","ranting and raving"

That list is by no means complete. It is just a flavour of the unthreatening, respectful, non-violent tone that emanates from Ancient Orange.

The man of whom his press secretary said had "condemned violence in all forms, has done that since day one, and will continue to do that."

To paraphrase Martin Sheen in Apocalypse Now, a film title that seems apt: the bull**** is piling up so fast, you need wings to stay above it.

25.10.18

Yes, we'll have no bananas.

Researchers at the University of Oxford have just released a warning that a 'hard Brexit' could kill thousands of people a year.

That's not so much Project Fear as Project Absolutely Bloomin' Terrifying.

The problem with a hard Brexit, that Mrs M's used to bang on about, is that we will not be freed of all rules about trade. That is the notion that the Brexiteer Ultras are pushing, that when we are out, it will be a lifting of rules like the last day of school before the summer holidays.

If we flounce out of the EU without kissing and making up first, we would revert to World Trade Organisation rules and extensive research on my part, that involved looking it up on Google, tells me that WTO tariffs on food average 22%.

They range from as much as 46% for Italian mozzarella to as low as 4% for French wine. At least we will be able to drink to forget that we can't afford pizza any more.

That cartoon top-hatted monocle wearer Jacob Rees-Mogg, the spokes-model of the super-rich far right claims that "no deal, no problem". Well, it won't be a problem for him. He will be able to afford an extra 22% on the price of food.

He could make up the difference by simply axing one of his butlers, or giving nanny a pay cut.

The problem with exiting the EU is that we are entwined with them like two octopuses making sweet briny love with each other.

By value, we get 90% of our fruit and vegetables from Europe, which means that the stuff they are trying to get us to eat more of will become much less affordable.

People think they cost too much already. Fruit and vegetables are always put right at the front door of any supermarket – they are what you see first. Supermarkets do this to kid on that they are all about freshness and good health.

Their customers take on board this virtuous idea subliminally and briefly feel good about themselves as they negotiate the fastest route through the aisles of spinach and sprouts and head straight for the crisps.

The government have been trying to get us to eat our 5-a-day for years now with little success. If the good stuff is about to get at least 22% more expensive, they've got no chance.

And by extension, neither do we stand a chance of living to an old age.

The scientists put a number on it: 5,600 extra dead people a year if we crash out of the EU without a deal.

Pricier fresh foods will put people off and the lure of ready meals and takeaways will become ever stronger for those that are already struggling to get by and it is those people that are most at risk of expiring mid-burger.

You can't get all the nutrition you need for a healthy life from food that comes in a bucket. You won't stay well on a diet of mystery meat from the kebab shop.

The only thing that causes more deaths than tobacco is our unhealthy diets. The pre-made rubbish we eat is filling up the grave yards as it is. They'll have to start burying us standing up if vegetables become even more expensive than they are now.

This is no idle speculation - the Global Burden of Disease Study, the most in-depth study of global mortality rates ever conducted, found last year that poor diets are linked to one in five deaths worldwide.

Not even driving round the M25 is that deadly.

Of course, these are only facts provided by experts, so no one is remotely interested in what they have to say.

Depending on which side of the debate you are on, a hard Brexit may be the death of us, or it might free us from the tyranny of the vegetable side dish and the agony of trying to get through a whole piece of fruit a day.

It might mean thousands of extra dead people a year, or none at all, if you don't believe in science.

03.11.18

Chewing through the competition.

If our plan is to rid ourselves of the competition for space and oxygen on this small planet, then we are doing very well.

We have managed to wipe out 60% of all the mammals, birds, fish and reptiles that were clogging up the place and we accomplished that in the few short decades since 1970.

At this rate we are well on course to annihilate all the wildlife on earth.

It's a tremendous success, three cheers for humanity – we win!

Unfortunately, killing all the fauna is now an emergency that threatens...well, nothing major...just our entire civilisation.

That's what a major report produced by World Wildlife Fund, involving 59 scientists from across the globe says, and I know what you're thinking.

You're thinking: scientists?

No one is remotely interested in scientists and their so called facts.

Not believing in them, however, does not make facts go away.

The report said that the exploitation of resources and our growing insatiable appetite for more and more food is destroying the web of life.

That web was billions of years in the making, and human society depends on it for clean air, water and everything else that keeps us alive.

Killing 60% of all the fauna on earth is a pretty amazing achievement but it is one which might be the end of us too.

The Executive Director of Science and Conservation at the World Wildlife Fund said, "If there was a 60% decline in the human population, that would be equivalent to emptying North America, South America, Africa, Europe, China and Oceania. This is far more than just being about losing the wonders of nature, this is actually now jeopardising the future of people.

Prof Johan Rockström, a global sustainability expert at the Potsdam Institute for Climate Impact Research in Germany said, "We are rapidly running out of time, only by addressing both ecosystems and climate do we stand a chance of safeguarding a stable planet for humanity's future on Earth."

These scientists say that we really need to change our way of life IMMEDIATELY in order to avoid a catastrophe later on.

They don't know us very well do they?

Our current leader is a giant ball of furious orange that does not believe in science and thinks animals are for shooting from the safety of a jeep on a holiday in Africa and that global warming is a Chinese hoax to stop him using so much hairspray.

Humankind has destroyed 83% of all mammals and half of all plants since the dawn of civilisation – we're not about to stop now that we only have another 17% of animals and half of all plants to get through and the planet will finally be ours.

Besides, it would cost us a lot in the short term to benefit the planet in the long term, so forget it. Delayed gratification is not really our thing, plus – we're hungry.

The biggest cause of wildlife losses is the destruction of natural habitats to create farmland.

What was once teeming with all forms of life are now vast fields of mono-cultures that are drenched in chemicals to increase yield while destroying anything that might take a fancy to it.

The second biggest cause of wildlife loss is that we've eaten it.

Three hundred mammal species are being eaten into extinction and the oceans are massively overfished.

We're a threat on land sea AND air.

There's chemical pollution, diseases spread by the pet trade, and we really must hate forests because in Brazil alone an area the size of Greater London is cleared every two months, if you can believe that.

The World Wildlife Fund said "We can no longer ignore the impact of current unsustainable production models and wasteful lifestyles."

But we're not listening because we can't hear them over the power saws cutting down the trees to build warehouses to keep all the dead animals we're planning to eat at Christmas and the presents we will be throwing away shortly afterwards.

Still, if God did not want us to ruin the environment he wouldn't have given us concrete and if he didn't want us to eat animals, he wouldn't have made them out of meat.

04.11.18

Out of kilter

Guess which country has got the worst work-life balance in western Europe?

That was an easy one, it has to be us.

The UK has the highest proportion of employees working more than 50 hours a week.

Every year we spend 325 more hours at work than the Germans who spend those extra hours enjoying typical Teutonic amusements, like unwinding to the sound of oompah bands while wearing lederhosen.

Stiff leather shorts and Bavarian tuba music. What a combination.

I'd rather be at work

And who has the best work life balance?.

That's right, the perfect six-foot blond people. Those bloomin' Scandinavians win again.

As with most things that add to the pleasure of life, they top the list of the world's industrialised nations with the best work-life balance.

This is probably why they are also top of the list every time one of those happiness indexes comes out.

I bet the Danes practically wake up laughing.

It's probably got a lot to do with all that hygge, that special feeling of cosy pleasure that the Scandis seem to be seeped in.

If you were having hot hygge with a 6 foot blonde perfect Scandinavian, you'd be laughing too.

What is odd is that we work harder than any country in western Europe but we're not very productive.

Last time I looked, the most productive country per hour worked was Luxembourg, followed by Ireland, Norway, Belgium, the USA, Denmark, France, Germany, the Netherlands, Switzerland, Austria, Sweden, Finland, Australia and then us.

We are fifteenth on the list.

We work our socks off and achieve very little. We are paddling furiously and going nowhere.

The researchers who compiled the work-life balance figures said, 'A healthy, happy workforce can drive productivity and creativity, but these figures reveal that Brits are among the most guilty of committing more time to their jobs rather than finding time to switch off.

Our work-life balance rating is almost the same as our productivity rating, we're 16th.

Only Greece, the US, Japan and South Korea do worse than we do.

Denmark topped the list, of course, followed by Norway and Sweden, just as you would expect.

The work-life index takes into account a range of factors like the average number of hours worked each year, annual leave available, time dedicated to leisure and taking care of yourself, and overall happiness.

And that's what it's all about isn't it, overall happiness?

I mean, we don't get to do our life over.

If we don't maximise our happiness the first time round, there IS no second time, unless you are a member of one of those religions that believes in reincarnation.

In which case, if you have been very good in this life, you may come back as a hot Danish hygge inspector.

Then you'd be happy.

10.11.18

Donny Does Paris

Donald Trump was prised out of the Whitehouse.

His handlers also managed to get him out of his Trump hotels, Trump golf courses, Trump country clubs and other assorted Trump property promotional opportunities that he spends most of his time in, when he's not at one of his demented rallies.

They flew him to where Make America Great Again hats are in short supply - France, to give him the chance to show the respect he has for the military.

The President had used the military in a mid-term election stunt by sending thousands of heavily armed troops to the border to repel the "invasion" of a bedraggled group of men, women and children that were, at the time, about 900 miles away, trudging through Mexico.

His cultists lapped it up.

Donny said he was protecting America from a horde of rapists and murderers who were going to eat their children...vote Republican.

The "threat" from the caravan dissipated as soon as the election was concluded, so Trump had to pick another fight in his perpetual rolling war of noise and impotent fury, just to keep his name at the top of the bulletins, and this time, it was France in his sights.

He fired the fist salvo before he had even landed. He does this a lot, to make sure that everyone is talking about him in advance of his arrival. All eyes on Donny, just the way he likes it.

The French President Emanuel Macron had tweeted, quite reasonably that "When I see President Trump announcing that he's quitting a major disarmament treaty which was formed after the 1980s euro-missile crisis that hit Europe, who is the main victim? Europe and its security."

Nothing wrong with that, it is just a statement of fact, but Donny don't like facts!

He tweeted that Macron's comments had been "very insulting", but some world class gold medal winning insulting behaviour was about to witnessed, and it would not be from the leader of France.

When the two met for the cameras, Trump sat beside the French president, did his usual pouty, risible, macho manspreading routine, and showed boredom, indifference or complete incomprehension when Macron spoke in English that was both grammatically and factually more accurate than Trump's.

When Donny's not talking, Donny ain't listening.

Ancient Orange had flown in for the marking of the centenary of the end of World War One, presumably because he couldn't get out of it.

He tweeted "Is there anything better to celebrate than the end of a war, in particular that one, which was one of the bloodiest and worst of all time?"

Leave aside that saying that it was vaguely "one of the bloodiest and worst of all time", made him sound like a school boy who hadn't done his homework and was winging it in front of the class when called on by his teacher: "It was a tremendously huge war and nobody ever saw such a war, and it was the biggest, I can tell you that, everybody says so."

The main issue with that missive, apart from it being on Twitter, which is not the place you immediately associate with respect, is that the occasion was not a celebration, it was a commemoration. The celebrations ended a hundred years ago.

Close, no cigar.

The key moment for a visiting American leader was to pay the respects of the nation at the US war cemetery Belleau Wood about 55 miles east of the French capital on Saturday afternoon.

Unfortunately, the weather was somewhat inclement, so to show the respect he really has for the military and for the service personnel that had laid down their lives for their country, Donny cancelled the trip.

It was raining, so the Screaming MeMe spent the afternoon in his hotel, probably calling down to reception bellowing that his TV can't get Fox News.

Trump's Whitehouse put out a statement that the weekend trip was "a historic opportunity to honor the sacrifices of those who gave their lives for our freedom in the war that ended 100 years ago on Sunday."

They should have added: "weather permitting".

The White House Chief of staff John Kelly braved the conditions in his stead.

For a man that revels in his tough-guy persona, Trump certainly is frightened of a lot of things: ramps, stairs, umbrellas, wives over 40, questions from journalists, things that aren't flattering and especially wind and rain.

The problem with standing to attention in the wind and rain is that there wouldn't be anything to stop his hair from unravelling.

Trump's people said the President couldn't make it because of logistical difficulties caused by the weather...which translates as Donny can't go out when its windy and raining in case his canary yellow hair-do unglues, flips up and lifts off his head like a kite.

The internet was awash with posts of a video highlighting the difference between Trump and the Canadian Prime Minster who took a soaking in Ottawa in August 2017, 75 years after Canadian and Allied troops rushed Dieppe in a futile attempt to free the French city of its German occupiers.

Justin Trudeau folded his umbrella to expose himself to the deluge and said, "Today, we honour those who fought with such grit and valour on the beaches of France. As we sit here in the rain, thinking how uncomfortable we must be these minutes as our suits get wet and our hair gets wet and our shoes get wet, I think it's all the more fitting we remember on that day in Dieppe, the rain wasn't rain. It was bullets.

Some contrast to the tough-guy president of the USA.

The Whitehouse, seeking to contain the damage, announced that Trump had actually refused to travel because the rain had made it difficult to get to the cemetery by helicopter and he did not want his motorcade to cause a traffic jam.

Nice try – no sale.

I will believe that he has respect for anyone or anything when wigs can fly.

11.11.18

Drinking in the competition.

You can't turn on your computer these days without seeing a story about someone who invented artificial intelligence or social media warning us about...er...artificial intelligence and social media.

Tim Wu is the Columbia Law professor who coined the term 'net neutrality'.

He has urged the US government to dissolve Facebook, Google and Amazon before they take over the entire economy, like a giant reptile emerging from the sea in a Japanese monster film.

Tim Wu says that the tech giants are faced with little competition and are acquiring more and more companies.

He's right – as soon as some company that threatens the dominant tech firms gains some traction, those same giants buy them out, absorb them into the mother-ship, gain more strength and power and carry on barrelling over the world, picking up things like a lint roller.

Wu says that the only way to control them is to sue them for breaking antitrust laws which regulate the conduct of business corporations to keep them honest and fair and end monopolies.

Good luck with that – they have all the money that the banks don't own and they seem not to be inclined to thinking about the consequences of their actions, as long as the money keeps coming in.

The tech giants have grown from nothing to influence nearly every aspect of our daily lives to the point that, if they were to fail, it would be as consequential as if electricity didn't work any more.

They have become so huge that they face no real competition and hold the most comprehensive collection of our personal data ever collected.

They know more about us than we do ourselves.

The harm they cause is very real. Just because they go to work in a T-shirt doesn't mean they're not evil.

Entire generations are hooked on social media like it is made of heroin. Kids can't walk five paces without checking their phone to see if they've missed anything.

The medical profession even has names for the various conditions that smartphone addiction can cause, from' Blackberry thumb' to 'iPhone neck' and 'texter's claw'.

What more evidence of harm do you need?

There is also the little matter of subverting democracy. Social media is awash with misinformation to the point that it is hard to tell what is true any more.

Up to now, they have got a pass because they are new and espouse hippy ideals and they are free at the point of use.

When Facebook was challenged by Instagram, they snapped them up with what, for them, amounted to spare change.

When WhatsApp became a concern, Facebook waved a cheque for $19bn and bought them too.

Facebook now faces no serious competition at all.

Google is so dominant that they have become the generic name for an internet search.

Add in Amazon, and pretty soon, there will be just three companies running everything.

Aided by genius-level accounting they can use the money they saved not paying tax to buy up anything that stands in their way of total world domination.

But it's not just tech giants that need to be broken up. Wu says that the pharmaceutical industry, cable television, the fertilizer industries and beer need to be broken up too.

He's right – just look at beer.

Anheuser-Busch make Budweiser, 'The king of beers'!

They also make: Michelob, Rolling Rock, Corona, Becks, Fosters and Stella Artois.

They are the biggest beer company in the world.

These days, there has been a move to craft beer. Punters are forsaking the delights of the largest sellers and plumping for a handmade beer in small batches from a family run brewery.

People are looking for something with heart and soul.

Good luck with that because when a craft beer company achieves success on a local scale, the mighty beer giants swoop in and pick them up like seagulls nicking chips.

When you scan the labels on the bar of your independent hostelry for something a little different from the mainstream, remember that Anheuser-Busch also make Natural, Landshark, Goose Island, Blue Point, 10 Barrel, Elysian, Golden Road, Four Peeks, Breckenridge, Karbach, Wicked Weed, King Cobra, Leffe, Lowenbrau, Camden Town, Skol, Oranjeboom, Labatt, Hoegaarden and Johnny Appleseed cider to name but a few.

This global mega-corporation makes beer with local names in Luxembourg, Brazil, Germany, India, Russia, Australia, Paraguay and China.

Where there's a thirst, you will find them. In fact it is rather difficult to avoid them, even if you are trying to.

Unlike the artificial intelligence tech giants, however, they won't steal your personal information while you enjoy their product.

Drink enough of it though and you might find you have lost all your real intelligence and are shouting that information to whoever is in earshot.

22.11.18

The cost of entertaining

The Duke and Duchess of Sussex are moving out of their London home and relocating to a modest sounding place called Frogmore Cottage in Windsor.

They will be raising their first child there, which the will do by hiving off all the difficult bits to nannies, cleaners, minders, groomers, burpers, nappy wranglers and various assorted serfs and servants as befits a couple who are too busy doing nothing for a living.

HRH Puff 'n' Stuff and Meghan Sparkles currently live in Nottingham Cottage in the grounds of Kensington Palace.

They were living there while we poor dopes who pay taxes tarted up a flat in the palace to their exact specifications.

It cost us about one and a half million pounds to fix up, and now they've decided not to live there.

How could a flat cost £1.5m to renovate, you might be wondering.

Well, they call it a flat but it is really an entire wing of a building big enough to be a hospital. That flat's got 21 rooms in it.

If the renovations are anything like Will's and Wotsits', who live in another 21 room flat in the palace, they will have spared no expense, because they're not paying for it, we are.

I bet they've plumped for one of those slightly colder fridges that cost as much as a house in Liverpool.

Why not? Free to those that can afford it, very expensive to those that can't.

Despite £1,500,000 of your money being spent, or in tabloidese: "splurged", their royal highnesses have now said they don't like it and they're off to live in another palace in Windsor that will probably also have to be renovated at vast expense paid for by us.

They're off to live on the Frogmore Estate in what is called a cottage but to you and me looks like house vast enough to be seen with the naked eye from the International Space Station.

It has been owned by the royal family since the 1500's when, presumably they took a fancy to it and annexed it.

Frogmore Cottage is not as big as the main house, though, which we'll probably have to tart up too, when they decide that a ten bedroom cottage doesn't quite cut it.

A royal source said 'Harry and Meghan want to move, and need more space, but they don't want to live next door to William and Catherine',

Why? Too boring? Hazza doesn't want Wills to steal his stash?

The source said 'There is no reason why their London home has to be at Kensington Palace. There are plenty of other options, including using their own money to buy their own place.

Ha! That'll be the day.

Why pay for anything yourself when you have a whole country of 65 million people who seem willing to pick up every bill?

Frogmore Cottage not only comes with 10 bedrooms, it also boasts a gym, spa, nursery, orangeries and yoga studio. Just like a normal cottage.

The much larger Frogmore House is a 17th-century English country house owned by the Crown.

That means the queen doesn't actually own it, we do. We pay for the upkeep and she gets to live in it. Actually, she doesn't even do that. She has so many houses, mansions, palaces, castles and estates to call home that the royal family only use Frogmore's big house for infrequent parties.

Of course, we can visit Frogmore House.

It is completely open to the public and we can look round any time we want, as long as it is one of the three days a year we are allowed in.

I'm not making that up. We can go and gawp at the place we pay for on three days in June: £19 per person for the house and garden, £35 if you want the tour.

No one has lived in the place since George V's cousin Grand Duchess Xenia Alexandrovna of Russia in 1937.

It had a £2.5 million restoration in 1990, and all they use it for is occasional entertaining.

Let's hope that Harry and Meghan are suitably entertained.

22 11 mail

The Thanksgiving turkey.

It is Thanksgiving in America and the press asked Donald Trump what he was thankful for.

As you would expect, he said he was most thankful for himself.

The President of the USA said, "I am thankful for my family - my current wife, my unbelievably hot daughter, she's so hot...boy if I wasn't her father...I am thankful for my two sons, or is it three? And I think there's another daughter somewhere that no-one talks about and perhaps some children that I may have conceived with women I had sign confidentiality agreements, but mostly I am thankful for me. I have made a tremendous difference to America and I am very thankful for that."

He may not have used those exact words but let's not get bogged down in facts. No one is interested in those any more.

He really said "I made a tremendous difference in the country. This country is so much stronger now than it was when I took office that you won't believe it. And I mean, you see it, but so much stronger that people can't even believe it."

That is true – people look at what is happening in America and they can't quite believe it. That is down to one man: the Tangerine Scream.

He said "I want to give thanks for my enormous hugeness...it is so huge...everybody says so...you talk to leaders of countries and they say why can't we get someone as great as you to run OUR country...it's true...I was speaking with God and God said to me 'Sir', he said, 'Mr Trump sir, you are even better than the tremendous job I did with Jesus. God said that to me ...it's totally true...he said Jesus was a loser compared to you, Mr Trump. I am His greatest success, a lot of people say that."

Trump said, "God told me that. He was very respectful, great guy, but I've met better frankly. I mean He's not SO great. Look at the mess God left for me to clear up, and I've done a tremendous job, better than anyone could have, believe me."

And while that sounds ridiculous, it is not too far from what he actually said, which was, "when I see foreign leaders they say they can't believe the difference in strength between the United States now and the United States two years ago."

Which leaders said that, he did not explain.

Trump is on holiday. He needs a break from getting up late and watching Fox News all day, so he is spending time at the Trump International Golf course at his exclusive country club Mar-a-Lago, where he had a dinner to celebrate himself.

The menu included but was not limited to: a full salad bar with Caesar, tomato, mozzarella, and Greek salads, devilled eggs, duck prosciutto & melon; a chilled seafood display with Florida stone crab, oysters, jumbo shrimp, and clams; a carving station with turkey and all the trimmings, beef tenderloin, lamb and salmon; main courses of Chilean Sea bass, red snapper, braised short ribs; sides of whipped potatoes, sweet potatoes, vegetables and traditional stuffing.

And assorted desserts.

Chefs served food in a corner of the room. Tables had long gold cloths with autumnal centrepieces and guests ate off of white plates edged in gold.

It is a good job that he keeps saying he is representing the poor people of America and is against the rich elites, because otherwise you wouldn't know.

The president started the day by speaking to various troops for about 25 minutes, as is the norm on Thanksgiving.

He had a script of the usual platitudes in front of him: thank you for your service, we are thinking of you, etc.

Of course, he couldn't stick to the prepared remarks because, as you know, he is a stable genius and very smart.

When he was talking to a Navy Commander, he couldn't stop himself from going on about the Navy's switch from steam to electromagnetic catapults on aircraft carriers.

The systems are used to launch planes off the decks and for some reason Trump is very anti-magnets.

Maybe he thinks they will make his hair go flat.

So, the Screaming MeMe is on the phone with this poor Naval Officer serving on an aircraft carrier and he says, "Would you go with steam or would you go with electromagnetic? Steam is very reliable. Electromagnetic – unfortunately you have to be Albert Einstein to really work it properly,'

After a slight pause, the officer responded: "Yes sir. You sort of have to be Albert Einstein to run the nuclear power plant that we have here as well, but we're doing that very well."

I don't know whether the officer was rolling his eyes during the call, but you can't prove he didn't so anyone who says otherwise is fake news.

Trump made the guy choose magnets or steam because Trump just wanted to hear someone say that he was right, that steam is better.

Unfortunately, the Naval officer is an expert, in possession of facts, and he said "Sir, Mr President, I would go electromagnetic. We do pay a heavy cost for transiting the steam around the ship."

And the steam went out of Donny, who did what he always does when he is told he is wrong and that is to say he always thought so.

He said "I'm actually happy about that answer, because at least they're doing what they're doing. That's actually a very good answer."

We can add "At least they're doing what they're doing" to the endless list of things the President says that makes no sense.

He's been on about this for years. He doesn't trust magnets, because that's science.

He likes things done the old ways – he likes coal, he likes steam, he likes it when America was white, in the period after the indigenous Americans got killed and before the African Americans arrived.

Last September Trump said the new system of launching planes off the deck of a carrier with magnets was too complex.

He may or may not have said, "Nobody ever saw anything so complicated, no one even heard of magnets before this"

He verifiably said to the Washington Post, 'It's like when you get a new car and you have to be a computer genius to fix your seat. The seat's moving all over the place, it's unbelievable.'

That is exactly correct – firing a fast jet fighter from the deck of an aircraft carrier is precisely like moving the seat in your new car so that you can squeeze your big orange gut behind the steering wheel.

By the way, the launching system is called EMALS and has been in development for the Navy's Gerald R. Ford-class aircraft carriers.

Aircraft are launched from the short deck of a carrier using a catapult that used to be powered by steam but which now uses a magnetic motor drive instead.

The magnet method is smoother, cheaper, more reliable, more flexible and causes less stress to the aircraft than steam.

But Donny doesn't like it because he's an expert on everything and no one around him seems to have the guts to tell him otherwise, apart from a man thousands of miles away, on a heavily protected war ship with a large selection of deadly weapons at his disposal.

24.11.18

<u>Turning it up to eleven.</u>

Have you ever heard of Witchrot?

It sounds like something embarrassing the doctor would give you an unguent for, the sort of thing that newspaper websites would publish a picture of beside the headline: "Warning, distressing content."

Let me be more specific - have you heard of a band called Witchrot?

No, of course you haven't...you're a music fan.

Well, there IS a band of that name. They are an a Canadian *a cappella* group that specialises in close harmonies.

Just kidding, they play the sort of heavy doom rock that sounds like something has crawled into your skull through your ear and is bashing your brains to bits with a metal bar.

They play songs called Devil's Dirt and Crypt Reaper and believe me, you don't want to hear them unless you think the only colour that clothes should come in is black and you sleep in a coffin.

And I apologise in advance for making light of this but outside of the film Spinal Tap, this is the most Spinal Tap thing I've ever heard.

A fellow from the band called Peter Turik went online this week and posted a message on Facebook that said, and I quote:

"Due to the unfortunate reality of our guitarist ****ing my girlfriend of almost 7 years WITCHROT will be taking an extended hiatus. I however will continue the band in another space and time, being ripe with hate the music is slowly flowing and without a doubt will become the most devastating, torturous music I have ever created. Thanks for the support, stay heavy – Peter. Also our drummer died."

Is it just me, or is that last part the most important?

Shouldn't that have come at the beginning, or in a separate post at least?

I mean, I don't want to make fun of someone's demise, even a drummer's, but that was top-notch professional comic timing - the band is breaking up because the guitarist slept with my girlfriend, and oh, by the way, the drummer's dead.

Peter Turik posted a picture to go with that message of a smashed guitar and empty beer cans thrown away outside under what could be snow or a massive delivery of cocaine.

But I bet that the band never partakes.

Not the group that released the song 'Druid Smoke'.

UPDATE: You will be pleased to know that Witchrot have risen above these two catastrophes and are scheduled to appear at their Resurrection concert in Toronto before the New Year.

They are sharing the bill with the bands Mount Cyanide and Whip Kisser.

At the time of writing, tickets were still available.

30 11 18

Playing games with our future.

You have probably heard a lot about the fishing industry in relation to Brexit: "we need to get out from under the thumb of the Evil European Unelected Overlords, 'cos they come over 'ere and nick our fish...", that sort of thing.

It seems odd that fish become our property when they stray over some arbitrary line in the moving waters of the sea. If we applied that thinking to everyday life, I could take possession of every car that drives past my house.

The real problem of drawing up plans for our future based on the desires of the professional angler is that there isn't very many of them and they don't make much money.

Harrods, the shiny retail palace in Knightsbridge, where if you have to ask the price, you can't afford it, actually employs more people and makes more money than all of our fishing fleet put together.

A shop earns more for the economy than British fisheries.

That may surprise you. Well, prepare to be stunned because the video gaming industry makes more than both put together.

And that industry doesn't want us to leave the EU

A hard or no-deal Brexit threatens to cause serious harm to Britain's gaming industry, which contributes almost £2bn a year to the economy, which is over double what the fishing industry contributes

If we crash out of the EU the gaming industry will fall flat on its face…game over…we lose.

A new report by a digital entertainment lawyer called Jas Purewal says, "UK interactive entertainment will be harmed by a hard Brexit … and devastated in a no-deal Brexit. This will make it harder to recruit talent into the UK and over the longer term may aid a brain drain of talent out of the UK and into the EU or elsewhere."

They'll be draining our brains, and squirting them up the EU.

If there's one thing that we can not afford to have less of in this country, it is brains.

But don't take Jas Purewal's word for it.

Ian Livingstone, the founder of Games Workshop and one of the leading lights of Britain's games industry, said that the business "ticks all the right boxes for the knowledge economy – high skills, high tech, high growth, IP-creating, regional, digital, 80% export in a global market worth $120bn per annum".

He said, "By removing certainty and many of the existing benefits of EU membership, it is feared that Brexit will hinder the UK industry's ambition to be the best in the world.

Hiring the best overseas talent does not displace British jobs, it helps protect them."

But he's only an expert so no one is remotely interested in what he has to say.

Gaming is a British success story, but as our aged elected politicians understand video games in the same way that they understand particle physics, the sector has been all but ignored and left out of government industrial strategy.

Who knew that the government even HAD a strategy on industry?

What is alarming is that this is what it's like when they HAVE a plan!

The figures are really quite amazing – it's a bigger business than films.

The global revenue from hit mobile game Golf Clash will exceed $100m in 2018. It was developed by a company in Wilmslow.

Rockstar North's Grand Theft Auto 5 generated $1bn in revenue in less than a week.

You can't even make that much money selling crack.

The Wikipedia founder, Jimmy Wales, said: "A good tech sector relies on an open and outward-facing business culture. But that's threatened by this Brexit deal, which pulls up the drawbridge and leaves us isolated."

Reportedly, 40% of UK games companies said they were considering relocating to the EU after Brexit, as they expected a skills shortage would follow.

We could pay attention to a voluble, small and ancient industry based on a dying and increasingly scarce resource, which in our waters is mostly mackerel, that we don't like, so we sell abroad, mostly to Europe.

Or we could bet our future on a much quieter business that deals in imagination, which is an unlimited resource, and seems to conjure money out of thin air and harms no animals in the making.

Which is it to be - Angry Birds or Captain Birdseye?

30.11.18

Bad news for Flipper

The Trump administration has given its approval for companies to conduct seismic surveys of the Atlantic Ocean, off the east coast of America.

They will do this by bouncing sound-waves off underground rock formations to see if there's any of that oil that fossil fuel fans like the old fossil in the Whitehouse get so giddy about.

Unfortunately, these deafening blasts could harm and potentially kill tens of thousands of dolphins, whales and other marine animals in the vicinity, about which Donald Trump cares not one jot, as you would expect.

It is part of the Tangerine Scream's attack on nature. If nature had treated you as badly as it has him, you'd be furious too.

Governors in states along the Eastern Seaboard, who represent people who have to live there are against it, the people themselves are against it, the ecology scientists are against it, the whales and the dolphins are most certainly against it, but the oil industry whispered sweet nothings in Ancient Orange's ear and he rolled over like a big fat lap dog.

In addition to harming sea life, acoustic tests — in which acoustic waves are sent through water 10 to 12 seconds apart to image the sea floor — can disrupt thriving commercial fisheries and if the tests lead to drilling, that would threaten beach tourism.

The President had to weigh up those concerns against the needs of the oil companies who gave him vast sums of money to fund his campaign and also told him he was handsome and smart, so what the fossil fuel industry wants, the fossil fuel industry gets.

Seismic testing maps the ocean floor and estimates the whereabouts of oil and gas, but only exploratory drilling can confirm their presence.

That phrase might sound familiar – it was exploratory drilling that caused the The 2010 Deepwater Horizon oil spill that soiled the Gulf of Mexico and resulted in a film starring Marky Mark and no one wants to have THAT happen again.

Another exploratory drill gulf disaster, The Taylor Energy spill, is almost as large – it's spewed oil for more than 14 years, up to an estimated 700 barrels a day after a hurricane ripped up production wells.

According the US government, it could continue for the rest of the century.

And besides all that, there's the small inconvenience of climate change, caused in large part by fossil fuels, which means we should be weaning ourselves off the black gold, not searching destructively for ever more of it.

But don't take my word for it - on the Friday after Thanksgiving, the administration published a report by 13 federal agencies projecting the severe economic costs of climate change as coastal flooding and wildfires worsen and hurricanes become more severe.

When asked about it by alert journalists, Trump dismissed it out of hand.

Of the threat of climate change, he actually said, "One of the problems that a lot of people like myself, we have very high levels of intelligence but we're not necessarily such believers."

According to one model prediction by the federal Bureau of Ocean Energy Management in 2014, nearly 2.5 million dolphins would be harassed or possibly killed by acoustic sound blasts each year in the middle and southern Atlantic, and nearly a half-million pilot whales would be affected.

Six of the mammals in the study area were endangered species, including four types of whales. The species most impacted would be the humpback whale.

But the giant hunched whale in the Whitehouse doesn't care about that.

He won't listen to anything that doesn't emanate from his own blow hole.

14.12.18

It's the real thing but nobody wants it.

From next June, advertising watchdogs are to ban gender stereotypes from TV commercials, like they used to run in the 'good old days' when they showed a harassed woman being a bad mother until she saw the light and bought the correct washing up liquid.

Depictions of a housewife tied to the stove are out.

From now on, a housewife must only be shown hunting down terrorists or having a sex change.

Companies will also not be able to suggest men are lazy or useless when it comes to doing things that they are lazy or useless at, like doing the washing up, dusting, cleaning, putting out the rubbish, hanging out the clothes, taking the kids to school, feeding the cat, walking the dog, making the dinner, combing their hair, or staging a coup against a Prime Minister.

This is because we are not living in 2017 any more...things have moved on...welcome to the new world.

It is a brave new world where no person must be pigeon-holed and which must be openly accessible to people who are not brave, or to people that do not identify as people.

This is good news because it will prevent boys and girls at a young age from being told how to play and what activities they should be interested in.

Girls that choose to play with dolls and horses and boys that put toy guns and racer cars on their list for Santa will be prosecuted to the fullest extent allowed by the law (no slapping).

Unfortunately, it might be true that boys want to play at being soldiers and girls want to play at being mummy not because evil advertising executives have brainwashed them into acting like that – it might be because that's what they are actually interested in.

It's part of our make up isn't it?

Make-up, by the way, will henceforth only be marketed at men, along with adverts for cushions and shoes that hurt your feet but make your legs look great.

The serious intent is to stop restricting certain jobs and activities to certain sexes – to open people's horizons and expand their opportunities.

No longer will we be subject to stereotypes in adverts which depict boys as daring and girls as caring, even if, by and large, boys ARE daring and girls ARE caring.

That's the way it is because long before our species could reproduce by making a deposit in a test tube, women tended to be the ones that made and cared for babies while men went out of the cave to hunt for buffalo.

The proposals will also outlaw adverts that suggest people may not be successful in love or life because they do not have what is considered an ideal physique.

Well, that's obviously not true is it? I mean Donald Trump has the body and hue of a Space Hopper and he has had so much luck in bed that he has to pay his exes money out of his campaign funds to keep them quiet about it.

As well as these edicts, traditional gender roles will not be tolerated in advertising either.

Adverts that used to show the mother in the kitchen cooking Christmas dinner for the family will now have the father doing half the work because, you know, that's just what happens these days.

No more depictions of a man popping down to the pub on Christmas day and getting home just in time to see the turkey come out of the oven.

From now on, he'll be shown crumbling a stock cube into hot water and THEN popping down to the pub to return just in time to see the turkey come out of the oven.

A few years ago, Asda was criticised over a Christmas TV ad that showed a mother doing all the work, buying presents and making the dinner, while everyone else relaxed and had fun.

But maybe Asda shouldn't have been criticised, maybe it should have been every family that has ever existed since the dawn of time, that let that become the norm, that should have been criticised.

Last year, Aptamil baby milk caused controversy by showing a girl growing up to become a ballerina and a boy becoming a rock climber.

This was despite the fact that the chances of the man becoming a ballet dancer and the woman becoming a rock climber are so slim.

It could happen that way round but the publisher of the climbing magazine Rock and Ice, said that his magazine's surveys showed that about 70 percent of the regular climbers in the United States were male and in 2014 the International Foundation for Women Artists says that 77% of US dancers are female.

So it could be that the boy grows up to be a ballet dancer and the girl grows up to be a rock climber, but that's not nearly as likely as the other way round.

Must adverts now only show scenarios that are unlikely in order to reverse years of stereotypical messages?

Well, no...because ads will still be able to show unnaturally good looking people doing glamorous things because they have picked the right holiday, toothpaste, coffee, bank, credit card, or butter substitute.

If adverts were really to drop damaging stereotypes they should show ugly, fat and old people enjoying the products they are trying to sell.

Get a bloated man with a gut so large he can't see his feet to sell beer.

Show a woman passed out drunk on the street with her shoes in her hands to sell alcopops.

How about a mother clearing up after her children that she doesn't really like, or a man using his new prescription eye glasses to ogle the woman behind his wife if you want reality.

Unfortunately, reality doesn't sell because people are buying those products to try to change their reality.

Boys buy body spray that could peel the paint off a car because they aren't getting any sex – they want to be chased by a bevy of babes just like that advert – if you showed some scrawny oik coating himself with that stuff, going out on the pull and failing to score anyway, that might be realistic, but it isn't going to sell much smell is it?

Show someone old and tired using rejuvenating cream without success if you want reality, and see how much of that goop you shift.

Depict an obese person trying to lose weight by eating some diet breakfast cereal and after months of that STILL can't squeeze their bulk behind the steering wheel to go down to the shops to get some more.

That's real life, but does anyone want to buy real life?

20.12.18

Stupid people

Jeremy Corbyn corrected some stupid journalists for asking him about whether he had said the Prime Minister of this stupid country was a stupid woman

He said the media were 'utterly obsessed', about whether he had or had not said 'stupid woman'.

What has been lost in this totally artificial row is that no one appears to be questioning that Theresa May is stupid.

What seems to be exercising people into a synthetic fury is that he used the word 'woman'. As though that is now, in itself, an insult.

Uncle Jezza was asked whether the language he used was 'respectful'.

That would not be quite as funny a question if it had not happened in that den of disrespect the Houses of Parliament

I mean, have people actually seen what goes on in there? Prime Minister's Questions is like a shouting match in an old peoples' home.

They scream and holler and make fun and wave their papers around like its a chimps' tea party

Drowning out people who are trying to speak is not respectful, laughing at those trying to make a point is not respectful.

They can dress it up in phoney phrases like 'the honourable gentleman' and 'my learned friend' but there is nothing honourable or learned about any of it.

PMQs is not a forum for debate, it is childish point scoring and pre-rehearsed put downs – what's respectful about that?

That the whole of British political life ground to a halt this week while experts were drafted in to read his lips and ministers were queuing up to go on TV to explain, oh yes he did, or oh no he didn't say 'stupid woman' just underlines what a charade it all is.

Apart from anything else, if the massed MPs shouting and fake-laughing and bullying and preening aren't drunk at Prime Minister's Questions, then we are in real trouble because we seem to be represented by a bunch of children, who all seem to having a terrific fun time at our expense.

You wouldn't be surprised if they all showed up in party hats expecting jelly and custard.

The press, of course, whipped itself up into a state of high-horse superiority over the potential for the word 'woman' to be used as misogynistic abuse.

They printed their fury right next to snaps of some nubile starlet photographed with a long lens on a beach with a 'top totty phwoar' type headline.

Look up the word hypocrite in the dictionary and it will have a link to that story.

Besides, isn't Theresa May a woman? Or is that now an illegal and discriminatory thing to say?

In bringing in the army and stockpiling medicines, the government are making no-deal Brexit preparations look like we're at war, and all the press and the politicians can talk about is a point of politeness.

How utterly, comically, stereotypically British is that?

Jeremy Corbyn tried to bring some perspective to all this by pointing out that a homeless man recently died outside Parliament, which is a little more important than who said what about whom in the din of the riotous cacophony that is PMQs.

Perspective is not Parliament's speciality however, and after a few day's acrimony, Andrea Leadsom turned it up to eleven by dragging Commons Speaker John Bercow into it saying that he had made the same 'stupid woman' comment about her.

You could debate whether or not the term stupid is accurate about Andrea Leadsom but the term 'woman' certainly is.

If calling someone a stupid man is not sexist , then why is it sexist to call someone a stupid woman?

A history of society's discrimination against women is not relevant – you can't prosecute someone for doing something that reminds you of something else.

Leadsom effectively accused Corbyn of lying by insisting he did brand the PM a 'stupid woman'.

If lying was grounds for punishment, then the entire House of Commons would on the naughty step thinking about what it had done.

Politicians lie all the time – its practically what they do for a living.

If the government is so against lying and insults, why is Theresa May so keen to cuddle up that orange ball of abusive, perfidious mendacity the President of the United States of America?

He changes his story on any given subject from one end of a sentence to the other and throws out insults like he chucks out kitchen rolls to flood victims.

The reason our politicians ignore the tsunami of lies that emanate from the Tangerine Scream, and from their own party, is that it suits them to do so.

It also suits them to clutch their pearls to their chests and go into a Victorian fainting fit when they think they can make a cheap score from attacking the opposition for doing the exact same thing.

Andrea Leadsom said standards of behaviour in the chamber had to improve.

Good luck with that.

It looks as though the MPs like it that way.

All that shouting and barracking is not debate for the benefit of the nation, it's a jolly game they play once a week before getting stuck into lunch.

It's part of being in the club. It goes with all that silly dressing up and the daft way they address each other: 'my honourable learned and gallant friend'...all that stuff.

The government is talking about food shortages, about industry closing, about medicines running out and about companies fleeing the ruins to set up abroad, and what is top of the agenda is whether calling someone a woman is sexist.

It is only thanks to the Tangerine Scream in the Whitehouse that we aren't the laughing stock of the world right now.

Thank you for being you Donny – if it weren't for you, WE would be the planet's comic relief.

21.12.18

Theresa gets the support she doesn't need.

Good news: Theresa May might not be getting much love from her fellow parliamentarians concerning her plans for Brexit but there is one world leader that is fully behind her.

Bad news: it is Vladimir Putin.

Vlad the Insaner has publicly backed Theresa May on Brexit.

As for the idea of having a second referendum, he said it would be undemocratic.

The chief election fixer himself said that.

What a sense of humour, what comic timing.

He's killing us...literally.

Vlad said the PM must 'fulfil the will of the people' and carry out the withdrawal from the EU.

This has nothing to do with the Russian desire to smash the EU, goodness me no, why would anyone think that?

He said he feels that way because, "is sense of fairness...very important to listen to peoples...I like listen to peoples as I torture them to death...is fun for me and for best friend king of Saudi Arabia – we have manly bro handshake – not like that Theresa May handshake, all wet like fish...or Donald Trump handshake...he have soft hands like lady"... or words to that effect.

Giving his annual televised press conference, the Russian president really said he 'understood' Mrs May's position in 'fighting for this Brexit'.

He said: 'The referendum was held. What can she do? She has to fulfil the will of the people expressed in the referendum.'

He did not mention that the will of the people might have been swayed by the Russian psych-ops team that pummelled us with lies about Brexit via social media, in order to swing the vote, just like they did to get the Screaming MeMe elected in America.

Vlad said: 'Was it not a referendum? Someone disliked the result, so repeat it over and over? Is this democracy? What then would be the point of the referendum in the first place?'

He said that while planning the disappearance of his political opponents and installing shredding machines on Russian ballot boxes.

When the autocratic leader of one of the least free countries in the world thinks you are on the right track, its probably time to get on another track.

Russia is 135th on the list of the Transparency International table of corruption, with number 1 being the least corrupt.

It is a worse place for corruption than Sierra Leone and Kyrgyzstan, wherever that is.

Kyrgyzstan looks like some random letters you pick out of a scrabble bag

Hey Kyrgyzstan...can I sell you a vowel?

If Vladimir Putin, the leader of a country that's so corrupt it won't tell itself its own pin number, is on our side, we've gone to the wrong side – the dark side.

If we are basically finishing the job that Vlad started by using Facebook against us, then Brexit looks less like freeing ourselves from the Evil Socialist European Superstate and more like drinking window cleaner and perfume and calling it a cocktail, just as they do in Siberia.

If that is what your people do to relax from their troubles, no wonder Putin wants the EU to fail.

If the EU looks weak and uninviting, then it might make his citizens feel better about their collapsing Russian homeland, especially if the medicinal bath soak they are drinking has lost its kick.

22 12 18

Handouts to the un-needy.

You know that thing called tax that the government takes from your wages to run the country?

Well, apparently it is optional.

Many of Britain's biggest companies paid not a penny of corporation tax in the UK last year.

The FTSE 100 is a list of the companies listed on the London Stock Exchange with the highest market capitalisation, which is accountant's speak for: they can afford to pay their ***ing taxes!

Unfortunately for us poor dopes who do, being able to pay also means that that they are able to avoid paying.

One in five of the 69 firms on that list that published their figures paid absolutely no corporation tax in this country.

Shall we assume that the remaining 31 who declined to make public what they paid did not refuse to publish their tax bill because they paid too much?

If you think that is bad, grip on to something firm, because it is about to get worse.

Not only do at least 20% of the richest firms in the land not pay tax, a good number of them managed to organise their affairs so efficiently that we ended up owing THEM money.

I am not making that up.

Companies that are worth billions, that made profits in the hundreds of millions, not only paid no corporation tax, they actually got a rebate.

That money the government takes from your income, that you imagine they might be spending on nurses, is going straight into the pockets of the super-rich that run multinational corporations.

This must be that fairer society that the government has told us so much about.

Usually, firms pay corporation tax of 19 per cent of their total profits, which doesn't seem too much.

But if you spend millions of pounds on genius accountants and lawyers, you can save billions of pounds by skipping lightly round the slow-footed regulator

BP made £5.6 billion in profit last year. You would think that we would be quids in, playing host to such a valuable enterprise.

Sadly, they did not pay corporation tax at 19%, they paid it at 0%.

In fact we paid them £134million in tax credits.

The country in which their stocks are listed, the country that provides its workforce, the streets they go to work on, the hospitals and doctors that tend to them, the police that keep order where they are located, the street lights that illuminate their way, the schools that teach their future workers and everything else that a government spends taxpayers cash on is providing all that for free to the companies that don't pay tax.

In fact, some of these firms pay their Chief Executive more than they pay in to the exchequer.

Isn't that totally unsurprising?

Take the Royal Mail. They made £39m in profit last year. That sounds like a pretty good achievement but less so when you learn that we paid the Royal Mail £93m in tax credits.

Presumably, without our generosity, they would have made a loss of £54m.

The boss of the company was so well regarded by his employer that they granted him £7.2m for his first year in charge.

If he could make it so the government deposited £93m in my account, he could be in charge of me too.

Many of the schemes companies use to produce these incredible results are so complicated that you would need to be a computer to understand them.

For example, say you had a business in this country and a business in Luxembourg.

You can get the business in Luxembourg to lend the business in this country enough money so that the interest you charged yourself would wipe out any profit you made here.

The money is still all yours – the profits you made here still exist, its just that now its called interest payments and it ends up in Luxembourg, which is a low tax jurisdiction.

You can create subsidiary companies that don't actually do anything except exist in name and shift profits from one to another till they appear to disappear.

It's like a magic trick, but when I say you can do this, what I mean is: you can't.

You don't earn remotely enough money to not pay tax.

If you as an individual tried something like that you'd go to jail because you need to earn a massive fortune to be able to save a massive fortune by not paying your taxes.

Of course, these organisations will say that they pay all the taxes that are due in every jurisdiction in which they operate.

They will say that exact phrase, like they all have the same lawyer, and that may be technically true but it is not morally true.

They will also say that they employ lots of people and THEY pay taxes, which is a pretty desperately hollow argument, as they wouldn't be able to run their business if they didn't employ those people.

Over time, the countries that they are leeching off become poorer, and their customers become poorer and eventually they can't afford to buy their products in the same numbers, but no one cares about 'eventually'.

The people who run these companies only care about the right now – their next bonus award, the value of their stocks at this minute.

The result is that they get ever more stratospherically rich and we can't afford to fund the NHS to operate on our knees and hips or to save people's sight, or for policepersons on the beat or for power stations to keep the lights on.

But at least the chief executives can take all that money that we would have frittered away on silly things like nurses and doctors and carers and go out and buy themselves a new Rolls Royce, or yacht, or Caribbean island.

Useful idiots will say: well, it's all legal and this is just the politics of envy and if you don't like the laws then change them.

Then they'll moan that they can't be seen by their consultant for 6 weeks and the council has just cancelled their weekly bin collection, as though those things aren't connected.

And besides, you can't change the tax laws to stop them because they can out-lawyer and out-accountant any government.

They've got tax specialists earning millions to save them billions.

They hire the best of the best and the government, starved of funds can't possibly keep up.

Plug one gap in the law and another will spring open that our threadbare HMRC could never have thought of.

I bet you everything I am wearing right now that when we are out of the EU we will be presenting ourselves to international business as a fine destination to avoid paying taxes that would be due in other countries.

Practically all the dodgy tax havens that exist on the planet have the British flag flying above their government buildings already.

The top ten tax havens for 2018, places to stash the cash with no questions asked are, apart from Luxembourg, Monaco and Switzerland, all either ex or current British colonies, crown dependencies or British overseas territories: The Bahamas, Hong Kong, The Cayman Islands, Malta, The Isle of Man, Mauritius and Singapore.

We taught the world the way round the rules, so it would be pretty surprising if we did not take our place at the top of the list once we are out of the EU.

Not everyone in government is on board though.

Dame Margaret Hodge, formerly chair of the Commons Public Accounts Committee, said: 'Tax avoidance by large corporations is a blight on this country. It means there is less money for our underfunded public services.

'The fact that some companies pay no corporation tax but grab our taxpayers' money through tax credits beggars belief.'

I am just an ignorant outsider, but it all seems less like an accident and more like undeclared policy.

24.12.18

Now it all makes sense!

Donald Trump is a manly man who appeals to the manly instincts of the manly men who follow him. You can tell they are many because they wear manly T-shirts with slogans like "Donald Trump: Finally someone with balls".

What could be manlier than a manly man wearing a reminder of a manly leader's personal manly area?

Well, as it turns out, a flower display at a Barbara Streisand concert could be manlier.

The problem is that his supporters are, perhaps, protesting too much.

If you have to act in a manly way and wear items of clothing to underscore your manliness, the chances are that you are not very manly.

Donny himself has frequently referred to his intimate manly part in glowing terms: "I have no problem in that department, believe me".

And like everything else he says that is followed by the phrase "believe me", we probably should not believe him.

Stormy Daniels is a porn star who Ancient Orange is said to have had a dalliance with. As she is a professional in this area, we should assume she knows what she is talking about when it comes to a male person's apparatus, and she described his in less than approving terms.

She also stated that her time with Donald was the least impressive sex she had ever had, an opinion, she said, clearly not shared by Trump himself.

I bet he gave himself an A+.

If Sigmund Freud was still alive, he would be able to explain all this to us, while we laid on his couch and tried not to fall asleep.

Unfortunately, he is still dead, so Eric Knowles, a social psychologist at New York University who studies the influence of group identities on political attitudes and behaviour and Sarah DiMuccio, a doctoral student in psychology at New York University whose research examines the role of masculinity in social and political behaviour have done the explaining for us.

They have a theory called the "fragile masculinity hypothesis" which states that Trump appeals to men that are secretly insecure about their manliness.

The President lurches about, firing off insults and threats and generally acts like someone who doesn't know how to be manly would act, if they were asked to fake it.

The men who are comfortable with their own masculinity find this a little comical, those that are not see someone they would like to be.

Even in our supposedly enlightened times, society places on boys and men the expectation of masculine behaviour.

It is a pretty unforgiving standard and many men worry that they do not measure up. Those men are said to experience fragile masculinity. To counter that, those men ally themselves to tough politicians and policies

That is a nice theory, and it feels true when you think of those people in the Make America White Again hats at Trump's safe space rallies.

They all look a bit desperate to impress.

To find proof of their theory, the researchers noted the search requests on Google for certain phrases and plotted them on maps of Trump support.

They selected phrases like: "erectile dysfunction," "hair loss," "how to get girls," "penis enlargement," "penis size," "steroids," "testosterone" and "Viagra."

They then measured where the searches for those terms were most prevalent.

Surprise, surprise, they found that internet searches for those topics were most frequent in areas that supported Donald Trump at the 2016 presidential election.

The more men searched for erectile dysfunction, the more likely they were to vote Trump.

This also held true for voters in the 2018 mid-term elections – the more they searched for penis enlargement, the more they were likely to vote Republican.

Trump fans have tiny weenies.

Maybe they should put THAT on a hat.

24 12 18

What's for Christmas dinner?

If you go down to the park today, you're in for a big surprise – there's stoned ducks all over the place.

That may surprise you, but if I tell you that it happened in a park in Southern California, it might be less of a shock.

There's nothing at all surprising about stoned ducks in a park near Los Angeles.

It happened in a place called Carr Park, which is a true fact, and not some name I just made up in a medically induced haze.

Recreational marijuana is now legal in California, but the birds were not high on the accumulated fog of the locals' smoke.

Those birds got wildly intoxicated after spying a cocktail of various medications dumped at the park.

They must have thought that they looked like the snack they could eat between meals without ruining their appetite.

Shortly after their feeding, a man walking through Carr Park in Huntington Beach noticed a goose and gull had abandoned air travel for walking.

They were staggering about, as though in slow motion, struggling to keep their necks up and their eyes open.

One of them collapsed onto its back, flat out, legs splayed in the air like something out of a Warner Brothers cartoon.

Bugs Bunny would have had a field day.

Apparently, some bright spark had dumped hundreds of pills in the grass, which is odd considering what medication costs in America.

The pills included, but were not limited to: medications for heart trouble, antidepressants, anti-anxiety and insomnia.

The birds found they could fit them in their mouths so ate them.

291

Those birds will eat anything. They're like gannets!

A concerned citizen took two of the most affected animals to a wetlands centre, where experts in avian welfare announced that they were treating a Canada Goose and a Ring-billed Gull that were exhibiting symptoms, such as loss of muscle control.

I often get that too when I have consumed a cocktail of mystery pills.

Don't worry though.

In a seasonally uplifting, positive end to this Christmas tale, they made a full recovery and were then roasted at 180 degrees for two hours and were served with roast potatoes, sprouts and an EpiPen.

Every year on my LBC show I ask the audience for the events, people and places of the past twelve months that correspond to the letters of the alphabet.

This year's A to Z was the biggest yet.

This is what 2018 looked like to us passengers along for the ride.

A-Z 2018

Abcde, child with that name mocked by Southwest Airlines who apologise

Apple – first publicly traded US company to reach $1 trillion valuation

Kofi Annan. former UN chief (d)

Charles Aznavour. French crooner (d)

Roman Abramovich didn't get UK visa, selling Chelsea?

Avengers: Infinity War. Highest opening weekend box office in history

Jim Acosta. CNN reporter has Whitehouse press pass rescinded

Jacinda Ardern, New Zealand PM, first leader to bring baby to UN general assembly

Alexa, AI PA starts randomly laughing and other weirdness

AI. the continued rise of artificial intelligence

Australian Dreamliner. Boeing 787 launched direct non-stop flight from Australia to UK

Amazon's effect on the high street

Amazon's harsh working practices in warehouses

Australia cricket team ball tampering scandal

Alt-Right

Austerity...still here

Paddy Ashdown, politician (d)

Abortion referendum Ireland

David Attenborough's plastic waste campaign

Aussie flu

Anti-vaccine movement grows, measles at highest in Europe for 20 years

Antibiotics and superbugs

Article 50

Ant and Dec – the end?

Avocados on toast

Abba joins Twitter. Comeback?

Avicii, musician (d)

Arctic Monkeys new LP fastest selling vinyl album in 25 years

Julian Assange sues Ecuador for violating his rights

Mike Ashley buys House of Fraser

Arm the teachers (Trump's answer to school shootings)

Activate, the Tory youth organisation closes

Adderall. Trump accused of snorting ADHD drug on set of The Apprentice

Anak Krakatau erupts, causes tsunami

Asda and Sainsbury's merger talks

Anti-Semitism in Labour Party etc.

Armistice 100th anniversary

Ashers bakery wins "gay cake" Supreme Court appeal

Angel of the North statue sports Christmas hat

Paul "Trouble" Anderson, DJ (d)

AR-15, weapon of choice for school shooters

"At your request" Jeff Sessions' resignation letter to Trump

Peter Armitage, actor (d)

Michael Anderson, film director, The Dam Busters (d)

Eddy Amoo, singer The Real Thing (d)

Jimmy Armfield, footballer (d)

Paul Allen, co-founder Microsoft (d)

Atheists outnumber Christians in Britain

Amazon Go, cashierless supermarket opens, Seattle

Apu racism row, The Simpsons

Avangard, Russian "unbeatable" missile

Abortion clinic protesters banned, Ealing

Acid attacks

Air fresheners, use refused in St George's Chapel for Harry/Meghan wedding

Air Force One spotted flying over Sheffield on Trump's secret trip to Iraq

Alcohol, study says all quantities bad for health

Amazon rainforest destroyed at fastest rate to date

Alba, only-known albino orangutan released into wild, Indonesia

Age related macular degeneration treatment "breakthrough"

Asda and Sainsbury's merger talks

Woody Allen sex abuse allegation

B

Trevor Bayliss, inventor (d)

Bump stocks banned in America

Blue Peter's 5000th show

Beast from the East cold spell

John Bluthal, actor (d)

Jim Bowen, TV presenter (d)

Benny the beluga whale in the Thames

Boris v Burkas (letter boxes)

Bell End, road name-change petition refused

Backstop, Irish border problem

Banksy's shredded artwork "Love is in the Bin"

Bitcoin rise and fall

The Bodyguard. TV show's massive ratings

Barbara Bush, ex-First Lady of USA (d)

George HW Bush, ex-President of USA (d)

The Beano, 80 years old

The Beano "accuses" Jacob Rees-Mogg of copying "Walter the Softy"

Jeff Bezos of Amazon became world's richest man.

Bridge collapse, Genoa, Italy

Big Brother, TV show ends?

Bullying in parliament

Border wall, USA/Mexico

Michel Barnier, EU's Brexit negotiator

Baby Blimp, Trump's insult balloon and Sadiq Khan's answer balloon

Richard Branson's Virgin Galactic's first successful test flight to space

Fiona Bruce new host of BBC Question Time

Brazil, far right Jair Bolsonaro elected president.

Big Ben (Elizabeth Tower) repairs

Richard Baker, newsreader (d)

Black Panther, film.

Roger Bannister, athlete (d)

Peter Boizot, founder of Pizza Express (d)

Nick Bailey, Detective Sgt infected with nerve agent in Salisbury.

Eric Bristow. darts player (d)

Alan Bean, US astronaut. 4th person on Moon (d)

Roseanne Barr, fired from own TV show

"Bicycle guy", Kenyan president "forgets" Boris Johnson's name

Buffalo Bottoms, banned from nature programmes in Iran.

Babs Beverley, Beverly Sisters (d)

Katie Boyle, Eurovision Song Contest host (d)

Big Envelope, letter from Kim Jong-un delivered to Trump.

Aaron Banks, Brexiteer investigated

Maria Bueno, Tennis player (d)

Stephen Barclay named new Brexit Secretary

Bernardo Bertolucci, director (d)

Rachael Bland, journalist (d)

Bank of England raise interest rates above emergency level

Olive Boar, Britain's oldest person aged 113 (d)

Black cats rejected as they "don't show up in selfies"

Beckham's house burglary

Henry Bolton axed as UKIP leader after five months

Gerard Batten elected new UKIP leader

Christine Ford abuse allegations against US Supreme Court nominee Brett Kavanaugh

Beer – "I like beer": US Supreme Court nominee Brett Kavanaugh

Blue wave – US mid-term elections

Zoe Ball announced as first female host of Radio 2 breakfast show

Burberry burns excess stock to protect brand's image

Benefit cuts breach human rights obligations says UN

Danny Boyle, director, quits new Bond film over Russian villain

Backpack Kid's mum sues Fortnite creators for using Floss dance

"Baby it's cold outside", song lyrics controversy

Jean Barker, Baroness Trumpington, Bletchley Park code-breaker (d)

Marty Balin, musician, Jefferson Airplane (d)

Kevin Beattie, footballer (d)

Anthony Bourdain, chef (d)

Baby Shark, song and dance

David Beckham employs "Mr Loophole", cleared of speeding

Bambi, US poacher sentenced to watch film every month for a year

Celia Brackenridge, athlete, campaigner (d)

Lindsey Buckingham dismissed from Fleetwood Mac tour, sues

Wendy Beckett, nun, art historian (d)

Michel Barnier, EU chief negotiator on Brexit

Budget cuts and council funding

Louis Blom-Cooper, lawyer, human rights campaigner (d)

Steve Bray, "Mr Stop Brexit" gatecrashes 100 TV interviews

C

Mark Carney, Governor of the Bank of England, Brexit predictions

Canada legalises recreational marijuana

Coup – Tory right-wingers' failure to unseat Theresa May

Tony Calder, record producer (d)

Colman's mustard, production shut down in Norwich.

Cadbury Creme Egg, find a white one, win a prize

Carillion, company collapses, UK's largest ever trading liquidation

John Cunliffe, creator Postman Pat (d)

Montserrat Cabale, opera singer (d)

Canadian national anthem, reworded to become gender neutral.

Cambridge Analytica, data mining company allegations

Caravan of migrants travel to U.S. border

Mike Coupe. CEO of Sainsbury's sings 'We're in the money' on TV re. Asda merger

Peter Carrington, 6th Baron Carrington (d)

Barry Chuckle, (nee Elliott) Chuckle Brothers (d)

Camels, disqualified from Saudi beauty contest for having botoxed lips.

California now world's 5th largest economy

California wildfires

Chas Hodges, Chas and Dave (d)

Cannabis, medicinal use legal in UK

Nick Clegg hired by Facebook

Jeremy Corbyn, hero/enemy of the people

Croatia 2 v 1 England, World Cup semi-final

Climate change

Chemical attack, Salisbury

Childish Gambino, This Is America video

John Allen Chau, missionary killed by Andaman Islanders (d)

Comcast, US cable giant takeover of broadcaster Sky in blind auction

Civil partnerships now available for heterosexuals

Capita, UK outsourcing group share collapse

Czech Republic 100 years old

Cyber-attacks, Russian

Croydon Cat Killer "does not exist" says Met Police

Chester Zoo fire

Emma Chambers, actor (d)

Michael Curry, American preacher at Harry and Meghan's wedding

"Crash out", Brexit

Contempt of Parliament, first time a UK government guilty

Calcutta Cup, Scotland win

Canada+, Brexit possibility

Cladding, flammable

Chequers deal, Brexit

Christopher Chope, MP, objects to "upskirting" bill

David Cassidy, singer (d)

Brendan Cox quits charity set up in murdered MP wife's memory

Crazy Rich Asians, first all-Asian cast in Hollywood film

Carbon Dioxide shortage affects beer manufacture

Carbon Dioxide in atmosphere exceeds 410ppm average across a month for first time

Caudrilla begins fracking

Eddie Clarke, musician, Motorhead (d)

Bill Cosby jailed for assault

Carol Cadwalladr, Guardian journalist exposes Cambridge Analytica scandal

Crossrail opening delayed

Crimea crisis, Russia

Jeremy Clarkson hosts Who Wants to be a Millionaire

Clown says comparing British politics to clowns is insulting to clowns

Beth Chatto, horticulturalist, (d)

Peter Carrington, politician (d)

Coffee cup charge "latte levy"

Jamie Carragher, footballer spits at girl from car

Michael Cohen, Trump lawyer jailed

Child separation, US border

Chelsea Ladies win Women's FA cup

Chelsea win FA Cup

County lines, drug gangs exploit children

D

Disaster, the Japanese symbol of the year

Drone intrusion at Gatwick

Dancing Queen, Theresa May.

David Dimbleby, quits question time

Danny Dyer, political sage

Paul Dacre left Daily Mail editorship

Divers rescue trapped footballers from cave in Thailand

Dover-Calais route's importance not understood by Brexit Sec Dominic Raab

Democratic Unionist Party's confidence and supply deal with Conservatives

Novak Djokovic wins Wimbledon Men's title

Stormy Daniels v Trump

Darts walk-on-girls axed

Duplex, Google's AI assistant

Dr Who, first female lead

Data breaches

Donegal, only constituency to vote No in Irish abortion referendum

De La Rue, lose British passport contract

Duke and Duchess of Sussex, Harry and Meghan's new titles

Ken Dodd, comedian (d)

Douma, Syria, chemical attack

Steve Ditko, co-creator Spider-Man (d)

Ed Doolan, broadcaster (d)

Ted Dabney, co-founder Atari (d)

Ruth Davidson, lesbian leader of Scottish Conservatives gives birth

James Dyson, Brexit supporter, chooses Singapore for new e-car factory

Nadine Dorries, MP, hard Brexiteer, asks for explanation of Customs Union

Tom Daley/ Lance Black have surrogate baby

Darts Grand Slam quarter-final farting controversy

Drill music blamed for violent crime

Daylight saving time, EU backs abolishment after survey

E

Earthrise, 50th anniversary of iconic image

Extinction rebellion, protesters block London bridges

Unai Emery, new Arsenal FC manager

European Research Group, Tory right-wing pressure group

Chris Evans leaves Radio 2

Energy drinks, supermarkets ban sales to under-16s

East Coast Rail Line put into public control

Education, Chancellor Hammond says funding will help buy "little extras"

Electric cars

Bella Emberg, actor (d)

Emma, storm, worst in 50 years

Ecosystem, massive discovery beneath earth's surface

Glynn Edwards, actor (d)

R. Lee Ermey, actor, Full Metal Jacket (d)

Dennis Edwards, singer, The Temptations (d)

Mount Etna erupts

Eugenie, Princess' wedding

8K TVs, the new 4K

Ebola in Democratic Republic of Congo

Noel Edmunds returns to TV on IACGMOOH

Duke of Edinburgh retires from public life

Earthquakes

Ross Edgley, first person to swim round Britain without stepping on land

Elton John announces farewell tour

Europe wins Ryder Cup

Enable, first Arc de Triomphe winner to win Breeders' Cup

F

France win World Cup

Fortnite, computer game

Floss, dance

Nigel Farage quits UKIP over Tommy Robinson appointment

DJ Fontana, musician, Elvis' drummer (d)

Christine Blasey Ford abuse allegations against Brett Kavanaugh

Falcon Heavy, reusable SpaceX rocket launches Tesla car into space

Florence, hurricane Trump says is "wettest...from the standpoint of water"

Millicent Fawcett, suffragist, first female subject statue in Parliament Square

Naomi Parker Fraley, Rosie the Riveter poster inspiration (d)

Franco's remains, Spanish parliament approves exhumation

Peter Fisher, homeopathic physician to the Queen (d)

G

Ruth Bader Ginsburg, US Supreme Court Justice hospitalised

Geordie Greig takes over as editor of the Daily Mail

Gemalto, French company to print British passports post Brexit

Gilets jaunes, French yellow vest protesters

Gingerbread persons, Scottish Parliament insists on gender neutrality

William Goldman, screenwriter (d)

Ray Galton, TV writer (d)

Leslie Grantham, actor (d)

Eunice Gayson, actor, first Bond girl (d)

Cathy Godbolt, actor (d)

Hubert de Givenchy, clothes designer (d)

Billy Graham, preacher (d)

Glasgow School of Art fire

General Data Protection Regulation, EU data rules

Gig economy

Global warming

Gibraltar's status agreed with Spain, re. Brexit

"Gammons", insult aimed at ruddy-faced Tories

Ariana Grande breaks YouTube record with "No tears left to cry", 45m views in 1 week

Philip Green, denies claims of "sexual or racist behaviour"

"Googly eye bandit", defaces US Revolution general's statue, Georgia USA

Good Friday Agreement, 20th anniversary

Gender fluidity

Great British Bake Off tops ratings for Channel 4

Golden Globes, women wore black, MeToo movement

Greece, wildfires

Guatemalan children die in US custody at border

"Gaslight", to manipulate others, on shortlist of word of the year

Global financial crisis predicted "imminent"

Matthew Hedges, student charged with spying by UAE, then pardoned

Heathrow third runway gets go-ahead

Heat wave, UK summer hottest on record

Lewis Hamilton wins 5th F1 world title

Peter Hain outs Philip Green as behind gagging orders on abuse allegations in Lords

Miss Helen, the horn shark, smuggled out of aquarium in pram, Texas

Hospital bed crisis

Hidden hunger crisis in UK

Healthcare Environmental Services, NHS waste scandal

Head teachers protest over funding

Roy Hargrove, musician (d)

Hole in International Space Station "drilled from inside"

Humble address, Keir Starmer's motion to force govt to publish Brexit studies

David Hockney, most expensive living artist

Huddersfield sexual exploitation trial

Hacked Off group loses judicial review of govt abandonment of Levinson 2

Homelessness

Nikki Haley resigns as US Ambassador to UN

Hakuna Matata, Disney accused of stealing Kenyan culture

Ada Hegerberg, footballer, Ballon d'Or winner asked to twerk

High Street, death of

Glenn Hoddle, footballer, has heart attack in TV studio

Gail Honeyman, author, best selling book of 2019, Eleanor Oliphant is Completely Fine

HMV goes into administration again

Hospital car parking fees rise

Helsinki Summit, Trump sides with Putin, against FBI

David Hogg, Parkland school shooting survivor, gun control activist

Genetically edited babies born, world's first, claim by Chinese scientist

Heinz Salad Cream renamed Sandwich Cream after 104 years

"Hostile environment" Theresa May's immigration policy, re. Windrush

Adolf Hitler, parents who named baby after Nazi leader jailed

Humbolt Broncos junior hockey team bus crash kills 16, injures 13, Canada

I

Indonesian tsunami

Irn Bru stockpiled ahead of recipe change

Ikea opens first store in India

Irish border question, Brexit

Irish backstop

The Island of Ireland

"I really don't care. Do U?" Melania Trump's jacket

Internet security

Iceland supermarket, anti-palm oil Xmas ad banned from TV

Identity politics and tribalism

IPCC climate change report: we have 12 years to save the planet

Immigration, new rules post Brexit

Israel 70th anniversary of independence

Interserve outsourcing firm's shares dive

Iran nuclear deal, Trump withdraws USA

Intermediate-Range Nuclear Forces Treaty, Trump withdraws USA

"It's coming home" premature World Cup chant

Impeachment talk, Trump

Idiot: search in Google images produces Trump as top answer

Italy budget rejected by EU

IBM pits Project Debater computer against humans

ISIS "beaten" in Syria: Trump

Iraq, first election since defeat declared of ISIS

Iraq, Trump visits troops, lies about their pay rise

Insects, edible, on sale at Sainsbury's

Interest rate rise

"I hear you" Trump's cue card for meeting school shooting survivors

ICON roller-coaster opens, Blackpool

J

Joe Jackson, father, Jackson 5 family (d)

Tessa Jowell, politician (d)

Jerusalem, new location for US embassy

Boris Johnson misses Heathrow 3rd runway vote

Boris Johnson burkha "letterbox" row

Boris Johnson failure to declare earnings

Boris Johnson resigns as Foreign Secretary

Jo Johnson resigns as transport minister

Johnston Press, i and Scotsman publisher bought by creditors

Japan to resume commercial whaling

"Just about managing", financial difficulties

Just-in-time manufacturing threatened by Brexit

Kylie Jenner tweet wipes $1.3bn off Snapchat parent company's market value

Jean-Claude Junker, EU Commission President

Japanese football fans clean stadium after defeat, World Cup

Junk food advert ban announced for London Underground

Sajid Javid appointed Home Secretary

Sajid Javid cuts short holiday to deal with migrant "crisis"

Anthony Joshua claims third "major" world-title belt, heavyweight

K

Angelique Kerber wins Wimbledon women's title

K-pop, rise of Korean music genre

Colin Kroll, co-founder of Vine (d)

Johnny Kingdom, wildlife filmmaker (d)

Clive King, author Stig of the Dump (d)

Margot Kidder, actor (d)

Brett Kavanaugh, assault allegations, "I like beer", gains Supreme Court seat

Harry Kane wins Golden Boot, World Cup's top scorer

Korean summits: U.S.&N. Korea; S.&N. Korea

North Korea repatriates dead US soldiers from Korean War

Korea submits united team for Winter Olympics

Imran Khan elected Prime Minister Pakistan

Kilogram definition changed from platinum weight to measure of current

Knife crime

Jamal Khashoggi, Saudi Arabian journalist (d)

Annegret Kramp-Karrenbauer elected Angela Merkel's successor, CDU

Kentucky Fried Chicken runs out of chicken

Korolev, Mars Express photograph shows crater topped with ice

Lindsey Kemp, dancer (d)

Kim Kardashian meets Trump in White House, discusses prison reform

Kew Gardens Temperate House, world's largest glasshouse, re-opens

KPMG/Carillion audit scandal

Koalas arrive at Longleat to protect species from Australian chlamydia threat

John Kelly no longer Trump's Chief of Staff

Colin Kaepernick, activist footballer's Nike advert

Morgana King, singer, actress (d)

Kim Jong-un takes portable toilet to Singapore summit

Knickers the giant Australian cow, twice normal size

Tom Jago, co-creator of Baileys Irish Cream (d)

L

Libby Lane, Bishop of Derby, first female C of E bishop

Liverpool FC, top of Premier League at Christmas

Tom Leonard, poet (d)

Stan Lee, comics artist (d)

Sandra Locke, actor (d)

Alan Longmuir, musician, Bay City Rollers (d)

Gillian Lynne, actor, dancer (d)

Tommy Lawrence, footballer (d)

"Leave means leave"

LadBaby, Christmas number one single

Lost Voice Guy wins Britain's Got Talent

Longest total lunar eclipse of the century, July

Leigh-on-Sea named happiest place to live in Britain

Legal aid cuts

Love Island, TV ratings hit

Luxembourg set to be first country to make all public transport free

Led Zeppelin 50th anniversary

Lies told by Trump average 9 per day, over 6400 since inauguration

Ken Livingstone quits Labour Party over anti-Semitism claims

Louis Arthur Charles, William and Kate's baby, 5th in line to throne

Kay Longstaff, cruise ship passenger jumps overboard

Nigella Lawson asks TV stations to stop airbrushing stomach

Iain Lee, radio host saves suicidal man live on air

Tim Martin, JD Weatherspoon's chairman, Brexiteer

Lion Air plane crash kills 189

Georges Loinger, WW2 resistance fighter, saved more than 350 children (d)

Louis C.K., allegations of sexual misconduct, says "these stories are true"

Lamp post powered electric vehicle charging points arrive

M

Meaningful vote on Brexit plan postponed

Theresa May

Jose Mourinho sacked by Manchester United

Esther McVey, resigns as Work and Pensions Sec over Brexit

#MeToo

Donald Moffat, actor (d)

Penny Marshall, actress, film director (d)

Mac Miller, rapper (d)

John McCain, US politician (d)

Michael Martin, former House of Commons Speaker (d)

Winnie Madikizela-Mandela , ex wife Nelson Mandela (d)

Bill Maynard, actor (d)

John Mahoney, actor, Frasier (d)

Elon Musk, entrepreneur smokes joint on camera, Tesla stocks dive

Terry Morgan, resigns from HS2 and Crossrail, expecting to be sacked

Luca Modric wins Golden Ball, World Cup's best player

James Mattiss, US Defence Secretary resigns over Trump's policies

"Myself", who Trump gives thanks to on Thanksgiving

Murder rate in London greater than New York

Emmanuel Macron

Robert Meuller, Special Counsel investigations

Paul Manafort, Trump "fixer" jailed

Mace, Labour MP Lloyd Russell-Moyle picks up Commons ornamental staff

Maplin closes last branch

Michael McIntyre mugged

Migrants crisis

Moped gangs

Marriott hotel hack hits 500m Starwood guests

"Mansize" tissues rebranded by Kleenex after complaints of sexism

Meghan Markle/ Kate "feud"

Thomas Markle says daughter Meghan has cut him out of her life

Hugh Masekela, musician (d)

Mental health campaigns

Microplastics found in 90% of bottled water

Esther McVey MP misleads parliament, resigns

Elon Musk smokes joint on camera, company loses $3.1bn share price

Elon Musk accuses Thai soccer boys rescue diver of paedophilia

Elon Musk accused of misleading investors re. taking company private

Mid-term elections, US, Democrats win Senate

Mid-terms, losing Wisconsin Republicans pass bill limiting winner Democrats' powers

Eddie Mair leaves Radio 4, joins LBC

Met Police lose Supreme Court case re. handling of John Worboys' victims

Emmanuel Macron

Angela Merkel announces she won't seek re-election

Emmerson Mnangagwa new President of Zimbabwe

H R McMaster fired as National Security advisor by Trump

Jerry Maren, last surviving Munchkin from Wizard of Oz (d)

Mormons rebrand as The Church of Jesus Christ of Latter-day Saints

McDonald's, Texas students put up inclusivity selfie poster, remains for 51 days

Chris McCabe locked in Devon freezer, escapes using sausage as battering ram

Shane Missler, 20, wins $451m on lottery, posts on Facebook "Oh. My. God"

Mary Poppins remake

MINERVA-II1, first mobile exploration robot to land on an asteroid (Ryugu)

Mars, NASA Curiosity rover finds organic matter

Madagascar pochard, 21 of world's rarest bird released into wild

Morrisons supermarket revives paper bags to combat plastic waste

Manchester City win Premier League with record point tally

Minimum pricing on alcohol, Scotland

N

Dennis Norden, TV presenter (d)

"Nebulous", Jean-Claude Junker to Theresa May on her demands

No-deal Brexit

V.S. Naipaul, writer (d)

Novichok, Salisbury nerve agent poison

New Zealand announces referendum on recreational marijuana for 2020

Nationalism, rise of

Netball, England's shock win at Commonwealth Games

Norway +, Brexit option

NASA 60th anniversary

Negotiations, ongoing, Brexit

NME goes digital only

Nobel Peace Prize, Denis Mukwege & Nadia Murad for fight re. sexual violence

Omarosa Manigault Newman, fired from White House, turns on Trump

NAFTA out, CUSMA in

Martina Navratilova "transphobic" row

Nigel the lonely gannet, New Zealand (d)

Oliver North named President of the NRA

Nitrites, cancer causing chemicals in bacon & ham, call for ban

Nomophobia, Cambridge dictionary word of the year, "fear of being without your mobile"

NHS hospital volunteer drive

Number plate cloning, car registration scam

O

Out of hours service, 2 doctors for 1.4m people, Kent

Jackson Odell, actor (d)

Alan O'Neill, actor (d)

Dolores O'Riordan, singer, The Cranberries (d)

Oscars Academy expels Bill Cosby and Roman Polansky

Jamie Oliver's "jerk rice" cultural appropriation accusation

Outsourcing company failures: Carillion, G4S, Interserve, Capita etc

O2 Network fails

Alexandra Ocasio-Cortez, youngest woman elected to US Congress

Roy Orbison hologram tour

Oxfam sex abuse scandal

Oligarchs, Russian visa crackdown after Salisbury poisoning

Fiona Onasanya MP, guilty of lying re. speeding

Kate Osamor, MP "I remain proud, not ashamed, to live in social housing"

Odeon Leicester Square cinema reopens with £40 top price seats

Ronnie O'Sullivan wins record 7th UK Championship, snooker

Overseas aid

Liam O'Flynn, musician (d)

Obesity, draft proposals re. calories in shops and restaurant meals

Joe Osborn, musician, Wrecking Crew (d)

Colin O'Brady, first person to cross Antarctica solo

George Osborne ads 9th job to his portfolio

Tracey-Ann Oberman, actress' husband eats napkin in "pretentious" restaurant

Oxbridge "over-recruits" from eight schools

Ocado, best performing stock in FTSE 350, up 93.4% on the year

Jimmy Osmond has stroke onstage during panto

P

Pound continues to fall

Penalty shoot-out, England wins first in World Cup

Presidents Club Charity Dinner, expose of sexual harassment

Pope visits Ireland, gets low turnout

Jacqueline Pearce, actor (d)

Vinnie Paul, musician, Pantera (d)

Errol Pickford, ballet dancer (d)

Plastic free zone, first supermarket to introduce: Budgens, Belsize Park

Logan Paul, YouTube star apologises for Japanese suicide spot video

Penguins, lesbian, New Zealand, Thelma and Louise, former lays egg

Katie Price, "Jordan", model, declares bankruptcy

Vladimir Putin wins 4th term in office

Pret a Manger sandwich, death from mislabelled allergy ingredients

Parkland school teens protest gun laws after shooting, Florida

"Project fear", Brexit

Poundworld falls into administration, closes

Poverty causing misery in UK says UN official Philip Alston

Prince of Wales Bridge, Second Severn Crossing re-named

Pompeii, new discoveries

Paradise, California destroyed by fire, Trump misnames it "Pleasure"

Parliamentary pairing row, Brexit vote

Pet shops to be banned from selling puppies and kittens, "Lucy's Law"

"Peoples' vote", Brexit

"Period poverty", school girls lack access to sanitary products

Philip, Prince, hip replacement surgery

Peppa Pig banned in China: "promotes gangster attitudes"

Nancy Pelosi nominated by Democrats to be next House Speaker

Parker Solar Probe heads to Sun

Peter Rabbit, film's blackberry allergy scene, Sony apologises

Emmeline Pankhurst statue unveiled Manchester 100 yrs after women first voted

Roxanne Pallett, "Punchgate", Celeb Big Brother

Postboxes that sing Xmas jingles launched by Post Office

Priti Patel suggests food shortage threat to Ireland to drop "backstop" demands

Pay gap between the sexes

Q

Queen gifted fake hand waving machine by Australian students

Queen decries poverty in Xmas speech in front of gold piano

QAnon, far-right conspiracy theory: "deep state" against Trump

Quorn opens world's biggest meat-substitute factory, County Durham

Quantum compass, accurate non-GPS locator invented

Question Time, David Dimbleby retires, Fiona Bruce appointed replacement

Qantas accused of sexism after calling female doctor "Miss"

Qantas fly direct London-Perth

R

Cliff Richard wins privacy case against BBC

Range anxiety, electric cars issue

Russian bots, cyber warfare

Nicolas Roeg, film director (d)

Burt Reynolds, actor (d)

Joel Robuchon, chef, most Michelin stars in history (d)

Philip Roth, writer (d)

Cyrille Regis, footballer (d)

Douglas Rain, actor, voice of Hal 9000 in 2001: A Space Odyssey (d)

Roger the muscular kangaroo (d)

Red Dead Redemption 2 game, outrage re. killing "annoying" feminist

Harry Redknapp wins IACGMOOH

Robert Redford retires

Referendum

Refugees

Remainers, Brexit

"Remoaners", Brexit

Jacob Rees-Mogg, failed coup attempt

RAF 100th anniversary

Riots in France

Christiano Ronaldo assault allegations

Raking the forests, Trump's answer to California wildfires

Rough sleeping, numbers rise

Rail timetable change chaos

Royal wedding

Lou Rudd, army officer, first Briton to cross Antarctica solo

"Rivers of Blood" speech, Enoch Powell, 50 years old

Amber Rudd, Home Secretary resigns over immigration policy

Cyril Ramaphosa, elected South African President

Tommy Robinson, far-right activist appointed political advisor to UKIP

Rocco, African grey parrot orders items on owner's Alexa

Robot Boris, "hi-tech" Russian dancing android is a man in a suit

Russian collusion re. Trump's win

Representation of the People Act, centenary

Emile Ratelband, 69, fails to legally alter age to 49 to get more Tinder dates

Restaurant closures, 10,000 people lose jobs

Redrock Stockport wins Carbuncle Cup, architecture's wooden spoon

S

Ole Gunnar Solskjaer, new caretaker manager at Manchester United

Kevin Spacey, assault allegations, releases "creepy video"

Scallop Wars, French and British boats clash

Vichai Srivaddhanaprabha, Leicester City FC owner helicopter crash (d)

Pete Shelley, Buzzcocks singer (d)

Harry Leslie Smith, activist (d)

Dudley Sutton, actor (d)

Ellie Souter, snowboarder (d)

Peter Stringfellow, nightclub owner (d)

David Ogden Stiers, actor, M*A*S*H (d)

Mark E. Smith, musician, The Fall (d)

Jon Paul Steuer, actor, Star Trek: Next Generation (d)

A Star is Born film remake

John Sulston, scientist, human genome (d)

Strictly Come Dancing beats X Factor in ratings for BBC1

Syria, Trump pulls out troops

Self-identifying, gender

Smart meter roll out

Nancy Sinatra Senior, Frank's first wife (d)

Salisbury poisoning

Sergei and Yulia Skripal, Salisbury poisoning

Dawn Sturgess, Salisbury poison victim (d)

"Snowflake", political insult

Shop closures

Alan Sugar denies accusations of homophobia, racism

Neil Simon, playwright (d)

Martin Sorrell quits WPP over misconduct allegations

Single use plastics

Straws, plastic ban

Second referendum proposals, Brexit

Sugar tax on soft drinks

Mohammed bin Salman bin Abdulaziz Al Saud

Marks and Spencer announce store closures

Separating families at US border

"Stupid woman/people" Corbyn mutters in Parliament

Jeff Sessions resigns as Attorney General at request of Trump

Abdel Fatah al-Sisi wins "sham" Egyptian election

Raheem Sterling, gun tattoo

Raheem Sterling racism row at Chelsea

David Schwimmer, Friends actor's double steals beer in Blackpool

Saddleworth Moor fire

Stormzy wins two Brit Awards

Stormzy launches Cambridge University scholarship for black students

Alex Salmond denies sexual misconduct allegations, quits SNP

Seaborne Freight, government awards ferry contract to firm with no ships

Larysa Switlyk, "hardcore huntress" shoots animals on Islay

Sandhurst Treaty, France and Britain agree deal on border security

Mohamed Salah named PFA Player of the Year

Alexis Sanchez highest paid in Premier League, £16.8m per year

Slayer, band splits

"Super-gonorrhea", superbug outbreak in UK

Space Force, Trump adds another branch to military

"S**tholes", Trump describes Haiti, El Salvador and African countries

"Sit down you disloyal twerp" Andrew Bridgen MP heckled in parliament

Seismic waves, unusual occurrence near Madagascar felt 11,000 miles away

Strasbourg Christmas market attack

Satanic group settles lawsuit with Netflix over goat deity copyright

Spice Girls announce reunion without Posh

"Sloppy Steve" Trump's nickname for Steve Bannon

Swaziland renamed Kingdom of eSwatini by King

Saudi Arabian women allowed to drive

Simon Shelton, actor, Tinky Winky (d)

Steven Seagal appointed "special representative" of Russia

Sexual assault allegations against very many male public figures

T

Tesla car sent to orbit Mars on SpaceX rocket

Morgan Tsvangirai, Zimbabwean politician (d)

Tommy Robinson, court case, joins UKIP as advisor

Peter Thomson, golfer (d)

Verne Troyer, actor, Austin Powers (d)

Thwart: Brexiteers' accusation against Remainers

3D printing

Trump popularity at all-time low at year end: 39% approval

Trump UK visit, walks in front of Queen

Trump on meddling: "I don't see any reason why it would(n't) be Russia"

Donald J Trump Foundation closed after "persistently illegal conduct"

Toilet paper on Trump's shoe as he ascends steps to Air Force One

Trade war, USA v China

Trump Baby blimp

Trump says his nuclear button "much bigger" than Kim Jong-un's

Trump declares himself "a very stable genius"

Trump visits Iraq, reveals secret info about Navy SEAL team

Thailand football Wild Boys team rescued from cave

Toys R Us closes

Titanic, musical's audience watches England penalty shoot-out on phones

Rex Tillerson, fired as Secretary of State, called "dumb as a rock" by Trump

Geraint Thomas wins Tour de France, has trophy stolen

Peter Tatchell, LGBT activist arrested in Russia prior to World Cup

Tuam mass baby grave found by ex nun-run unmarried mothers' home, Ireland

"Tactical contact" police ram moped criminals

Train timetable change chaos

Tsunami hits Indonesia

Ray Thomas, singer, Moody Blues (d)

"They shall not grow old", Peter Jackson transforms WW1 footage

"Trotters up", Danny Dyer describes David Cameron in Nice

Telephones in prison cells, government initiative to stem illegal mobiles

Thai boys' football team cave rescue

Tiangong-1, Chinese space station falls to Earth

Twiglet, Cambridge student's de-stress dog, signed off sick for stress

Toblerone reverts to original shape

Turner Prize show features no painting or sculpture

U

UKIP annual conference condoms feature Nigel Farage, urge hard Brexit

Ultra Low Emission Zone announced for London

USA v China trade war

US government shutdown

Upskirting bill derailed by Christopher Chope MP

UN Relief and Works Agency, USA stops funding

Universal Basic Income, trial ends in Finland, debate continues

UN poverty report condemns "callous" UK government

Umbrella left at top of steps to Air Force One by Trump

"Unicorns and rainbows", Brexit wishful thinking

Ursid meteor shower, Winter Solstice and full moon coincide, next in 2094

Unilever scrap move of HQ to

Uber and minicabs to pay Congestion Charge

UAE helicopter crashes near world's longest zipline, kills four

Universal Credit, controversial roll-out

"Unhappy Meal" sculpture by Carol May, thrown out as rubbish, Hong Kong

V

Virgin Trains and Stagecoach hand over East Coast Rail Line franchise

Big Van Vader, wrestler (d)

Virtue signalling

Leo Varadkar, Irish PM

Vodka, world's most expensive bottle at £960,000 stolen from Copenhagen bar

Voter ID, elections in U.S. And U.K.

Virgin Trains deploy staff in pink vests to manage football fans

Virgin Galactic rocket plane reaches edge of space

Vaping

Jeremy Vine replaces Matthew Wright on Channel 5 after 18 years

Viagra goes on sale over the counter

"Vassal state", Brexit

Venice to charge admission fee to combat "over-tourism"

V&A Dundee opens

VAR, video assistant referee debuts

W

Arsene Wenger, longest serving manager leaves Arsenal

Harvey Weinstein, assault allegations

Nancy Wilson, singer (d)

Kanye West, various meltdowns

Ray Wilkins, footballer (d)

Tom Wolfe, writer (d)

Dale Winton, TV presenter (d)

Peter Wyngarde, actor, Jason King (d)

Wall, Trump's wish

Holly Willoughby replaces Ant on IACGMOOH

Winter Olympics, Pyeongchang, South Korea

Serena Williams rows with umpire, loses US Open

John Worboys, Black cab rapist loses parole hearing

Kanye West meets Trump in White House, melts down

Sean White wins half-pipe final thriller, Winter Olympics

Windrush scandal

Gareth Southgate, England Manager sparks M&S waistcoat sales boom

June Whitfield, actor (d)

Winnie the Pooh film banned in China as bear is compared to leader Xi

Willow, Queen's corgi dies

Wind on Mars, sound recorded by NASA

World Cup held in Russia

Gillian Wearing, 1st female artist to create statue for Parliament Square

"Wet noodle", Schwarzenegger on Trump at press conference with Putin

Whiskey, over 33% of rare bottles found to be fake

"Will of the people", Brexit

Water cannon, Boris Johnson's sold for scrap at £300,000 loss

Wombat poop, scientists discover why it's cube-shaped

WTO rules, Brexit

Wonga payday lender collapses

"Whiffyleaks", Julian Assange, Ecuador Embassy staff complain of smell

Tony Joe White, musician (d)

Michael White, musician, Thompson Twins, author (d)

JW Waterhouse's naked nymphs painting removed from Manchester Art Gallery

Whooping cough on the rise

Wembley Stadium, Shahid Khan withdraws offer to buy

"We're in the money", Sainsbury's CEO sings in TV studio re. Asda merger

X

XR, short for Extinction Rebellion

Xi Jinping allowed to become President of China for life

Xenophobia, rise of

Disease X, WHO name for as yet unknown pathogen

Y

John Young, astronaut, 9th man on Moon (d)

Yemen civil war

Yanni/Laurel debate

Toby Young resigns from university regulator after sexist comments

Yarl's Wood detention centre, inmates' hunger strike over poor conditions

Z

Nazanin Zaghari-Ratcliffe, prisoner in Iran, release held up over payments

Mark Zuckerberg, Facebook boss bats away criticisms

Zsa Zsa, bulldog named World's Ugliest Dog

Jacob Zuma resigns as President of South Africa, takes up music career

Ryan Zinke, U.S. Secretary of the Interior resigns after many scandals

Zero hours contracts

Zippy, Britain's second ever zonkey born

Zero tolerance, Trump's immigration policy

ZTE, Chinese telecom firm deemed national security risk to UK

Printed in Great Britain
by Amazon